THE CAMBRIDGE COMPANION TO ALICE MUNRO

This *Companion* is a thorough introduction to the writings of the Nobel Prize winner Alice Munro. Uniting the talents of distinguished creative writers and noted academics, David Staines has put together a comprehensive, exploratory account of Munro's biography, her position as a feminist, her evocation of life in small-town Ontario, her non-fictional writings as well as her short stories, and her artistic achievement. Considering a wide range of topics – including Munro's style, life writing, her personal development, and her use of Greek myths, Celtic ballads, Norse sagas, and popular songs – this volume will appeal to keen readers of Munro's fiction as well as students and scholars of literature and Canadian and gender studies.

David Staines is Professor of English at the University of Ottawa. A scholar of medieval culture and literature, as well as Canadian culture and literature, he has authored or edited more than fifteen books, including *The Canadian Imagination: Dimensions of a Literary Culture*, *Tennyson's Camelot: the Idylls of the King and its Medieval Sources*, and *The Letters of Stephen Leacock*.

THE CAMBRIDGE COMPANION TO
ALICE MUNRO

EDITED BY
DAVID STAINES

CAMBRIDGE
UNIVERSITY PRESS

CAMBRIDGE
UNIVERSITY PRESS

University Printing House, Cambridge CB2 8BS, United Kingdom

Cambridge University Press is part of the University of Cambridge.

It furthers the University's mission by disseminating knowledge in the pursuit of education, learning and research at the highest international levels of excellence.

www.cambridge.org
Information on this title: www.cambridge.org/9781107472020

© Cambridge University Press 2016
Chapter 6, 'Lives of Girls and Women: a portrait of the artist as a young woman' by Margaret Atwood © O. W. Toad Ltd 2016

This publication is in copyright. Subject to statutory exception and to the provisions of relevant collective licensing agreements, no reproduction of any part may take place without the written permission of Cambridge University Press.

First published 2016

Printed in the United Kingdom by Clays, St Ives plc

A catalogue record for this publication is available from the British Library

Library of Congress Cataloguing in Publication Data
Names: Staines, David, 1946– editor.
Title: The Cambridge companion to Alice Munro / edited by David Staines.
Description: Cambridge ; New York : Cambridge University Press, 2016. | Includes bibliographical references and index.
Identifiers: LCCN 2015038209| ISBN 9781107093270 (Hardback) | ISBN 9781107472020 (Paperback)
Subjects: LCSH: Munro, Alice, 1931–Criticism and interpretation.
Classification: LCC PR9199.3.M8 Z576 2016 | DDC 813/.54–dc23 LC record available at http://lccn.loc.gov/2015038209

ISBN 978-1-107-09327-0 Hardback
ISBN 978-1-107-47202-0 Paperback

Cambridge University Press has no responsibility for the persistence or accuracy of URLs for external or third-party internet websites referred to in this publication, and does not guarantee that any content on such websites is, or will remain, accurate or appropriate.

CONTENTS

Notes on contributors		*page* vii
Note on editions used		ix
Chronology		x
Introduction DAVID STAINES		1
1	From Wingham to Clinton: Alice Munro in her Canadian context DAVID STAINES	7
2	Where do you think you are? Place in the short stories of Alice Munro MERILYN SIMONDS	26
3	The style of Alice Munro DOUGLAS GLOVER	45
4	'Oranges *and* apples': Alice Munro's undogmatic feminism MARIA LÖSCHNIGG	60
5	Alice Munro and her life writing CORAL ANN HOWELLS	79
6	*Lives of Girls and Women*: a portrait of the artist as a young woman MARGARET ATWOOD	96
7	Re-reading *The Moons of Jupiter* W.H. NEW	116

CONTENTS

8	Alice Munro and personal development ROBERT MCGILL	136
9	The female bard: retrieving Greek myths, Celtic ballads, Norse sagas, and popular songs HÉLIANE VENTURA	154
10	The mother as material ELIZABETH HAY	178
	Bibliography	193
	Index	197

NOTES ON CONTRIBUTORS

MARGARET ATWOOD is the author of more than forty volumes of children's literature, fiction and non-fiction, and poetry. Her novels include *The Edible Woman*, *The Handmaid's Tale*, the Giller Prize-winning *Alias Grace*, *Blind Assassin*, which won the Booker Prize in 2000, and her most recent, *The Heart Goes Last*. Her most recent volume of poetry, *The Door*, was published in 2007. *In Other Worlds: SF and the Human Imagination*, a collection of non-fiction essays, appeared in 2011. She is a Companion of the Order of Canada.

DOUGLAS GLOVER is the author of four novels, five short story collections, and three works of non-fiction, including *The Enamoured Knight*, a study of *Don Quixote* and novel form. He won the Governor General's Award for his novel *Elle* (2003) and he was a finalist for the International IMPAC Dublin Literary Award in 2005. His most recent book is the collection *Savage Love*. Editor of the annual *Best Canadian Stories* from 1996 until 2006, he currently teaches writing at the Vermont College of Fine Arts and edits the online literary magazine *Numéro Cinq*.

ELIZABETH HAY is the author of one collection of short fiction, *Small Change*, three books of creative non-fiction about her travels outside Canada, and five novels: *A Student of Weather*, *Garbo Laughs*, the Giller Prize-winning *Late Nights on Air*, *Alone in the Classroom*, and *His Whole Life*. Formerly a radio broadcaster, she spent a number of years in Mexico and New York City before returning to Canada.

CORAL ANN HOWELLS is Professor Emerita of English and Canadian Literature, University of Reading, and Senior Research Fellow, Institute of English Studies, University of London. She has published extensively on contemporary Canadian fiction, especially writing by women. Her many books include *Margaret Atwood*, *Alice Munro*, and *Contemporary Canadian Women's Fiction: Refiguring Identities*. She edited the *Cambridge Companion to Margaret Atwood* and co-edited, with Eva-Marie Kroller, the *Cambridge History of Canadian Literature*. She is a Fellow of the Royal Society of Canada.

NOTES ON CONTRIBUTORS

MARIA LÖSCHNIGG is Professor of English, University of Graz, Austria. Her publications include *The Contemporary Canadian Short Story in English: Continuity and Change*; she also co-edited *Migration and Fiction: Narratives of Migration in Contemporary Canadian Literature* and co-wrote the first history of Canadian Literature in German, *Kurze Geschichte der kanadischen Literatur* (both with Martin Löschnigg). Her most recent work looks at postcolonial literature from an eco-critical point of view.

ROBERT MCGILL is Associate Professor of English, University of Toronto. He is the author of two novels, *The Mysteries* and *Once We Had a Country*, as well as a book of literary criticism, *The Treacherous Imagination: Intimacy, Ethics, and Autobiographical Fiction*. His articles on Alice Munro have appeared in *a/b: Auto/Biography*, *Canadian Literature*, *The Journal of Commonwealth Literature*, *Mosaic*, and *University of Toronto Quarterly*.

W. H. NEW is University Killam Professor Emeritus, University of British Columbia. A critic and editor, poet and children's writer, he is the author of *A History of Canadian Literature*, *Borderlands*, *Land Sliding*, and *Grandchild of Empire*, and editor of *Encyclopedia of Literature in Canada*, among other works. His studies of the short story include *Dreams of Speech and Violence* and *Reading Mansfield and Metaphors of Form*. Among his books for children is the prize-winning *The Year I Was Grounded*. His *New & Selected Poems* appeared in 2015. He is an Officer of the Order of Canada.

MERILYN SIMONDS is the author of sixteen books, including the novel *The Holding*, a *New York Times Book Review* Editors' choice, and the creative non-fiction *The Convict Lover*, a Governor General's Award finalist. Her recent releases are a collection of personal essays, *A New Leaf*, a travel memoir, *Breakfast at the Exit Café*, and *The Paradise Project*, flash fiction published in a hand-printed edition. In 2015 the National Arts Centre Orchestra premiered *Dear Life*, a symphony by Zosha di Castri based on Simonds's adaptation of the Alice Munro story.

DAVID STAINES is Professor of English, University of Ottawa. He divides his time between medieval culture and literature and Canadian culture and literature. Among the many books he has authored and/or edited are *The Canadian Imagination: Dimensions of a Literary Culture*, *Tennyson's Camelot: the Idylls of the King and its Medieval Sources*, *The Complete Romances of Chrétien de Troyes*, and *The Letters of Stephen Leacock*. He is a Member of the Order of Canada.

HÉLIANE VENTURA is Professor of Contemporary Literature in English at the University of Toulouse-Jean Jaurès, France. Her area of specialization is the contemporary short story in the Anglophone world with special emphasis on the rewriting of the canon, intermedial relationships, and the emergence of transatlantic literatures. She has published two monographs on Margaret Atwood and Alice Munro and written more than ninety articles published in Britain, Canada, and France, principally on female short story writers from Britain, Canada, and New Zealand as well as on Aboriginal writers.

NOTE ON EDITIONS USED

In quoting from Alice Munro's writings, contributors to this volume have used a variety of American, British, and Canadian editions. Details of editions used are included in the endnotes to each chapter.

CHRONOLOGY

1931   Alice Laidlaw [Munro] born 10 July in Wingham, Ontario, Canada, the first child of Robert Eric Laidlaw (1901–76) and Anne Clarke Chamney Laidlaw (1898–1959).

1936   Alice's only brother, William, born 13 March.

1937   Alice's only sister, Sheila, born 1 April.

1937–49   Attends Lower Town School, Wingham (1937–9), Wingham Public School (1939–44), and Wingham and District High School, graduating in 1949 at the top of her class and winning a two-year scholarship to the University of Western Ontario with the top marks in English of all incoming students.

1949–51   Attends the University of Western Ontario on a two-year scholarship, majoring first in journalism, then changing her major to English. While at university, she writes stories, her first one, 'The Dimensions of a Shadow', appearing in the April 1950 issue of *Folio*, the university's undergraduate literary magazine. Two more stories, 'Story for Sunday' and 'The Widower', appear in the December 1950 and April 1951 issues. Robert Weaver, who becomes a mentor and a support, buys one of her stories for radio broadcast on *Canadian Short Stories* on the Canadian Broadcasting Company. Marries James Munro in Wingham on 29 December.

1952   Moves with her husband to Vancouver, British Columbia, where he holds a position in the textile section of Eaton's department store and Alice works as a part-time assistant at the Kitsilano branch of the Vancouver Public Library. From the autumn of that year until June 1953 she works as a full-time assistant, then, after the birth of her first child, she is part-time again until her next pregnancy in 1955.

1953   Sheila Munro born 5 October. Alice Munro's first sold story is published in the Canadian magazine *Mayfair* (November). Over

the following decade she contributes to other Canadian publications: *Canadian Forum, Queen's Quarterly, Chatelaine, Tamarack Review*, and *The Montrealer*.
1955 Catherine Munro born 28 July – died the same day.
1957 Jenny Munro born 4 June.
1958 Applies for a grant from the Canada Council; the application is rejected.
1959 Her mother, Anne, dies after suffering from severe Parkinson's disease for nearly twenty years.
1963 Moves with her family to Victoria, British Columbia, to found Munro's Books.
1966 Andrea Munro born 8 September.
1968 With the encouragement of Earle Toppings, an editor from Ryerson Press, *Dance of the Happy Shades* is published, winning the Governor General's Award for Fiction.
1969 Her father, Robert, marries Mary Etta Laidlaw, the widow of one of his cousins.
1971 *Lives of Girls and Women* is published, winning the first Canadian Booksellers Association/International Book Year Award and becoming an alternate selection for the Literary Guild's Book-of-the-Month Club in Canada and the United States.
1972 Named Outstanding Fiction Writer by the British Columbia Library Association.
1973 Separates from her husband. Teaches summer school at Notre Dame University in Nelson, British Columbia. Moves from Victoria to London, Ontario, from where she commutes by train one day a week to Toronto to teach for the fall term at York University. Receives a Canada Council Senior Arts Grant.
1974 *Something I've Been Meaning to Tell You* is published, winning the Province of Ontario Council for the Arts Award. Receives the Great Lakes Colleges Association Award for the American publication of *Dance of the Happy Shades*. Reunites with Gerald Fremlin, a retired geographer, whom she knew slightly in her undergraduate years. Appointed writer-in-residence at the University of Western Ontario (1974–5).
1975 Gerald Fremlin and Munro settle in Clinton, Ontario.
1976 Receives an honorary degree from the University of Western Ontario. Engages as her agent Virginia Barber, who becomes a close friend and sells 'Royal Beatings', the opening story of *Who*

Do You Think You Are?, to *The New Yorker*. Munro's divorce is finalized. Robert Laidlaw dies.

1977 National Magazine Foundation Gold Medal Award for 'Accident', collected later in *The Moons of Jupiter*. Signs a contract for right-of-first-refusal with *The New Yorker*. Screenplay, *1847: the Irish*, is filmed.

1978 Wins the Canada–Australia Literary Prize. *Who Do You Think You Are?* is published, winning the Governor General's Award for Fiction, and is shortlisted for Britain's Booker Prize. The Canadian Booksellers Association chooses it as Book of the Year; it is also selected for the Book-of-the-Month Club in Canada.

1979 Robert Laidlaw's novel, *The McGregors: a Novel of an Ontario Pioneer Family*, is published posthumously.

1980 Writer-in-residence at the University of British Columbia (January–April). Writer-in-residence at the University of Queensland (September–December).

1981 July trip to China with six other Canadian writers as guests of the Chinese Writers' Association.

1982 February trip to Norway and Sweden to promote the publication of the Norwegian translation of *Who Do You Think You Are?* *The Moons of Jupiter* is published.

1983 National Magazine Foundation Gold Medal Award for 'Mrs Cross and Mrs Kidd', collected in *The Moons of Jupiter*.

1986 Wins the inaugural Marian Engel Award. *The Progress of Love* is published, winning the Governor General's Award for Fiction.

1988 One of the three-member Editorial Board of McClelland & Stewart's New Canadian Library.

1990 Spends three months in Scotland. *Friend of My Youth* is published, winning the Province of Ontario Trillium Award for Fiction. It is a finalist for the Governor General's Award and shortlisted for the Irish Times–Aer Lingus Fiction Prize. Winner of the Canada Council Molson Prize for 'outstanding lifetime contributions to the cultural and intellectual life of Canada'.

1994 Receives the Order of Ontario. *Open Secrets* is published, winning the W. H. Smith Award for 'the best book of the year'. Jury member for the first Giller Prize for Fiction and serves as a member of the Giller Foundation.

1995 Spends six months in Ireland.

CHRONOLOGY

1996	*Selected Stories* is published.
1997	Wins the PEN/Malamud Award for Excellence in Short Fiction.
1998	*The Love of a Good Woman* is published, winning the Giller Prize for Fiction, the Province of Ontario Trillium Award for Fiction, and the National Book Critics Circle Award.
2001	Wins Rea Award for Lifetime Achievement and O. Henry Award for Continuing Achievement in Short Fiction. *Hateship, Friendship, Loveship, Courtship, Marriage* is published.
2003	*No Love Lost* is published.
2004	*Runaway* is published, winning the Rogers Writers' Trust Fiction Prize.
2005	Terasen Lifetime Achievement Award for an Outstanding Literary Career in British Columbia.
2006	*The View from Castle Rock: Stories* is published. *Alice Munro's Best* (with an introduction by Margaret Atwood) is published.
2008	Wins the Flaiano Prize in Italy.
2009	*Too Much Happiness* is published. Munro wins the Man Booker International Prize 'for a body of work that has contributed to an achievement in fiction on the world stage'.
2012	*Dear Life* is published.
2013	*Dear Life* wins the Province of Ontario Trillium Award for Fiction. Gerald Fremlin dies. Munro wins the Nobel Prize for Literature, heralding her as 'the master of the contemporary short story'.

DAVID STAINES

Introduction

On 14 November 2004, Jonathan Franzen reviewed Alice Munro's *Runaway*, her tenth collection of short stories, in the *New York Times Book Review*; his article began:

> Alice Munro has a strong claim to being the best fiction writer now working in North America, but outside of Canada, where her books are No. 1 best sellers, she has never had a large readership ... I want to circle around Munro's latest marvel of a book, 'Runaway,' by taking some guesses as to why her excellence so dismayingly exceeds her fame.[1]

Two years later, Margaret Atwood opened her collection *Alice Munro's Best: Selected Stories* with the statement:

> Alice Munro is among the major writers of English fiction of our time. She's been accorded armfuls of super-superlatives by critics in both North America and the United Kingdom, she's won many awards, and she has a devoted international readership. Among writers themselves, her name is spoken in hushed tones. Most recently she's been used as a stick to flog the enemy with, in various inter-writerly combats. 'You call this writing?' the floggers say, in effect. 'Alice Munro! Now *that's* writing!' She's the kind of writer about whom it is often said – no matter how well-known she becomes – that she ought to be better known.[2]

In the *Guardian*'s account of the development of the short story genre on 11 September 2013, Tessa Hadley heralded Munro as one of the ten finest short fiction writers of all time. 'Munro has changed our sense of what the short story can do as radically as Chekhov and Mansfield did at the beginning of the 20th century', she stated. 'There's never a false or fussy note, as Munro penetrates in words into the hidden roots of how we choose to live, and why we act.'[3]

And then on 10 December 2013, Munro was awarded the Nobel Prize for Literature. 'It is a challenge to find an unessential word or a superfluous phrase. Reading one of her texts is like watching a cat walk across a laid dinner table', Peter Englund, Permanent Secretary of the Swedish Academy, stated in his presentation speech:

> A brief short story can often cover decades, summarizing a life, as she moves deftly between different periods. No wonder Alice Munro is often able to say more in thirty pages than an ordinary novelist is capable of in three hundred. She is a virtuoso of the elliptical and – as the Academy said in its brief prize citation – the master of the contemporary short story.[4]

'The master of the contemporary short story', Alice Munro has devoted her writing career to a careful exploration of the genre of the short story, questioning its boundaries, expanding its length (her early stories were ten pages long, her later stories up to seventy), and challenging the common understanding of its purpose and power. From her first collection, *Dance of the Happy Shades*, published in 1968, to her most recent, *Dear Life*, published in 2012, she has explored the many dimensions of human life. As the Nobel Prize presentation speech made explicit, she has 'come close to solving the greatest mystery of them all: the human heart and its caprices'. And all this within the supposed confines of the short story.

For Munro, reading a short story is like entering a house. 'I don't take up a story and follow it as if it were a road, taking me somewhere, with views and neat diversions along the way. I go into it, and move back and forth and settle here and there, and stay in it for a while', she stated in 1982. 'It's more like a house. Everybody knows what a house does, how it encloses space and makes connections between one enclosed space and another and presents what is outside in a new way. This is the nearest I can come to explaining what a story does for me, and what I want my stories to do for other people.'[5] Her fiction reveals the recurring problems of everyday life, everyday life being the focus of the mature narrator in *Lives of Girls and Women*: 'People's lives, in Jubilee as elsewhere, were dull, simple, amazing and unfathomable – deep caves paved with kitchen linoleum.' Her stories are kitchen linoleum with the deep caves of people's aspirations and failings just beneath the surface. 'It's a drama in people's lives that I think a writer is naturally attracted to', she observed in 1991,[6] and when she spoke at the shortlist announcement for the Giller Prize in 1994, she reiterated her particular perspective: 'I chose the writers who seemed to me to have the truest voices and the most reliable skills and who gave me as a reader the most lively and constant pleasure.' In November 2013, she reflected, in her official interview about the Nobel Prize, 'I want my stories to move people. I don't care if they're men or women or children. I want my stories to be something about life that causes people not to say "Oh, isn't that the truth," but to feel some kind of reward from the writing.'

Introduction

This *Companion* presents a kaleidoscope of critical views on Alice Munro and her fictional and non-fictional works. Distinguished and informed authorities write about the excellence of her writings, offering their original insights into her unique universe.

Opening the collection is 'From Wingham to Clinton: Alice Munro in her Canadian Context', David Staines's bio-critical chapter, which explores the roots of her writings in rural Huron County in southwestern Ontario. Born in Wingham and residing now in Clinton, about thirty-five kilometres to the south, Munro fashions her work from the people and incidents of the county. Initially scorned by some townspeople for her studies of the narrow and restricted lives of the county people she creates, she is now an acknowledged figure of international importance, and the restricted lives speak to the larger human experience beyond the local settings. Tracing Munro's writing life from her childhood readings, including the works of Lucy Maud Montgomery and Emily Brontë, through her delight in discovering the writers of the American South, especially Eudora Welty, the chapter chronicles her steady vision of the infinite wonders, both positive and negative, of the small town. Growing up herself on the margins of her rural society, Munro finds her own understanding of life mirrored in the fiction of female southern writers. And Canada, where she has lived all her life, is her artistic and personal home, the centre of her life, and she is the careful and perceptive observer and chronicler of life in Huron County and, by extension, in the world.

Complementing the opening chapter is Merilyn Simonds's chapter, 'Where Do You Think You Are? Place in the Short Stories of Alice Munro', a steady and sympathetic look at Munro's treatment of place in her fiction and non-fiction. Regarding the world as 'an imperfect Eden, hanging with fruit but writhing with snakes', Munro depicts her people against the background of rural life. And though her 'place' expands to encompass the immediate worlds beyond Huron County, including Stratford, Kitchener, and Toronto, the larger distances within Canada, including Kingston, Ottawa, Vancouver, and Victoria, and the distant lands of Albania, Australia, Indonesia, and Scotland, she always returns to her own 'place', here instead of there, to understand the complicated attitudes in her writings to the often bewildering 'local' sense.

The third chapter, 'The Style of Alice Munro', focuses on Munro's style: 'style as the basket of syntactic moves habitual to an author, but also style as tilt, the characteristic lean or bearing of the author as she represents herself through her writing'. Using 'Lives of Girls and Women' from the book of the same name as his analytical text, Douglas Glover argues that Munro reaches for complexity and irony over interpretation, preferring to note distinctions rather than similarities in her constant struggle to resist closure. A statement provokes a counter-statement or a further complication, and the stories progress through the accumulation of such contraventions.

In Chapter 4, '"Oranges *and* Apples": Alice Munro's Undogmatic Feminism', Maria Löschnigg analyses the feminism of Munro and her fiction. Munro's stories are not explicitly addressed to female readers, the fiction being written for 'men or women or children', and though Munro has never thought of herself as being anything but a woman, Löschnigg argues that she is both a feminist and *not* a feminist author, drawing her evidence through readings of her fiction.

The next three chapters look directly at Munro's individual artistic achievements. In Chapter 5, 'Alice Munro and her Life Writing', Coral Ann Howells, herself the author of *Alice Munro*, a pioneering 1998 study, examines Munro's literary non-fiction, isolating it as much as is feasible from her fiction. Observing the various treatments of Munro's life in successive renditions, she finds that Munro's literary non-fiction 'is as full of gaps, shifting perspectives, fleeting moments of revelations, and as endlessly open to revision as her fictions'.

In the sixth chapter, Margaret Atwood turns her critical eye to a study of Munro's second book, *Lives of Girls and Women*, seeing it as a *Bildungsroman* and a *Künstlerroman* depicting the growth of a young artist into her maturity. She analyses the book under four headings – the Drowned Maiden, the Crazy Person, the Failure, and the Storyteller – using a fifth heading, Performance, for her study of the Epilogue. This female version of an artist's portrait leaves its protagonist, Del Jordan, 'at the threshold', the same position where James Joyce left his hero in *A Portrait of the Artist as a Young Man*: 'The door is open, and the young writer is about to step through it.'

Unlike *Lives of Girls and Women*, which has a unifying protagonist, *The Moons of Jupiter*, Munro's fifth book, is a collection of her short stories. In 'Re-reading *The Moons of Jupiter*', the seventh chapter of this *Companion*, W. H. New describes the painstaking care with which Munro fashions her individual books. From his account of the history of composition of the volume, he traces its growth into a collection, 'a coherent and interactive, formally adventurous inquiry'. Like other contributors to this volume, he finds the book refusing unilateral closure: 'it calls for a different kind of recognition: to realize that going back – re-reading – means beginning again'.

In the final chapters, three critics stand back and wonder about the thematic power of Munro's fiction. Looking at her whole corpus, Robert McGill examines an anti-progressive strain in her writing in Chapter 8,

'Alice Munro and Personal Development'. Based on his understanding of the shape of her career, which is distinguished by recursion more than by transformation or straightforward 'improvement', he argues that her fiction self-reflexively calls attention to its poetics of return and review, a poetics that also turns out to be a hermeneutics, for her stories encourage readers not only to look closely at life itself but also to look at it repeatedly.

In Chapter 9, 'The Female Bard: Retrieving Greek Myths, Celtic Ballads, Norse Sagas, and Popular Songs', Héliane Ventura begins with *Dance of the Happy Shades* and continues through to Munro's last volume, examining her bardic affiliation through her 'covert or overt references to Homeric songs, Scottish minstrelsy, Nordic sagas, American folklore, and Canadian songs'. These many references reveal her strong power of recall, a facet of her character strongly criticized in her own childhood, and they suggest an astonishing range of literary allusions throughout her writings.

In the concluding chapter, 'The Mother as Material', Elizabeth Hay examines the prominent figure of the mother in Munro's fiction from the early story 'The Peace of Utrecht', through 'The Ottawa Valley', to the final lines of the final story in *Dear Life*. Exploring Munro's guilty use of such personal material, Hay shows how Munro tries to escape her mother as subject matter. Throughout her long writing career Munro probes this topic, 'branches out from it, leaves it behind, returns to it once again'. In this way she continues to employ her narrative strategy of revisiting similar situations in order to observe them from fresh angles, all the while pressing against the limitations of the subject.

In light of Munro's receipt of the Nobel Prize for Literature, these ten writers have read and re-read her corpus many times, each occasion bringing new insights into the nature of her fictional worlds. And each reading brings fresh and revealing thoughts on her complex writing.

Fifty years ago, at the same time that Munro was organizing her first collection of short fiction, Allen Tate, the American poet and critic, gathered twenty-six distinguished writers to reflect on *T. S. Eliot: the Man and his Work*. One of the writers was Ezra Pound, who could capture, in four paragraphs, only a fragment of Eliot. 'His was the true Dantescan voice – not honoured enough, and deserving more than I ever gave him,' commented Pound. 'Am I to write "about" the poet Thomas Stearns Eliot? Or my friend "the Possum"? Let him rest in peace. I can only repeat, but with the urgency of 50 years ago: READ HIM.'

Reflecting on the significant achievements of Munro, the ten contributors believe that the most important thing to do – in terms of her remarkable fiction and non-fiction – is to read her. And then, after reading, one can re-read her to begin to understand the power of her literary creations. 'If you read a lot of Munro's works carefully', as the Nobel Prize presentation speech stated, 'sooner or later, in one of her short stories, you will come face to face with yourself; this is an encounter that always leaves you shaken and often changed, but never crushed.'

Notes

1 '"Runaway": Alice's Wonderland', *New York Times Book Review* (14 November 2004), 1.
2 Alice Munro, *Alice Munro's Best: Selected Stories*, with an Introduction by Margaret Atwood (Toronto: McClelland & Stewart, 2006), vii.
3 'Tessa Hadley's Top 10 Short Stories', *The Guardian* (11 September 2013).
4 Alice Munro, *Vintage Munro* (New York: Vintage, 2014), 209.
5 Alice Munro, 'What Is Real?', in John Metcalf (ed.), *Making it New: Contemporary Canadian Stories* (Toronto: Methuen, 1982), 224.
6 Eleanor Wachtel, 'An Interview with Alice Munro', *Brick* 40 (winter 1991), 53.

I

DAVID STAINES

From Wingham to Clinton

Alice Munro in her Canadian context

Huron County lies in rural southwestern Ontario, nestled along the southeastern shore of Lake Huron, one of the five interconnected Great Lakes of North America. A beautiful lake, it is 'no piddling pond in the rocks and pines but a grand freshwater sea, with a foreign country invisible on the other side. There all the time – unchanging. Bountiful Lake Huron that spreads a blessing on the day. Behind the farms and fences and swamp and bush and roads and highways and brick towns – there all the time.'[1]

According to the first official records of the Huron District Assessment Rolls of 1842, the total population of the townships that later were included in modern Huron County was 3,894. Now, along with its many villages and hamlets, the county is home to five towns, the port town and county seat of Goderich on Lake Huron (approximate population 7,500), and four smaller towns: Clinton towards the centre of the county (approximate population 3,200), Exeter towards the south (approximate population 4,800), Seaforth towards the east (approximate population 2,300), and Wingham towards the north (approximate population 2,900). The most agriculturally productive county in Ontario, Huron is a lush landscape of hills and valleys, prosperous farms and farms now for sale or abandoned, and home to a host of small rural communities dotting the horizon.

Huron County is also home to Alice Munro, a writer who lived for twenty years in British Columbia and has travelled as far away as Australia and the Scandinavian countries, but a writer who usually makes her artistic and her personal home in this rural Ontario world. Born in Wingham on 10 July 1931 and residing now in Clinton, about thirty-five kilometres to the south, she crafts her remarkable stories from the people and incidents of the county, making her ordinary world extraordinary through her art.

'I think of houses and streets and rooms and faces as what I put into the stories', she said in 1983. 'But I never think I am writing a story about Wingham or I'm writing a story about a Southwestern Ontario small town.

Ever. I just use that stuff because it is familiar to me. It's what I know about.'[2] Fifteen years later, she reflected:

> The reason I write so often about the country to the east of Lake Huron is just that I love it. It means something to me that no other country can – no matter how important historically that other country may be, how 'beautiful,' how lively and interesting. I am intoxicated by this particular landscape, by the almost flat fields, the swamps, the hardwood bush lots, by the continental climate with its extravagant winters. I am at home with the brick houses, the falling-down barns, the occasional farms that have swimming pools and airplanes, the trailer parks, burdensome old churches, Wal-Mart, and Canadian Tire. I speak the language.[3]

That same year, she added, 'I love the landscape here. We go for long walks; they're the most wonderful walks you can imagine.'[4]

Huron County, 'a closed rural society with a pretty homogeneous Scotch-Irish racial strain going slowly to decay',[5] fostered the narrow values of many of its people. Munro lived in

> a culture that has become fairly stagnant. With a big sense of righteousness. But with big bustings-out and grotesque crime. And ferocious sexual humour and the habit of getting drunk and killing each other off the roads. There's always this sort of boiling life going on. I'm always surprised when people say your stories are about such – ohhhh – well they don't say *dull*. That wouldn't be polite, but *restricted* lives and people. I always think the country I was born and brought up in is full of event and emotions and amazing things going on all the time.[6]

Parochialism, mean-spiritedness, and vengeance on those who would rise above its narrow confines, what could these attitudes promote? 'In the community where I grew up, books were a time-waster and reading is a bad habit, and so if even reading is a bad habit, writing is an incomprehensible thing to do.'[7] 'My home town is hostile', she reflected in 1982. 'The newspaper actually came out with an editorial against me. This official viewpoint gave carte blanche to a lot of kooks. I have actually received letters that say things like who do you think you are, or we're sick and tired of seeing your old mug in the paper. They are sad, black letters, full of anger, and almost illiterate.'[8] She later commented:

> The *Wingham Advance Times* wrote a blistering editorial criticizing me, calling me a 'warped personality'. It didn't surprise me or hurt me because you know what you can expect if you try to do anything that comes out of your real self. If you've grown up in this kind of community you should know that you're not going to be rewarded for doing something honest or real.[9]

Yet that negativity has slowly changed to pride in Munro's achievement. In 2002 the town of Wingham opened the Alice Munro Literary Garden, a tribute to its most illustrious native. As recently as 2013, Munro reflected on her longstanding fascination with the area: 'To me, it's the most interesting place in the world. I suppose that's because I know more about it. I find it endlessly fascinating.'[10]

Though born in Wingham, Alice Laidlaw, later Munro, was raised outside the town's boundaries on a farm two kilometres west of the town. 'Our nine-acre farm', she remembers,

> had an unusual location. To the east was the town, the church towers and the tower of the Town Hall visible when the leaves were off the trees, and on the mile or so of road between us and the main street there was a gradual thickening of houses, a turning of dirt paths into sidewalks, an appearance of a lone streetlight, so that you might say we were at the town's farthest edges, though beyond its legal municipal boundaries. But to the west there was only one farmhouse to be seen, and that one far away, at the top of a hill almost at the midpoint in the western horizon.[11]

The farm was a dangerous locale. 'We lived outside the whole social structure because we didn't live in the town and we didn't live in the country', she recalls. 'We lived in this kind of little ghetto where all the bootleggers and prostitutes and hangers-on lived. Those were the people I knew. It was a community of outcasts. I had that feeling about myself.'[12]

Munro's father, Robert Laidlaw (1901–76), born near the village of Blyth – about midway between Wingham and Clinton – was a shy only child, the product of a prosperous marriage of Presbyterian Scots. Although his parents wanted him to attend university, he dropped out of school to pursue a life of hunting and trapping in the bush, selling pelts of foxes, muskrat, and mink. In 1925 he purchased his first pair of Norwegian silver foxes and started to breed them in pens he built on his father's farm. Munro's mother, Anne Clarke Chamney (1898–1959), came 'from a much poorer home, a poorer farm' than her father's residence, this one in Scotch Corners not far from Carleton Place in the Ottawa Valley. A member of the Church of England, she had escaped a confining home life to complete high school in Carleton Place and 'become a schoolteacher by her own desperate efforts',[13] both in Alberta and in Ontario. The two married in 1927, and money from Anne's teaching helped to purchase the nine-acre farm outside Wingham: 'they came and picked out the place where they would live for the rest of their lives, on the Maitland River just west of Wingham in Turnberry Township in the County of Huron'.[14] As they embarked on fox-farming, they had too few monetary resources, and the era of such farming – given the imminent depression and, later, the Second World War – was almost ending.

For the first five years of her life, Alice was the cherished only child. Then her brother, Bill, was born in 1936, her sister, Sheila, in 1937. Her long walks to school were a time of passionate daydreaming; indeed her childhood was a time of fantasies, though her fantasies would become more formal, more detached, less personal daydreams. 'When I was quite young I got a feeling about Wingham', she reflected,

> which is only possible, I think, for a child and an outsider. I was an outsider; I came into town every day to go to school, but I didn't belong there. So everything seemed a bit foreign, and particularly clear and important to me. Some houses were mean and threatening, some splendid, showing many urban refinements of life. Certain store-fronts, corners, even sections of sidewalk, took on a powerful, not easily defined, significance. It is not too much to say that every block in that town was some sort of emotional atmosphere for me.[15]

Munro read Hans Christian Andersen's 'The Little Mermaid' when she was seven: 'I started making up a happy ending and I made up an ending that I liked a lot better.'[16] She read Lucy Maud Montgomery for the first time when she was nine or ten years old, and although she devoured *Anne of Green Gables*, Montgomery's first novel, she was more pleased by *Emily of New Moon*, her later novel:

> I decided that it was 'good but different.' By 'good' I meant that it kept me reading at a speedy clip through a series of home-and-school adventures, provided me with a fair number of fearful thrills, and ended with upsets righted and the child-heroine vindicated after her trials, optimistically facing adolescence and a sequel. That was the kind of book I liked, and I read plenty of them. By 'different' I meant that there were other things about the book that got in my way, slowed me down, even annoyed me, because I sensed a different weight about them, a demand for another kind of attention, the possibility of some new balance between myself and a book, between reader and writing, which took me, the reader, by surprise, and did not let me off so easily.[17]

Munro finds ultimately that she cannot address the essence of Montgomery's world:

> I've been trying to say what it was that the ten-year-old reader found that was 'different.' These are the same things the eleven- and twelve- and even the fourteen-year-old reader kept going back for. But I have a sense of things I haven't said that are perhaps the most important. In this book, as in all the books I've loved, there's so much going on behind, or beyond, the proper story. There's life spreading out behind the story – the book's life – and we see it out of the corner of the eye. The mail pails in the dairy-house. Aunt Elizabeth pouring the tallow for the candles. The slightly repulsive splendour of the parlour at Wyther Grange. The corners of the kitchen at New Moon. What

mattered to me finally in this book, what was to matter most to me in books from then on, was knowing more about that life than I'd been told, and more than I can tell.[18]

This is Munro looking back from her adult perspective on her earlier world as a child immersed and troubled by her readings. About Montgomery, who fascinated her, she would later remark:

> Montgomery's writing life I consider a tragedy because it's what happens to the real writer under certain circumstances where she feels her position as a minister's wife only allows her to get away with certain things where she couldn't overcome things in her own background and in herself, probably, and where she did write most successfully for the market.[19]

As a young child, Munro read many, many other books, including, for example, western writer Zane Grey; when she encountered him, she began to invent many stories in which she was a shooting-from-the-hip western showgirl.

> When I was eleven or twelve I had worked out – mostly in my walks to and from school – an adventure-narrative inspired mostly by *The Last of the Mohicans*, and by the true story of the fourteen-year-old heroine Madeleine de Verchères, who held her family farm against the Iroquois near Montreal in 1692. The devouring woods, the bears, and the Indians, the perilous fields outside the palisades.[20]

Then, in her early teens, Munro read *Wuthering Heights*, which 'really excited me beyond anything that was happening in my real life. I think I probably read it thereafter constantly for four or five years. I was really reading it all the time.'[21] In these years, Emily Brontë's novel was a source of constant inspiration:

> I know other things in *Wuthering Heights* delighted me, not the romanticism but the things that she did about the farm, the house, the fields. I remember something about the little brooks where the snow was melting and all that kind of detail which I think you have to do if you want to make up a novel of strong emotions that's credible. And that is one of the things I loved about it. It was the way I could visualize everything – the way I was really living in that house.[22]

The power of the novel consumed Munro. 'Its long shadow fell over all the remaining years of my adolescence, and I carried in my head a whole demonic tragedy in which people were riven by love, blasted by curses, and died young, all in a landscape of windy moors inserted into Huron County.'[23]

In high school, where students who brought their lunches gained noon-time access to classrooms should they wish to study, Munro began writing a novel, *Charlotte Muir*. 'It was imitation *Wuthering Heights*', she recalls. 'Strange and occult, all about love that is stronger than death. I was wonderfully satisfied with it at the time.'[24] 'When I started to write the dreadful things I did write when I was about fifteen', she said, 'I made the glorious leap from being a victim of my own ineptness and self-conscious miseries to being a godlike arranger of patterns and destinies, even if they were all in my head; I have never leapt back.'[25] Years later, her stepmother threw out Munro's old school notebooks and her early novel, too.

Although Canada has a distinguished history of short story writers, beginning at least as early as the animal stories of Charles G. D. Roberts and Ernest Thompson Seton and continuing with the stories of Morley Callaghan, Munro found her early inspiration in the writers of the American South, who reverberated with her because she recognized that they came from a similar region:

> The writers who first excited me were the writers of the American South, because I felt there a country being depicted that was like my own. I can think of several writers now who are working out of Southwestern Ontario. It is rich in possibilities in this way. I mean the part of the country I come from is absolutely Gothic. You can't get it all down ... It's a very rooted kind of place. I think the kind of writing I do is almost anachronistic, because it's so rooted in one place, and most people, even of my own age, do not have a place like this any more, and it's something that may not have meaning very much longer. I mean this kind of writing.[26]

Twenty years later, she observed:

> The writers of the American South were the first writers who really moved me because they showed me that you could write about small towns, rural people, and that kind of life I knew very well. But the thing about the Southern writers that interested me, without my really being aware of it, was that all the Southern writers whom I really loved were women. I didn't really like Faulkner that much. I loved Eudora Welty, Flannery O'Connor, Katherine Ann Porter, Carson McCullers. There was a feeling that women could write about the freakish, the marginal ... I came to feel that was our territory, whereas the mainstream big novel about real life was men's territory. I don't know how I got that feeling of being on the margins, it wasn't that I was *pushed* there. Maybe it was because I grew up on a margin. I knew there was something about the great writers I felt shut out from, but I didn't know quite what it was.[27]

The writer she admired most was not O'Connor, a fiction writer with a strong Christian point of view, but Welty: 'her work has always seemed more intimately real to me than any other writer's'.[28] 'The writer I adored', she confessed in 2012, 'was Eudora Welty. I still do. I would never try to copy her – she's too good and too much herself.'[29]

Munro's family was Protestant, her father growing up in a Presbyterian family and her mother coming from an Irish-Protestant background. During her youth, her family belonged to the United Church, which was established in 1925, though they were not actively involved in a church which typically catered to middle-class families living in town. A teenager within the loosely structured folds of the United Church, Munro abandoned her church affiliation in her growing devotion to art.

In her graduating high school class, Munro came first, winning a two-year scholarship to the University of Western Ontario with the top marks in English of all incoming students. She enrolled in journalism, publishing her first story in the April 1950 issue of the student publication *Folio*, then switched to English in her second year. At the end of the year, she received an award for obtaining the highest marks in English.

During her time at university, she met Jim Munro, a right-wing, upper-middle-class student from Oakville, Ontario; his father was an auditor for Eaton's department store in Toronto. 'I was nineteen years old when I became engaged, twenty on my wedding day', she writes. 'My husband was the first boyfriend I ever had.'[30] After the pair married on 29 December 1951, in 'a quiet ceremony at the home of the bride's parents' in Wingham,[31] they departed for Vancouver, where Jim had a job in the textile department of Eaton's and Alice worked as an assistant in the Vancouver Public Library.

Although Munro wished to continue at the University of Western Ontario, her two-year scholarship ended. She applied to have it extended – her request was turned down. Nor was she 'allowed to take out books, because I did not graduate, but I can use my husband's card'.[32]

In Wingham, her mother, who had shown signs of Parkinson's disease from the early 1940s, was steadily declining in her ability to walk and to talk. She died in 1959. 'I did not go home for my mother's last illness or for her funeral', recalls Munro. 'I had two small children and nobody in Vancouver to leave them with.'[33] After his wife's death, her father married Mary Etta Laidlaw in 1969, the widow of one of his cousins; she ran a store in Blyth, while he took employment at the local foundry, then raised turkeys till he was past seventy. 'It was after giving up such work that he took up writing. He began to write reminiscent pieces and to turn some of them into stories, which were published in an excellent though short-lived local magazine', Munro remembers. 'And not long before his death he completed a novel about pioneer life, called *The Macgregors*.'[34] Her father died in 1976.

During her years in Vancouver (a daughter, Sheila, was born in 1953; a second, Catherine, who lived only one day, in 1955; a third daughter, Jenny, in 1957) and after her move to Victoria in 1963 (a further daughter, Andrea, was born in 1966), where she and her husband founded Munro's

Books, Munro wrote steadily when she had the time. 'Jim Munro', she said, 'helped me, just by believing I was a writer. Not that I would become one, that I was one.'³⁵

In this period Robert Weaver (1921–85), a radio programmer for the Canadian Broadcasting Corporation, featured some then relatively unknown Canadian writers for his programme, *Canadian Short Stories*. Munro sold him a story in 1951, and for the next ten years and more he provided her with literary support.

> He was almost the only person I knew who had anything to do with the world of writing. He was one of the two – or possibly three – people who took my writing seriously. Sometimes he would reconsider a story in which no changes had been made, and occasionally reverse an opinion, finding some power or grace in it he hadn't been able to see before. He also wrote me letters when I hadn't sent him anything, when I hadn't written anything, and it was these letters, especially, that gave me nourishment and hope.³⁶

In 1956 Weaver founded the literary magazine *Tamarack Review*, which featured such new writers as Margaret Atwood and Mordecai Richler, and published many of Munro's early stories; an esteemed magazine, it lasted until 1982. Munro later dedicated *The Moons of Jupiter* to Weaver.

Through the 1950s, 'Mostly, all through my twenties all I did was read. I read most of the writers of the twentieth century that you're supposed to have read.'³⁷ And she 'sold [to] – or I should say I was *published* in' – a variety of Canadian magazines. 'All through the '50's there were just dribbles. There weren't many markets, none that I knew about. Of course I wasn't in touch with any other people who were writing during that decade either. It never bothered me.'³⁸ At this time, she applied for a Canada Council grant, 'when I really needed it', she recalls.

> I said it was to get a cleaning woman and babysitters. I did not get it, and I heard via the grapevine that – I do not know how true it was – part of the reason was that a demand like this just was not taken seriously. I imagine that men who said they had to go to Morocco or Japan would get grants. Women who said they needed babysitters would not, and this is true from my own experience.³⁹

During this period, Munro attended some events in the writing community. On 28 January 1956, for example, she attended a session at the University of British Columbia on 'How Does a Writer Reach his Audience?' The speaker, Ethel Wilson, was a writer she revered, and the lecture was the first extended paper Wilson had read in public; the young writer did not introduce herself to the older writer, though she knew her writings. 'I was *enormously* excited by her work because the style was such an enormous pleasure in itself', she reflected. 'It was important to me that a Canadian writer was using so elegant a style. You know I don't mean style in the superficial sense, but that a point of view so complex and ironic was possible in Canadian literature.'[40] Six years later, interestingly, Wilson happened to read Munro's 'The Office', which she applauded: 'I have read and re-read with sympathetic pleasure a piece named *The Office*, by Alice Munro, appearing in *The Montrealer*. Why my heart warmed and expanded towards Mrs Munro is because I have never before seen in print an admission of a frailty, a peculiarity, a folly, or an honesty which I share with her.'[41] Explaining how difficult it is for a woman to assert her writing talent in a social context, the story spoke directly to Wilson's own reticence: 'What an *excellent* thing by Alice Munro. I don't know when I've read a short piece that so pleased me. Isn't she *good!*'[42]

The Munros became friends with Jack and Margaret Laurence, who had come to Vancouver after their African sojourn. Munro met Laurence in 1960 at the launch of Laurence's first novel, *This Side Jordan*, and they saw each other socially. 'We became very friendly almost immediately, but not close friends in the sense that we tried to see more of each other a lot, because I think we were both desperate for time', recalls Munro.[43]

In 1967 an editor at Ryerson Press, Earle Toppings, who had been carefully following Munro's writing, invited her to put together some of her stories:

> I'd been writing these stories over the years and finally an editor at Ryerson Press, a Canadian publisher that has since been taken over by McGraw-Hill, wrote and asked me if I had enough stories for a book. Originally he was going to put me in a book with two or three other writers. That fell through, but he still had a bunch of my stories. Then he quit but passed me onto another editor, who said, 'If you could write three more stories, we'd have a book.' And so I wrote 'Images,' 'Walker Brothers Cowboy,' and 'Postcard' during the last year before the book was published.[44]

'Ryerson was pretty good about publishing Canadian books', she acknowledges. 'They weren't very good about marketing them. In fact they had no notion at all of marketing, but they did take chances.'[45] Dedicated to her father, *Dance of the Happy Shades* won the Governor General's Award, the highest fiction award in Canada.

While *Dance of the Happy Shades* reflects a young writer looking at the world outside herself, *Lives of Girls and Women*, Munro's next collection and 'the only sort of thing approaching a novel that I've done,'[46] reflects the writer looking inside herself to map her own personal growth. The first edition states on the copyright page, 'This novel is autobiographical in form but not in fact. My family, neighbours and friends did not serve as models', and Munro observes that the book 'could be called an autobiographical novel ... most of the incidents are changed versions of real incidents. *Some* are completely invented but the emotional reality, the girl's feeling for her mother, for men, for life is all ... it's all solidly autobiographical. I would not disclaim this at all.'[47] The narrator of the stories, now in her thirties, tells of growing up in the small provincial town of Jubilee, Ontario, the expressed setting of some of *Dance of the Happy Shades*. As she stands back and wonders about her coming-of-age in this stultifying but strangely interesting town, she writes her own *Bildungsroman*: 'I wanted to write the kind of thing about a young girl's sexual experience that had often been written about boys.'[48] Dedicated to Jim Munro, *Lives of Girls and Women* won the first Canadian Booksellers Award and was an alternate selection for the Literary Guild's Book-of-the-Month Club in both Canada and the United States, the first piece of Canadian fiction ever selected by the Guild.

For Munro, the early 1970s were a period of artistic achievement and personal development. With the slow dissolution of her marriage, she accepted in 1973 a proposal to teach a summer-school creative writing course at Notre Dame University in Nelson, British Columbia, her three daughters accompanying her. When she returned to Victoria later that summer, she stayed with her children in a motel. She then accepted an offer from York University in Toronto to teach one day a week. She commuted there by train, while living with her two younger daughters in London, Ontario. In 1973, too, she received a Canada Council Senior Arts Grant, only the second time she had applied to the Council.

In January 1974 Munro resigned her York job, agreeing to be the writer-in-residence at the University of Western Ontario for 1974–5. While she was there, Brandon Conron of the Department of English nominated her for an honorary doctor of letters, which was awarded on 9 June 1976: 'Here, Mr Chancellor, is an Alice who, from everyday experience, has created her own Wonderland, making of it a looking glass through which we begin to identify vital aspects of our world and of ourselves.' The degree, which she accepted because she had never received an undergraduate degree, is her sole honorary degree. 'What good is an honorary degree?' she wonders aloud to anyone who raises the subject. In 1974, too, Munro published a new collection of stories, *Something I've Been Meaning to Tell You*, dedicated to her three daughters.

The academic world was no home for Munro. 'You have to be available to people, that's part of the problem', she said.

The information you give people they could find in a library. You have to give a lot and after a while no matter how hard you try not to, you play a role. You have an Alice Munro character that you play, and you've found out that people accept it. I wind up feeling like a total fraud. I like the students, but I think if I had to work regularly I would rather get a job in a store.[49]

She confessed: 'I'm not at all good in classroom work because I don't, I can't talk generally and I can't talk to the group. And I don't like doing anybody's story when there are other people around. I don't like the workshop situation. I like the one-to-one situation.'[50] Later still, when Joseph Kertes, director of the Humber School for Writers, invited her to teach in a 1994 summer workshop, joining such authors as Tim O'Brien and Carol Shields, she politely but firmly declined: 'I really have no wisdom at all about writing, except that it doesn't get easier.'

Gerald Fremlin, a senior at the University of Western Ontario and a war veteran when Munro was a freshman student, had received one of her early stories, being mistaken for the editor of the student journal. When the story was published, he wrote her a fan letter comparing her writing to Chekhov's. In 1974, as yet unmarried, he happened to hear a radio interview with her where she mentioned that she was separated from her husband. Retired from his job as a government geographer – he was one of the editors of the *National Atlas of Canada* – he telephoned her and suggested that they meet for a drink. By the end of 1974 Munro knew that she wanted to live with him, and in the summer of 1975 she moved into the house where he was born so that they could care for his ageing mother; when his mother entered a nursing home, he visited her every day, Munro visited her every other day. Clinton was also close enough to Wingham that the couple could keep a watchful eye on Munro's ageing father and her stepmother. She recalls:

> I met this man I had known a long time ago who came from the area I came from, and we decided to live together and to go back to this rural community because his mother was alone and couldn't manage on her own, and my father was old and my stepmother was old, and we went back for these people and we thought we'd stay about a year or until such time as they were not around any more ... And of course they've been dead for quite a while, and we're still there.[51]

Moreover, Huron County continued to have a tremendous hold on her and her artistic imagination:

> One of the reasons to stay now is that the landscape is so important to both of us. It's a great thing that we have in common. And thanks to Gerry I appreciate it in such a different way. I couldn't possess any other landscape or country or lake or town in this way. And I realize that now, so I'll never leave.[52]

To return to Huron County. To live about thirty-five kilometres south of her birthplace. Events had come full circle, and Munro was now securely settled in another town in Huron County where she could write of the landscape and its people. After twenty years in the west, she had come home. One day she was visiting her home town, taking the bus from London to Wingham, as she did when she was a student at the University of Western Ontario. Now grey-haired, the bus driver was the same one from twenty years ago. As she presented her ticket, he remarked: 'Hello, Alice. Where have you been?'

On her return to her own county, Munro became an avid supporter of the summer Blyth Festival, founded in 1975 to develop plays that reflect the culture and concerns of the people of southwestern Ontario. In 1976 the festival produced her drama, *How I Met My Husband*, and she continued to be a staunch supporter of the festival, attending the plays, helping to serve dinners before the theatre, and, from time to time, acting and even substituting when a cast member was indisposed. Michael Ondaatje remembers driving to Blyth in 1982 to see Janet Amos's play, *Down Under*, only to find a notice in the programme: 'For today's performance of *Down Under*, Janet Amos will play the part of Henriette Deveau and Alice Munro will play the part of Felice Lachance.' Though often mentioned during the play, Lachance entered only at the end and had a single line of dialogue.

In 1974 Virginia Barber wrote to Munro to ask if she could be her agent; Munro declined the request. Two years later, she accepted Barber's offer, and Barber sold 'Royal Beatings', the opening story of *Who Do You Think You Are?*, to *The New Yorker*, thus beginning a relationship which, the following year, included a contract for right-of-first-refusal. '*The New Yorker* has the right of first refusal of my stories; they don't fiddle around much with style or content except that they're fastidious about punctuation and fidelity to fact and they have a feeling of propriety about raw sex scenes,' she commented in 1986. 'Anyway, I don't write with an eye to the so-called New Yorker house style; it's a mistake for writers to gear their stories for a certain market.'[53]

In 1977 Munro's screenplay *1847: the Irish* was filmed and broadcast the following year as part of the television series *The Newcomers*. In the same year, she became the first Canadian winner of the Canada–Australia Literary Prize, presented jointly by the Australia Council and Canada's Department of External Affairs.

Munro published *Who Do You Think You Are?* in 1978; the road to the book's completion was not easy. Another series of interconnected stories of growing up and, more importantly, finding one's way in the world, a darker version of *Lives of Girls and Women*, the book caused Munro immense trouble and financial hardship. Originally a book of stories about Janet and about Rose, the stories gradually came together as a series of stories about Rose. She recalls:

> [A]ll of a sudden I saw how all these would go together as Rose stories ... The book was already in galleys. So I got them to pull it out at my expense, which was over $2,000. I then rewrote it. I wrote 'Who Do You Think You Are?' in a weekend and rewrote everything else in a week. So that with the printers working overtime, which I paid for, they could get the book out into the fall season. A book cannot go on the Canadian market later than about mid-November, or its chances for Christmas sales are just dead. So we had to get it out by that time. All of which things, having been a bookseller, I understand.[54]

She confesses: 'I was just very determined. Even if it had cost me twice as much I would have done it. You see, I knew all along the book wasn't right.'[55] Dedicated to Gerald Fremlin, *Who Do You Think You Are?* won another Governor General's Award.

Who Do You Think You Are? received a new title, *The Beggar Maid: Stories of Flo and Rose*, when it was published in the United States. The American publisher, Munro recalls, 'felt the colloquial put-down was not familiar to Americans. I had to accept that, though I think it probably is in certain parts of the US anyway.'[56] The British edition appeared with the American title, too.

It was in the autumn of 1979 that I first met Munro. She accepted my invitation to give a reading at the University of Ottawa where her friend Jack Hodgins was writer-in-residence. When she arrived that October, I went to the Holiday Inn to meet her. As we made our way to the reading, she told me she wanted to read 'The Ottawa Valley', a story she had never read before an audience; she did not know if she could read the entire story, including its remarkable conclusion. She did read it from its beginning to its painful ending. Our friendship began that afternoon, and a personal appreciation of this remarkable writer has continued to develop and to deepen to this day.

Munro knew what she wanted to do: write short stories, which would become increasingly long and increasingly complex, out of her Huron County home. 'When I first went back to Clinton, I remembered a lot of things that I had forgotten; and that's why I wrote some of the earlier material in *Who Do You Think You Are?*. It seemed to me that I wasn't finished with this', she says. 'I *was* conscious of attitudes that I wanted to do more with, and the shape of people's lives, the shape of their stories, the whole business of how life is made into a story by the people who live it, and then the whole town sort of makes its own story.'[57]

In 1981 Munro travelled with six other Canadian writers to the People's Republic of China, where she spent her fiftieth birthday. 'There is no *alone* in China', she commented.

> You know, the way the streets are just full of people, day and night; there was just this moving river of people in and out of the buildings, on the streets. I'd never, never had that feeling of crowds, especially crowded fields where so many people were working. The first week when I was back in Ontario and would look into a field and see one enormous machine instead of a hundred people, it seemed very strange; and the streets seemed terribly empty.[58]

In 1982 she joined me in Norway and Sweden to promote the Norwegian translation of *Who Do You Think You Are?*, and in the autumn her fifth collection, *The Moons of Jupiter*, was published. Four years later, her sixth collection, *The Progress of Love*, appeared, winning a third Governor General's Award. In the same year, Munro became the first winner of the Marian Engel Award, a prize of $10,000 for a Canadian woman who has created a distinguished and continuing body of work; Engel herself had died of cancer the preceding year. The award meant a great deal to Munro:

> Part of that is my memories of Marian and a sort of pride in getting the first award that has her name on it – but it also means something because it is a sizable award that we are starting in Canada, where there has not been much like this for writers. It is the fact of the award existing that pleases me a lot – and if my getting it is a sort of start to it, then that's great.[59]

In the later 1980s Munro extended her influence on Canadian literature. In February 1988 I accepted an invitation to become General Editor of the New Canadian Library. As part of the redesign of the series, I envisioned a three-person Advisory Board. The first person I telephoned was Munro. I told her about the 'new' series, each book containing a biography and a bibliography I would compile and an afterword by a distinguished critic or writer. She agreed to serve on the Advisory Board, adding ironically, 'And, I suppose, you will want me to write an afterword?' 'Yes', I replied, 'if I can get the rights to *Emily of New Moon*.' The other members of the Board are critic William New and novelist and short-story author Guy Vanderhaeghe. Our few meetings have taken place in Toronto and Vancouver, Halifax, Calgary, and Victoria, and for each meeting, Munro read every title we were considering, giving penetrating critiques of all the books. In addition to being a great fiction writer, she is an astute and discerning reader of fiction, too.

Meanwhile, Munro continued to garner further acclaim for her fiction. *Friend of My Youth* appeared in 1990, four years after *The Progress of Love*, winning the Trillium Book Award for the best book published by an Ontario author. The following April, Munro received the $50,000 Molson Prize for her 'outstanding lifetime contributions to the cultural and intellectual life of Canada'.

In the 1990s, too, Munro expanded her influence on Canadian fiction. In September 1993 I had to telephone her again. Jack Rabinovitch wished to establish the Giller Prize, honouring the best volume of Canadian fiction (novel or collection of short stories) published in English or translated into English. At his invitation, Mordecai Richler and I agreed to serve as jurors for the first three years of the prize: we sought to establish a quality award for quality work. A third juror was needed, and the two of us wished to ask Munro. I initiated a few telephone discussions. She informed me that she had a book coming out the following year, *Open Secrets*, her ninth collection; she agreed to join us so that her own book would not qualify for the prize. At the announcement of our shortlist, Munro observed: 'I chose the writers who seemed to me to have the truest voices and the most reliable skills and who gave me as a reader the most lively and constant pleasure.' On the evening of the prize giving, Richler and I joked about giving the award to Munro despite her disqualification, for she had written the finest work of fiction in that year.[60]

Open Secrets received the W. H. Smith Award in Britain as the best book of the year, and in the United States Munro became the first non-American to receive the PEN/Malamud Award for Excellence in Short Fiction. The following year, she received the Lannan Foundation Literary Award for Fiction for the exceptional quality of her writing. Her next collection, *The Love of a Good Woman* (1998), won the year's Giller Prize as well as the National Book Critics Circle Award for Fiction, making Munro the first Canadian to win the American honour.

In this century, Munro has continued her practice of writing, publishing five more collections: *Hateship, Friendship, Courtship, Loveship, Marriage* (2001), *Runaway* (2004), *The View from Castle Rock* (2006), *Too Much Happiness* (2009), and *Dear Life* (2012). Each volume finds her probing more deeply, analysing more penetratingly the foibles and the fates of individual people caught in the dilemmas of their own contemporary world. And sometimes, as in the partly autobiographical *The View from Castle Rock* and in the four brief vignettes that close *Dear Life*, the individual people become the author herself.

In a 1973 interview Munro gave to a young graduate student at the University of New Brunswick, she reflected on what she was doing in her fiction:

> The adult narrator has the ability to detect and talk about the confusion. I don't feel that the confusion is ever resolved. And there is some kind of a central mystery, as in 'Walker Brothers Cowboy,' that is there for the adult narrator as well as it was for the child. I feel that all life becomes even *more* mysterious

and difficult. And the whole act of writing is more an attempt at recognition than of understanding, because I don't understand many things. I feel a kind of satisfaction in just approaching something that is mysterious and important. Then writing is the act of approach and recognition. I believe that we don't solve these things – in fact our explanations take us further away.[61]

This is precisely what Munro has done and continues to do in her writing: the act of recognition rather than the act of explanation. She seeks to approach the 'mysterious and difficult' and recognize the complexity of the human condition. To offer explanations is beyond the realm of her art; 'in fact our explanations take us further away'. And what she shows in her fiction is the irresolvability and yet the sustainability of life itself. 'What I have is people going on. Just as if every day had its own pitfalls and discoveries and it doesn't make much difference whether the heroine ends up married or living in a room by herself. Or how she ends up at all. Because we finally end up dead', she commented in 1982.

> There are just flashes of things we know and find out. I don't see life very much in terms of progress. I don't feel at all pessimistic. I rather like the idea that we go on and we don't know what's happening and we don't know what we'll find. We think we've got things figured out and then they turn around on us. No state of mind is permanent. It just all has to be there.[62]

And ten years later, she exclaimed:

> If you ask me what I believe as a person, I'd say I do think life gets better, or one's ability to put up with it gets better. But I think things change. That's really one of the things that interest me so much in writing, and in observing people, is that things keep changing. Cherished beliefs change. Ways of dealing with life change. The importance of certain things in life changes. All this seems to me endlessly interesting. I think that is the thing that doesn't change, or that I certainly hope doesn't change. If you find life interesting, it just goes on being so.[63]

While publishing her five collections, Munro has also accepted numerous honours. In 2001 she won the Rea Award for Lifetime Achievement and the O. Henry Award for Continuing Achievement in Short Fiction. For *Runaway*, she received her second Giller Prize; at her own request, her subsequent books were not entered in the annual competition. In 2009 she won the Man Booker International Prize for her lifetime body of work. And in 2013 she received the Nobel Prize for Literature, heralded as 'the master of the contemporary short story'.

On our first meeting in 1979, Munro talked about *Who Do You Think You Are?*, her latest and, she then said, her last collection; she found disconcerting the consternation and stress of a new book and its attendant publicity. She had already expressed this desire after the publication of *Something I've Been*

Meaning to Tell You, and she has reiterated these feelings after each subsequent book's publication. With the publication of *Dear Life*, however, she is putting down her pen for the final time. 'What I feel now is that I don't have the energy anymore', she stated. 'Starting off as I did at a time when women didn't do much else besides bring up children – it's very hard, and you get very tired. I feel a bit tired now – pleasantly tired. There is a nice feeling about being just like everyone else now.' Writing was a mainstay of her life. When Gerald Fremlin died on 17 April 2013, Munro lost her other mainstay. 'The most important thing in my life is gone. No, not the most important thing. The most important was my husband, and now they're both gone', she said.[64]

'It seems to me this is what writing is, when it's real', Munro commented back in 1970, 'a straining of something immense and varied, a whole dense vision of the world, into whatever confines the writer has learned to make for it, and this process, unless you are Shakespeare or Tolstoy, must be accompanied by regret; fortunately it is often accompanied by gleeful satisfactions as well.'[65]

Sitting in her late nineteenth-century home on a dead-end avenue off the main streets of Clinton, Munro remains quiet and reticent but not shy. The recipient of every major fiction award in Canada and abroad, she is still the careful and perceptive observer and chronicler of life as it takes place in the world of Huron County. 'I feel that I've done what I wanted to do', she says, 'and that makes me feel fairly content.'[66]

Notes

1 Alice Munro, 'Going to the Lake', *Ontario: a Bicentennial Tribute* (Toronto: Key Porter Books, 1983), 52.
2 J. R. (Tim) Struthers, 'The Real Material: an Interview with Alice Munro', in Louis K. MacKendrick (ed.), *Probable Fictions: Alice Munro's Narrative Acts* (Downsview, Ont.: ECW Press, 1983), 33.
3 Alice Munro, 'Introduction', in *Selected Stories* (Toronto: Penguin, 1998), x–xi.
4 Patricia Hluchy, 'Alice Munro', *Maclean's* (21 December 1998), 67.
5 Mari Stainsby, 'Alice Munro Talks with Mari Stainsby', *British Columbia Library Quarterly* 35, 1 (July 1971), 30.
6 Geoff Hancock, 'An Interview with Alice Munro', *Canadian Fiction Magazine* 43 (1982), 93.
7 Graeme Gibson, *Eleven Canadian Novelists* (Toronto: House of Anansi Press, 1973), 246.
8 'Writing's Something I Did, Like the Ironing', *Globe and Mail* (11 December 1982), ET1.
9 J. A. Wainwright (ed.), *A Very Large Soul: Selected Letters of Margaret Laurence to Canadian Writers* (Dunvegan, Ont.: Cormorant Books, 1995), 143.
10 Charles McGrath, 'Putting Down her Pen to Let the World In', *New York Times* (2 July 2013), C7.

11 'Working for a Living', in *The View from Castle Rock* (Toronto: McClelland & Stewart, 2006), 147.
12 'What Is', in Alan Twigg (ed.), *For Openers* (Madeira Park, BC: Harbour Publishing, 1981), 18.
13 'Working for a Living', 138.
14 Ibid., 139–40.
15 'An Open Letter', *Jubilee* 1 [1974], 6.
16 'An Interview with Alice Munro', *Canadian Children's Literature* 53 (1989), 21.
17 'Afterword', in *Emily of New Moon* (Toronto: McClelland & Stewart, 1989), 357.
18 Ibid., 360–1.
19 Struthers, 'The Real Material', 19.
20 'Introduction', *Selected Stories*, xi.
21 'An Interview with Alice Munro', *Canadian Children's Literature*, 18.
22 Harold Horwood, 'Interview with Alice Munro', in Judith Miller (ed.), *The Art of Alice Munro: Saying the Unsayable* (Waterloo, Ont.: University of Waterloo Press, 1984), 124.
23 'Introduction', *Selected Stories*, xi.
24 Martin Knelman, 'The Past, the Present, and Alice Munro', *Saturday Night* 94, 9 (November 1979), 18.
25 'Author's Commentary', in John Metcalf (ed.), *Sixteen by Twelve: Short Stories by Canadian Writers* (Toronto: Ryerson, 1970), 125.
26 Gibson, *Eleven Canadian Novelists*, 248–9.
27 Alice Munro, 'The Art of Fiction', *The Paris Review* 36, 131 (Summer 1994), 255–6.
28 Jill Gardiner, 'The Early Short Stories of Alice Munro', MA thesis, University of New Brunswick, 1973, 'Appendix', 172.
29 Deborah Treisman, 'On "Dear Life": an Interview with Alice Munro', *The New Yorker* (20 November 2012).
30 'The Ticket', in *Dear Life* (Toronto: McClelland & Stewart, 2012), 258.
31 *Wingham Advance Times*, 2 January 1952.
32 'What Do You Want For?' in *The View from Castle Rock*, 325.
33 'Dear Life', in *Dear Life*, 319.
34 'Working for a Living', 167.
35 Hancock, 'An Interview with Alice Munro', 80.
36 Alice Munro, 'Foreword', in Robert Weaver (ed.), *The Anthology Anthology: Selection from 30 Years of CBC Radio's 'Anthology'* (Toronto: Macmillan, 1984), ix.
37 Robert Thacker, *Alice Munro: Writing her Lives* (Toronto: McClelland & Stewart, 2005), 116.
38 Horwood, 'Interview with Alice Munro', 127.
39 'An Intimate Appeal', *Maclean's* (17 November 1986), 12j.
40 Struthers, 'The Real Material', 18.
41 'Admissions, Seabirds, and People', in David Stouck (ed.), *Ethel Wilson: Stories, Essays, and Letters* (Vancouver, BC: University of British Columbia Press, 1987), 107.
42 Quoted in David Stouck, *Ethel Wilson: a Critical Biography* (University of Toronto Press, 2003), 268–9.

43 Wainwright, *A Very Large Soul*, 142.
44 Munro, 'The Art of Fiction', 235.
45 Horwood, 'Interview with Alice Munro', 127.
46 Ibid., 131.
47 John Metcalf, 'A Conversation with Alice Munro', *Journal of Canadian Fiction* 1, 4 (1972), 58.
48 Hancock, 'An Interview with Alice Munro', 112.
49 Knelman, 'The Past, the Present, and Alice Munro', 22.
50 Hancock, 'An Interview with Alice Munro', 107.
51 Mervyn Rothstein, 'Canada's Alice Munro Finds Excitement in Short-Story Form', *The New York Times* (10 November 1986), C17.
52 *The Paris Review*, 249.
53 Ken Adachi, 'Alice Munro: At the Very Top of her Form', *The Sunday Star* (21 September 1986), G11.
54 Struthers, 'The Real Material', 30.
55 Knelman, 'The Past, the Present, and Alice Munro', 16.
56 Struthers, 'The Real Material', 29.
57 Ibid., 33.
58 'Through the Jade Curtain', in Gary Geddes, Robert Kroetsch, Adele Wiseman, Patrick Lane, Alice Munro, Suzanne Paradis and Geoffrey Hancock, *Chinada: Memoirs of the Gang of Seven* (Dunvegan, Ont.: Quadrant, 1982), 51–2.
59 'An Intimate Appeal', 12j.
60 Munro did get revenge, however. In a profile of her that autumn, she commented about me: 'No one else can get me to do anything, no one else can. It's a good thing he doesn't want me to be a cocaine runner.' (Val Ross, 'A Writer called Alice', *Globe and Mail* (1 October 1994), C1.)
61 Gardiner, *The Early Short Stories of Alice Munro*, 178.
62 Hancock, 'An Interview with Alice Munro', 102.
63 Eleanor Wachtel, 'An Interview with Alice Munro', *Brick* 40 (Winter 1991), 52.
64 McGrath, 'Putting Down her Pen to Let the World In', C7.
65 'Author's Commentary', *Sixteen by Twelve*, 126.
66 McGrath, 'Putting Down her Pen to Let the World In', C7.

2

MERILYN SIMONDS

Where do you think you are?

Place in the short stories of Alice Munro

> After supper my father says, 'Want to go down and see if the Lake's still there?'[1]

From the opening line of the first story in Alice Munro's inaugural collection of short fiction, there it is: place. The narrator leaves her mother sewing in the dining room and her little brother calling mournfully for his sister to bring back an ice cream cone – homely details that balance her father's remarkable and terrifying question: Is the Lake still there?

Might it have shifted in the night? Might they?

If you had asked me about place in Alice Munro's fiction when I first read this story – it was 1968 and I was 19, living in a village populated by five generations of my family (within the cemetery and without), not more than an hour cross-country from Munro's home town – I would have said that her stories were portraits of small-town southwestern Ontario. Deadly accurate, horrifying, Alex Colville-like representations of a place that I, too, couldn't wait to escape. But over the past three months, as I re-read not only the stories of that first collection, *Dance of the Happy Shades*, but every story she has published since, I shivered with an entirely different dread. Place, in Alice Munro, is a chimera: deceptive, implausible, sometimes one thing, sometimes another, made up of scales, woolly skin, a lion's roar, and a feral laugh that, once heard, haunts forever.

'*La Mer Douce*, the French had called this lake', Munro writes in *Friend of My Youth*, mistranslating *douce* as sweet and mild, instead of fresh water. 'But of course it could change colour in an hour; it could turn ugly, according to the wind and what was stirred up from the bottom.'[2]

The undercurrents and what they stir up: that is what attracts Munro's writerly attention.

Going on the road

Munro's first story, 'Walker Brothers Cowboy', takes place in Tuppertown, 'an old town on Lake Huron, an old grain port'.[3] As the narrator and her father walk towards the lake, 'the town falls away in a defeated jumble of sheds and small junkyards, the sidewalk gives up and we are walking on a sandy path with burdocks, plantains, humble nameless weeds all around'.[4]

This walk into the unfamiliar is a prelude to another, less innocent journey into the unknown. The father is a Walker Brothers salesman (modelled on the travellers who sold Watkins baking products and health tonics door to door in rural Ontario until the end of the last century, now available on the Internet and at Wal-Mart). One day, his daughter is invited to travel with him when he goes on the road. Unexpectedly, he drives out of his territory where he becomes a different person, a man with a past and a former girlfriend, Miss Cronin, who, shockingly, serves him whiskey in his teacup and invites him to dance. As they head home, the daughter says,

> I feel my father's life flowing back from our car in the last of the afternoon, darkening and turning strange, like a landscape that has an enchantment on it, making it kindly, ordinary and familiar while you are looking at it, but changing it, once your back is turned, into something you will never know, with all kinds of weathers, and distances you cannot imagine.[5]

Not only might the lake have shifted, but her father shifts, too, with the landscape.

In 'Images', a story later in that first collection, the father is a traveller of different sort, a trapper who works a line along the Wawanash River. The girl moves through her father's territory with him, checking the traps for muskrat. 'The river curved, I lost my sense of direction', she says, and a man appears, dark-skinned, long-haired, with a hatchet gleaming in his hand. 'All my life I had known there was a man like this and he was behind doors, around the corner at the dark end of the hall.'[6] She stands frozen, electrified, as the man slips through the bushes to her father, who speaks softly to the hermit, calming him. The girl returns home, like Gilgamesh, 'dazed and powerful with secrets'.[7]

There are other travellers, too: a mother who sells encyclopedias, one who travels the countryside in search of antiques, a man named Mr Fullerton who has simply 'gone off on his travels'.[8] Place creates a here and a there. The possibility of travel, of movement into the unknown. And it is in the unknown – there – that Alice Munro's stories reveal their truths.

The wrong side of the river

Alice Munro is not from Wingham, Ontario, as long-time local residents of that town are quick to point out. She was born in the hospital in Wingham, yes, but she grew up across the river, in Morris-Turnberry Township. The poor side of town.

In *Lives of Girls and Women*, the town is called Jubliee. In *Who Do You Think You Are?*, it is Hanratty. In other stories in other collections, it is variously Carstairs, Dalgleish, Gallagher. The names hardly matter. The pattern of settlement is the same: the first homesteaders built their shacks on the banks of fast-flowing rivers that supplied not only transportation and sustenance but power to drive the grain and woollen mills, the engines of future industry.

With a few exceptions – 'Meneseteung', 'A Wilderness Station', 'Too Much Happiness', and the first half of *The View from Castle Rock* – Alice Munro sets her stories in the relatively recent past of the last hundred years. The original pioneers have long since died or moved on; the town has settled firmly into the shape of itself. Spanned now with bridges, the river is no longer a physical barrier, although it defines a real and barely navigable economic and social divide.

> In Hanratty the social structure ran from doctors and dentists and lawyers down to foundry workers and factory workers and draymen; in West Hanratty [on the other side of the river] it ran from factory workers and foundry workers down to large improvident families of casual bootleggers and prostitutes and unsuccessful thieves. Rose thought of her own family as straddling the river, belonging nowhere.[9]

Ironically, the towns in Munro's fiction began on the wrong side of the river. 'This was where the town set out to be, over a hundred years ago,' the narrator explains in 'Spaceships Have Landed', as if the town itself had exercised an intention.

> Mills and hostelries were here. But the river floods persuaded people to move to higher ground. House-plots remained on the map, and roads laid out, but only the one row of houses where people lived was still there, people who were too poor or in some way too stubborn to change – or, at the other extreme, too temporary in their living arrangements to object to the invasion of water.[10]

The young protagonists of these stories don't live in the houses where spring floods watermark the walls. They most often live, as Alice Munro herself did, beyond the flood plain, first at the end of the Flats Road, then at the end of River Street, fictionally described as Del's house in *Lives of Girls and Women*. In 'Dear Life', the last of four stories in that eponymous collection that she introduces as 'the closest ... things I have to say about my own life', Munro writes,

> I lived when I was young at the end of a long road, or a road that seemed long to me. Back behind me ... was the real town with its activity and its sidewalks and its streetlights for after dark. Marking the end of town were two bridges over the Maitland River ... Then there was a slight hollow, a couple of rickety houses that got flooded every spring, but that people – different people – always came and lived in anyway ... After that, the road divided, one part of it going south up a hill and over the river again to become a genuine highway, and the other jogging around the old fairgrounds to turn west.
> That westward road was mine.[11]

At the end of that road was – and still is – the house where Alice Munro grew up. It is a classic southwestern Ontario two-storey red-brick building with a second-floor door that opens on to thin air, one of thousands just like it that wait at the end of long lanes throughout Ontario. A fanciful alternation of light and dark brick decorates the corners of this particular house, but otherwise it sits on the land as stolidly as its nineteenth-century builders intended, a bulwark against the west wind with its heavy burden of winter snow and searing summer heat.

The isolation of such houses creates the intimate setting for some of Alice Munro's darkest stories: kitchens where toddlers are scalded and ex-husbands expose the private parts of their new loves; dining rooms where young girls are belted by angry fathers overseen by vengeful stepmothers; outhouses where menstrual blood gushes forth; basements where foxes are skinned; livingrooms where infant sons are strangled and sexual predators are beaten to death. The isolation itself doesn't prompt the acts (human nature takes care of that), but the secrecy that isolation allows creates the moral dilemmas that Munro explores so ruthlessly in her fiction. For example, in the title story of *The Love of a Good Woman*, Rupert has just murdered the optometrist Mr Willens, who was making advances to his wife. 'Their yard couldn't be seen from the road, that was lucky. Just the peak of the roof and the upstairs window. Mr Willens's car couldn't be seen.' Rupert has figured out how to dispose of the body, but

> the trouble was it meant driving out their lane and along the road to the Jutland turn. But nobody lived down there and it was a dead end after the Jutland turn, so just the half mile or so to pray you never met anybody. Then Rupert would get Mr Willens over in the driver's seat and push the car right off down the bank into the water.[12]

Years later, Rupert's dying wife tells the story to her practical nurse, Enid, who decides to confront the murderer. She plans her argument: 'I am not going to tell, but you are. You can't live on with that kind of secret.'[13] But then she wonders, 'Could a person make up something so detailed and diabolical? The answer is yes.'[14]

Crossing the divide

Alice Munro grew up in the 1930s, at a time when the population of Canada was fairly evenly split between city and country. The halfway mark was hit in 1919, but even in 1941, when Munro was ten, 45 per cent of the population lived, as she did, in small rural communities and on farms. This was before the suburban sprawl provoked by the automobile, a time when the divide between rural and urban was clearly marked into solitudes as distinct as English and French, black and white, rich and poor.

In *The View from Castle Rock*, the collection in which Alice Munro's fictions veer most sharply towards personal essays, she writes: 'In those days people in town did generally look upon the people from the country as more apt to be slow-witted, tongue-tied, uncivilized, than themselves ... And farmers saw people who lived in towns as having an easy life and being unlikely to survive in situations calling for fortitude, self-reliance, hard work.'[15]

Town and country were not just distinct, they were different worlds.

'Their house became like a tiny sealed-off country, with its own ornate customs and elegantly, ridiculously complicated language', the narrator says in the second chapter of *Lives of Girls and Women*, describing the house at Jenkin's Bend where her two aunts and uncle live, 'where true news of the outside world was not exactly forbidden, but became more and more impossible to deliver'.[16] The narrator, as the designated keeper of the family history, is handed a box that, like the Ark of the Convenant, contains their most precious documents. 'Aunt Elspeth and Auntie Grace stood in their doorway, ceremoniously, to watch me go, and I felt as if I were a ship with their hopes on it, dropping down over the horizon.'[17]

When elderly aunts send a card at Christmas, as reported in a later story, 'Chaddeleys and Flemings',

> it was an act of faith for them to write and send those sentences to any place as unimaginable as Vancouver, to someone of their own blood leading a life so strange to them, someone who would read the card with such a feeling of bewilderment and unexplainable guilt. It did make me guilty and bewildered to think that they were still there, still attached to me. But any message from home, in those days, could let me know I was a traitor.[18]

That whiplash shift in point of view, mid-sentence, from faithful aunts to traitorous niece, turns on the knife-edge of the rural/urban divide. Even when I was growing up, twenty years after Alice Munro, almost no one in my Grade Seven class had been to Toronto, hardly more than an hour's drive away. Having made that journey was, in itself, reason enough to be shunned.

Munro spells this out clearly in 'Family Furnishings'. Alfrida

> was a city person. And the city, when it was spoken of in this way, meant the one she lived and worked in. But it meant something else as well – not just a distinct configuration of buildings and sidewalks and streetcar lines or even a crowding together of individual people. It meant something more abstract that could be repeated over and over, something like a hive of bees, stormy but organized, not useless or deluded exactly, but disturbing and sometimes dangerous. People went into such a place when they had to and were glad when they got out.[19]

People living in the country rarely went to the city, and those who escaped rarely came back. 'Town' was a more familiar place, although it, too, had its particular customs and language, as described in 'A Queer Streak', a place where 'the curtains were called drapes, and had pull cords'; where the little hedged-in back yard, which only Violet had the use of, 'was as tidily enclosed, as susceptible to arrangement and decoration, as any living room'.[20]

Through the years that Munro was writing her fictional worlds, out in the real world the rural/urban divide was shifting. By the 1970s, less than a third of the population of Canada lived in the country. By 2000, four out of five Canadians were urban. In Ontario, the figure was even higher: almost nine out of ten. As Munro herself says in the frontispiece of the 1983 King Penguin paperback edition of *Dance of the Happy Shades*, 'I guess that maybe as a writer I'm kind of an anachronism ... because I write about places where your roots are and most people don't live that kind of life any more at all.'

It's true that many of Munro's early stories are resolutely rural, the division between town and country so sharp that the church in 'The Queer Streak' has two doors.

> One door was used by country people – the reason for this originally being that it was nearer to the drive shed – and the other by town people. Inside, the pattern was maintained: town people on one side of the church, country people on the other ... Even country people who had retired and moved to town made a point of not using the town door.

When Violet moves into town, she switches to the town door, which alienates her from her family. 'Choosing the country side would have shown loyalty, and a certain kind of pride, a forgoing of privilege.'[21]

From the outset, Munro leavened her Huron County tales with stories that had urban settings, one or two per collection at first and increasingly more, set mostly in Vancouver, Victoria and Toronto, occasionally in Ottawa and Kingston, all places with which she was personally familiar. In these city stories, place functions differently, less like an active player in the story, more like a stage set: the small writing room the narrator rents in 'The Office' (*Dance of the Happy Shades*); the basement apartment in a city where it rains non-stop in 'Material' (*Something I've Been Meaning to Tell You*); the Victoria bookstore in 'The Albanian Virgin' (*Open Secrets*); the rented rooms in 'Queenie' and the west coast house in 'Post and Beam' (*Hateship, Friendship, Courtship, Loveship, Marriage*); Mr Purvis's mansion in 'Wenlock Edge' (*Too Much Happiness*).

Sometimes, outside Huron County, place becomes frankly symbolic: the suspended purgatory of trains, planes and cruise ships; the white dump of that eponymous story in *The Progress of Love*, where hardened marshmallow and vanilla icing are heaped behind a small-town biscuit factory. 'It was like a kid's dream', says Isabel. 'The most wonderful promising thing you could ever see.' To which her ironic, cuckolded husband replies, 'Mother and the Socialists would take it all away in the dead of night ... and give you oranges instead.'[22]

For those who move from city to country, however, the rural landscape continues to exert its relentless, ruthless force. In 'My Mother's Dream', Jill sits outside the house, listening to her inconsolable baby scream.

> If you walked three blocks east from here or five blocks west, six blocks south or ten blocks north, you would come to walls of summer crops already sprung high out of the earth ... Nowhere to breathe for the reek of thrusting crops and barnyards and jostling munching animals. Woodlots at a distance beckoning like pools of shade, of peace and shelter, but in reality they were boiling up with bugs.[23]

As the Canadian population became increasingly urbanized, 'rural' gained a certain gloss, a transition Munro captures perfectly in the story 'Home'. 'Contempt was what I imagined to be always waiting ... just under the skin and just behind the perceptions of people like the Montjoys',[24] the city people for whom the young country girl works. By the time that girl becomes a middle-aged woman, she, like the rest of her city generation, is wearing water-buffalo sandals and primitive peasant skirts.

On a visit home, she pitches hay down to her father's sheep, thinking, 'People I know say that work like this is restorative and has a peculiar dignity, but I was born to it and feel it differently.'[25]

Drudgery or dignity: it depends on who is looking at the rural landscape.

An imperfect Eden

May in *Dance of the Happy Shades*, Del in *Lives of Girls and Women*, Rose in *Who Do You Think You Are?*, Jesse in *The Progress of Love*, Robin in *Runaway*: Munro's girls and women ache to leave 'here' for 'there'. In 'A Trip to the Coast', May sits 'with her legs folded under her looking out at the road where she might walk now in any direction she liked, and the world which lay flat and accessible and full of silence in front of her'.[26]

But embedded in that silence and solitude is a shard of something else.

'Nobody had spoken for this day yet; its purity astonished her. She had a delicate premonition of freedom and danger, like a streak of dawn across that sky.'[27]

The world, in Munro's stories, is an imperfect Eden, hanging with fruit but writhing with snakes. Freedom and danger are inevitably intertwined, waiting, *out there*.

When Rose in 'Wild Swans' leaves town on the train, she is 'extraordinarily happy. She felt Flo receding, West Hanratty flying away from her, her own wearying self discarded as easily as everything else ... They were travelling ... into ... a tenderer sort of landscape.'[28] The viper in this case is a minister who, under cover of his wide-spread newspaper, explores the hills and valleys of her nether flesh. When Juliet, in 'Chance' (*Runaway*), escapes by train, a man she rebuffs commits suicide on the tracks. The mother in 'Miles City, Montana' happily sheds her house in Vancouver for the drive east, then narrowly escapes losing her little girl, Meg, in a near-drowning.

In Munro's early collections, 'there' might mean the next town, 'towns which derived their magic from being places we did not know and were not known in ... Walking in the streets of one of these towns I felt my anonymity like a decoration, like a peacock's train.'[29]

Through the 1980s and '90s, as travel in the world became easier, the distance between 'here' and 'there' in Alice Munro's stories widens. 'There' becomes increasingly exotic: Scotland, Australia, Albania, Indonesia. But regardless of how distant the destination, the balance of potential pleasure and deadly risk remains the same.

For instance, in 'Pictures of the Ice', the elderly Austin pretends to his over-vigilant daughter that he is travelling to Hawaii to remarry but instead heads off to minister to a small community in the far north, where his float plane crashes into the aptly named Shaft Lake. In 'The Albanian Virgin', Charlotte escapes her boring companions, veering into the mountains on her own, where her capture by hill tribes changes her life forever.

Occasionally, a journey turns out well, as in 'A Real Life', when Dorrie travels to Australia where she shoots crocodiles and learns to fly a plane. But the real question raised in this story is: Can a person, given the chance to leave, refuse? 'Nobody had any business living a life out "here" if they had been offered what Dorrie had', her friend Millicent says. 'It was a kind of sin to refuse such an offer. Out of mulishness, out of fearfulness, and idiocy.'[30]

But the danger cannot be underestimated: a journey through any landscape, even a familiar one, can hold unexpected threats. In 'Save the Reaper', a grandmother takes her grandson for a drive and ends up at a place where she is sure that, as a child, she saw a fantastic wall decorated with 'tropical-colored birds half as big as the trees, a fat horse with dinky legs and burning red eyes ... All of this made of pieces of colored glass set into cement or plaster.'[31] The journey turns grotesque, perilous, as the grandmother and child enter a farmhouse occupied by a captive girl and ageing, naked hippies. As she makes her escape, she glimpses a fragment of wall but abandons it in the rush to return to the known.

Not all Munro protagonists are so fortunate.

The fourth dimension

'What is your world, Mary Jo?'[32] the lover's daughter asks in 'Eskimo'.

This is not an easy question. How can a person know where 'here' is when even home territory can be a 'foreign' place, when lakes can disappear overnight?

In the fictional world of Alice Munro, place is a shifty thing.

'The road wasn't the main road out of Hanratty to the Lake, any more', the narrator observes in *Who Do You Think You Are?*: 'there was a highway bypass. And it was paved, now, with wide gutters, new mercury vapor street lights. The old bridge was gone and a new, wide bridge, much less emphatic, had taken its place.'[33]

The old stove foundry has been converted into a crafts centre 'where people blew glass and wove shawls and made birdhouses, which they sold on the premises'.[34] Sprawling mansions have become nursing homes. Porches have been stripped from houses in a frenzy of modernization, then the children's children nail the verandahs back in place. As Joan notes in 'Oh, What Avails', 'the town of her childhood – that haphazard, dreamy Logan – was just Logan going through a phase. Its leaning board fences and sun-blistered walls and flowering weeds were no permanent expression of what the town could be.'[35]

Nothing is immune to the constancy of change, not even waste land. In 'Visitors', the old farmsteads are bought up by back-to-the-landers who tear down the barns and renovate the houses out of existence. Some of the farms disappear, too, obliterated by a government that drains the swamp and expropriates the land in the name of conservation.

> Albert walked up and down in the grass. He made a turn, he stopped and looked around and started again. He was trying to get the outline of the house. Wilfred frowned at the grass, and said, 'They don't leave you much.'
> 'Who?' said Mildred faintly. She fanned herself with goldenrod.
> 'Conservation people. They don't leave one stone of the foundation, or the cellar hole, or one brick or beam. They dig it all out and fill it all in and haul it all away.'[36]

Only a lilac bush remains to mark the human lives that unfolded there.

As the houses, barns, fields, even the rivers, swamps, and lakes – all the bellwethers of Munro's landscapes – are spruced up, grow decrepit, are cleared and treed, rerouted and drained, place becomes a marker of time as well as of space: a visible fourth dimension through which she reveals the past and present and future, sometimes all at once.

Versions

In an Alice Munro story, there is almost always more than one version of a place.

When Del goes for a drive with the predatory Mr Chamberlain in *Lives of Girls and Women*, 'the countryside I knew was altered by his presence, his voice, overpowering foreknowledge of the errand we were going on together. For a year or two I had been looking at trees, fields, landscape with a secret, strong exaltation ... now with Mr Chamberlain I saw that the whole of nature became debased, maddeningly erotic.'[37]

Love transforms a landscape; the withdrawal of love restores a landscape to itself.

In 'Simon's Luck', Rose drives west from Kingston, escaping a soured love affair. She drives and drives until, somewhere in Alberta's Cypress Hills, she sees dishes in a diner and realizes she is saved: 'She saw them in a way that wouldn't be possible to a person in any stage of love ... it seemed the world had stopped being a stage where she might meet him, and gone back to being itself.'[38]

How fragile are these versions of place! Like tissue-paper palimpsests. When Del takes her American uncle into town, she sees 'the whole street, differently. Jubilee seemed not unique and permanent as I had thought but almost makeshift, and shabby; it would barely do.'[39]

This, of course, is what artists do: remake the world. Munro alludes to this in her epilogue to *Lives of Girls and Women*, where Del describes a novel she is writing.

> For this novel I had changed Jubilee, too, or picked out some features of it and ignored others. It became an older, darker, more decaying town ... The main thing was that it seemed true to me, not real but true, as if I had discovered, not made up, such people and such a story, as if that town was lying close behind the one I walked through every day.[40]

Munro makes the world seem a tentative, uncertain place. It occurs to me that in presenting these multiple versions, she is striving for a kind of balance, the same impulse that underlies the rural habit of telling the worst and the best about a person, all in the same breath. I grew up with this, and it only seems unusual to me now, framed in a Munro story, 'The Ottawa Valley'. 'My mother would say of a family we knew that they had everything money could buy but their only son was an epileptic, or that the parents of the only person from our town who had become moderately famous ... had said that they would give all their daughter's fame for a pair of baby hands.' In the mother's universe and in Munro's, too, 'luck was not without its shadow'.[41]

'Time and place can close in on me', the woman says in 'Home'; 'it can so easily seem as if I have never got away, that I have stayed here my whole life. As if my life as an adult was some kind of dream that never took hold of me ... like one of those misfits, captives – nearly useless, celibate, rusting – who should have left but didn't, couldn't, and are now unfit for any place.'[42]

Where is here?

In the story 'Mischief', Rose moves from Huron County to Vancouver, then back again. Wherever she is, she struggles to remember the place she has left.

> When Rose lived in Capilano Heights she used to spend a lot of time remembering the parts of Ontario where she had lived, being faithful, in a way, to that earlier landscape. Now that she was living in Ontario she put the same sort of effort into remembering things about Vancouver, puzzling to get the details straight that were in themselves quite ordinary.[43]

I'm puzzled by the details, too. The Maitland River, for instance, which flows through Wingham on its way to empty into Lake Huron at Goderich, is called the Tiplady in one story, the Wawanash in several others (a misspelling of Wawanosh, which is not a river but a Huron County township, the only one named for an aboriginal). The Maitland River, which flows through Wingham and skirts Wawanosh township, was named for Sir Peregrine Maitland, Lieutenant Governor of Upper Canada from 1818 to 1828. Alice Munro selects his given name, Peregrine, as the pseudonym for the Maitland River in 'Wood' (*Too Much Happiness*) and in 'Open Secrets', an inspired choice, since 'Peregrine' shares its Latin root with 'pilgrim', an apt description of the young Canadian Girls in Training who hike to the river falls and into the foreign territory of womanhood.

I recently stumbled on the source of Alice Munro's Peregrine River when I was driving through Huron County, and it made me wonder whether Munro's other pseudonyms for real places were accidental or if they, too, have a secret provenance. Did she choose Walley, one of her names for Goderich, because of the Walleye, the main fish harvested from Lake Huron? What about Goderich's other pseudonym, Tuppertown? Or the string of aliases she concocts for Wingham? Jubilee, Carstairs, Dalgleish, Hanratty.

Munro invites such contemplations. She rings her fictional Huron County towns with the actual communities of Kitchener, Stratford, Owen Sound, London, Kincardine, Sarnia. Even the tiny places she mentions can be found on Google Maps: Logan, Clover, Ripley, the Greenoch Swamp, which she renames the Grenoch in *Lives of Girls and Women*. It is tempting to try to catch her out. She leaves clues to the Wingham doppelgangers – the town hall with its oddly ornate tower, the cinema, the post office, the river – but does she also embed errors to trip us up? That would seem to fit with her sly wit, the mischievousness, the lack of sentimentality that sometimes skirts close to cruelty, saved by a wink and a laugh.

Halfway through Munro's writing career, a change becomes apparent: places are as likely not to be named as they are to be named, even when it is fairly clear where they are. The proportion of unnamed places increases until in her last collection, *Dear Life*, twelve of the fourteen stories take place in unnamed locations, though occasionally a marker or two is noticeable in the landscape.

What I find particularly curious is that, overall, some 20 per cent of Munro's stories are titled with names related to place. In *Dear Life*, three-quarters of the fictional stories are named for landscape in some way: 'To Reach Japan', 'Amundsen', 'Leaving Maverley', 'Haven', 'In Sight of the Lake'.

I wonder about this move to namelessness. Between 1968 and 1998, there was a similar move away from the settings of Huron County, what is now known as Alice Munro Country. In *Dance of the Happy Shades* twelve of the stories are sited in Huron County, whereas a decade later in *Who Do You Think You Are?*, only five are, and by 1998, in *The Love of a Good Woman*, only three are, which remains roughly the proportion in all the rest of her collections except for *Runaway*. Did the criticism of locals, unhappy at seeing their town in print, prompt her to give up on both the frankness of actual place names and the subterfuge of changing them? Did she perhaps run out of plausible pseudonyms? Is all this coincidental?

In 'Home', the narrator, whose travels away from and back to her rural home are so much like Alice Munro's that it is difficult to keep author and narrator separate, says, 'For a long time, I lived more than a thousand miles away and would go for years without seeing this house. I thought of it then as a place I might never see again and I was greatly moved by the memory of it. I would walk through its rooms in my mind.'[44] When she moves closer and is able to visit more often, she finds 'the house does not mean as much to me as it once did ... I am not sure now whether I love any place ... it seems to me it was myself that I loved here – some self that I have finished with, and none too soon.'[45] She thinks all this in response to her father's renovations, but 'the town, unlike the house, stays very much the same ... Nevertheless it has changed for me. I have written about it and used it up ... all their secret, plentiful messages for me have drained away.'[46]

Into the wild

In an Alice Munro story, you never know exactly where you are or what it is you are looking at. Even the natural world is slippery. At the beginning of 'Winter Wind', the narrator looks out over a wide stretch of the Wawanash River, all winter ice now and untracked snow, and sees not agricultural Huron County but an unfamiliar place. 'Like Siberia, my grandmother said, offended, you would think we were living on the edge of the wilderness. It was all farms, of course, and tame bush, no wilderness at all, but winter buried the fence posts.'[47]

An appreciation of nature is something relegated to young girls in these stories. In 'Nettles', the narrator remembers her childhood home, where 'each of the trees on the place had likewise an attitude and a presence – the elm looked serene and the oak threatening, the maples friendly and workaday, the hawthorn old and crabby'.[48]

In 'Hired Girl', the adolescent working at the Montjoys' cottage is thrilled by nature, 'the silky water, dark underneath but flashing back from its surface the light of the sky'. At the same time, she becomes aware of a barrier between her and this newly discovered natural world.

> Perhaps *barrier* is too strong a word – there was not a warning so much as something like a shimmer in the air, an indolent reminder. *Not for you.* It wasn't a thing that had to be said. Or put on a sign ... And to tell the truth, this wasn't so different from the way things were at home, where taking any impractical notice of the out-of-doors, or mooning around about Nature, even using that word, *Nature* – could get you laughed at.[49]

What a revelation! Nature, like a town, a house, a room, could *belong* to someone, could be denied to a person. Nature, as Jinny discovers in 'Floating

Bridge', was like everything else in the physical world, 'just a peg to hang the unruly sensations of your body on, and the bits and pieces of your mind'.[50]

In that sense, places become interchangeable, a notion underscored in 'A Wilderness Station', where the minister quotes Thomas Boston, a Scottish philosopher and theologian who was, ironically, an ancestor of Alice Munro's. *'This world is a wilderness, in which we may indeed get our station changed, but the move will be out of one wilderness station into another.'*[51]

But there is a larger Nature, too, one that, now and then, Munro allows us to glimpse. A place that has little to do with either adolescent exaltation or the harder emotional pull of roots. A place that is not impractical at all. We see it in 'The Bear Came over the Mountain'. Grant is returning from visiting his wife, Fiona, whose dementia has put her in a nursing home.

> Driving home, he noticed that the swamp hollow that had been filled with snow and the formal shadows of tree trunks was now lighted up with skunk lilies. Their fresh, edible-looking leaves were the size of platters. The flowers sprang straight up like candle flames, and there were so many of them, so pure a yellow, that they set a light shooting up from the earth on this cloudy day. Fiona had told him that they generated a heat of their own as well. Rummaging around in one of her concealed pockets of information, she said that you were supposed to be able to put your hand inside the curled petal and feel the heat. She said that she had tried it, but she couldn't be sure if what she felt was heat or her imagination. The heat attracted bugs.

Grant remembers what Fiona said: 'Nature doesn't fool around just being decorative.'[52] Neither does Munro.

Mapping Alice Munro

A landscape, natural or manmade, can be read with maps. Although it hardly matters where 'Tricks' takes place – the encounter with the immigrant Albanian clockmaker could have happened anywhere – still Robin pores over maps

> where it was hard enough to find the country itself, but possible finally with a magnifying glass, to become familiar with the names of various towns ... and with the rivers ... and the shaded mountain ranges ... Her need to follow this investigation was hard to explain ... What she must have been trying to do – and what she at least half succeeded in doing – was to settle Danilo into some real place and a real past.[53]

But maps in Alice Munro stories are most often unreadable, unreliable, or a matter of dispute. In 'The Children Stay', there is a map under glass between the cottages where Brian and his wife, children, and parents are holidaying together.

> You can stand there looking at the map, then looking at what's in front of you, looking back at the map again, until you get things sorted out. The grandfather and Brian do this every day, usually getting into an argument – though you'd think there would not be much room for disagreement with the map right there ... Brian's mother won't look at the map. She says it boggles her mind.[54]

The map in 'Differently' is equally uncertain. 'The map of the city that she has held in her mind up till now, with its routes to shops and work and friends' houses, was overlaid with another map, of circuitous routes followed in fear (not shame) and excitement, of flimsy shelters, temporary hiding places.'[55]

And in *Lives of Girls and Women*, when Benny goes to the city to look for the runaway Madeleine and her daughter, he asks at a gas station for a map, but that station didn't have it so he thought none would. He asks for directions and discovers it's very risky asking people. 'You're tellin' me, he says. Lying alongside our world was Uncle Benny's world like a troubling, distorted reflection, the same but never at all the same.'[56]

When Alice Munro (then Laidlaw) escaped from Wingham to the University of Western Ontario and then to British Columbia with her first husband, she could hardly have imagined she would end up back in Huron County, in the town of Clinton, just a forty-minute drive south of her home town.

She had already published three collections of stories when she settled in Clinton in the mid-1970s with her second husband, Gerald Fremlin, a cartographer and geographer who had edited the fourth edition of the *National Atlas of Canada*. In *The View from Castle Rock*, Munro writes about the drives she and Fremlin would routinely take through Huron County and beyond.

'It was a pleasure, as always, to be together in this part of the world looking at the countryside that we think we know so well and that is always springing some sort of surprise on us. The landscape here is a record of ancient events', she writes in 'What Do You Want to Know For?' She mentions the ice age, advancing and withdrawing, retreating for the last time 15,000 years ago.

> Quite recently, you might say. Quite recently now that I have got used to a certain way of reckoning history.
>
> A glacial landscape such as this is vulnerable ... So you have to keep checking, taking in the changes, seeing things while they last.[57]

She continues:

> I didn't learn any of this at school ... I learned it when I came to live here with my second husband, a geographer.

Where do you think you are? Place in Alice Munro

They travel with special maps marked with towns and roads but also coloured to show drumlins and moraines, eskers and spillways, bevelled till and kame, which is her favourite kind of landscape, 'all wild and bumpy, unpredictable, with a look of chance and secrets'.[58]

Gerald Fremlin published *Maps as Mediated Seeing: Fundamentals of Cartography*, first as a monograph in 1999, then as a book for geographers and general readers in 2004. The cover shows a face, its features contoured like a topographical map. In the book, he proposes cartography as a 'system for seeing that mediates between the seer and the thing to be seen'.[59] 'Seeing via representation is a form of seeing, alternative to direct seeing. It allows us to see in times and places we are not in and in projections other than those provided by the lens of eye. It is the only way some things can be seen.'[60]

Alice Munro's stories are a kind of mediated seeing, too.

'Geography begins with an outing in a stroller – a primal urge to see what's next along the route', writes Fremlin, who is described in his 17 April 2013 obituary in the *Clinton News Record* as 'a philosopher, painter and poet with a taste for the absurd'. 'At its core', he says of geography, 'is an injunction to *explain* the landscape that its name commits it to depict.'[61]

In 'What Do You Want to Know For?' Munro tells a story about a crypt that the narrator and her geographer husband glimpse on one of their back-country rambles. Curious, they look for it again and after several attempts, finally locate the place as well as a local woman who remembers the last time the crypt was opened.

> Sitting there the same today, all sealed up and nobody going to see it ever again.
> 'Nobody knows why they did it. They just did.'
> She smiles at me with a sociable sort of perplexity, her almost colorless eyes enlarged, made owlish, by her glasses. She gives a couple of tremulous nods. As if to say, it's beyond us, isn't it? A multitude of things, beyond us. Yes.[62]

Later, in the Epilogue of *The View from Castle Rock*, in a piece called 'Messenger', the narrator visits a number of cemeteries, including one in Illinois marked 'Unknown Cemetery', which turns out to be a vacant lot gone wild.

> I could pursue this. It's what people do. Once they get started they'll follow any lead ... We are beguiled. It happens mostly in our old age, when our personal futures close down and we cannot imagine – sometimes cannot believe in – the future of our children's children. We can't resist this rifling around in the past, sifting the untrustworthy evidence, linking stray names and questionable dates and anecdotes together, hanging on to threads, insisting on being joined to dead people and therefore to life.[63]

Place is so fundamental to Munro that she draws on it for a metaphor to describe her writing process:

> A story is not like a road to follow ... it's more like a house. You go inside and stay there for a while, wandering back and forth and settling where you like and discovering how the room and corridors relate to each other, how the world outside is altered by being viewed from these windows. And you, the visitor, the reader, are altered as well by being in this enclosed space, whether it is ample and easy or full of crooked turns, or sparsely or opulently furnished. You can go back again and again, and the house, the story, always contains more than you saw the last time. It also has a sturdy sense of itself of being built out of its own necessity, not just to shelter or beguile you.[64]

The struggle to engage with place – and to simultaneously be free of it – is a constant in the stories of Alice Munro. As she peels back the skin of her characters, she excavates, too, the places where they live, not just in Huron County, but everywhere, anywhere, that humans have tried to put down – and pull up – roots.

At first glance it may seem as though place as a cross-section of physical geography hardly exists in Munro's literary world, but I believe the opposite is true: place forms a kind of bedrock to her stories, wild and unpredictable as kame. Beguiling. Ephemeral and everlasting.

As one of Alice Munro's ancestors writes in the fictional memoir 'The Wilds of Morris Township': 'And the place that now knows us, will soon know us no more.'[65] It is unclear whether this is because of its demise or ours. Munro goads us to keep checking: Is the Lake still there?

Notes

1. 'Walker Brothers Cowboy', in *Dance of the Happy Shades* (New York: McGraw-Hill, 1973), 1.
2. 'Oranges and Apples', in *Friend of My Youth* (Toronto: McClelland & Stewart, 1990), 134.
3. 'Walker Brothers Cowboy', 1.
4. Ibid., 2.
5. Ibid., 18.
6. 'Images', in *Dance of the Happy Shades*, 37–8.
7. Ibid., 43.
8. 'The Shining Houses', in *Dance of the Happy Shades*, 20.
9. 'Royal Beatings', in *Who Do You Think You Are?* (Toronto: Macmillan, 1978), 4.
10. 'Spaceships Have Landed', in *Open Secrets* (Toronto: McClelland & Stewart, 1994), 234.
11. 'Dear Life', in *Family Furnishings: Selected Stories 1995–2014* (Toronto: McClelland & Stewart, 2014), 605.
12. 'The Love of a Good Woman', in *The Love of a Good Woman* (Toronto: McClelland & Stewart 1998), 59–60.
13. Ibid., 72.

14 Ibid., 74.
15 'Working for a Living', in *The View from Castle Rock* (Toronto: McClelland & Stewart, 2006), 128-9.
16 'Heirs of the Living Body', in *Lives of Girls and Women* (Toronto: McGraw-Hill Ryerson, 1971), 59-60.
17 Ibid., 62.
18 'Chaddeleys and Flemings: the Stone in the Field', in *The Moons of Jupiter* (Toronto: Macmillan of Canada, 1982), 31.
19 'Family Furnishings', in *Hateship, Friendship, Courtship, Loveship, Marriage* (Toronto: McClelland & Stewart, 2001), 87.
20 'A Queer Streak', in *The Progress of Love* (Toronto: McClelland & Stewart, 2001), 236.
21 Ibid., 237.
22 'White Dump', in *The Progress of Love*, 306.
23 'My Mother's Dream', in *The Love of a Good Woman*, 318-19.
24 'Hired Girl', in *The View from Castle Rock*, 240.
25 'Home', in *The View from Castle Rock*, 312.
26 'A Trip to the Coast', in *Dance of the Happy Shades*, 189.
27 Ibid., 174.
28 'Wild Swans', in *Who Do You Think You Are?*, 58.
29 'Princess Ida', in *Lives of Girls and Women*, 68.
30 'A Real Life', in *Open Secrets*, 76.
31 'Save the Reaper', in *The Love of a Good Woman*, 163.
32 'Eskimo', in *The Progress of Love*, 191.
33 'Spelling', in *Who Do You Think You Are?*, 176.
34 'White Dump', in *The Progress of Love*, 282.
35 'Oh, What Avails', in *Friend of My Youth*, 196.
36 'Visitors', in *The Moons of Jupiter*, 211-12.
37 'Lives of Girls and Women', in *Lives of Girls and Women*, 168.
38 'Simon's Luck', in *Who Do You Think You Are?*, 170.
39 'Princess Ida', in *Lives of Girls and Women*, 84-5.
40 'Epilogue: The Photographer', in *Lives of Girls and Women*, 247-8.
41 'The Ottawa Valley', in *Something I've Been Meaning to Tell You* (Toronto: McGraw-Hill Ryerson, 1974), 227-8.
42 'Home', in *The View from Castle Rock*, 312.
43 'Mischief', in *Who Do You Think You Are?*, 129-30.
44 'Home', in *The View from Castle Rock*, 288.
45 Ibid., 290.
46 Ibid., 300.
47 'Winter Wind', in *Something I've Been Meaning to Tell You*, 192.
48 'Nettles', in *Hateship, Friendship, Courtship, Loveship, Marriage*, 157.
49 'Hired Girl', in *The View from Castle Rock*, 231-3.
50 'Floating Bridge', in *Hateship, Friendship, Courtship, Loveship, Marriage*, 57.
51 'A Wilderness Station', in *Open Secrets*, 204.
52 'The Bear Came over the Mountain', in *Hateship, Friendship, Courtship, Loveship, Marriage*, 315-16.
53 'Tricks', in *Runaway* (Toronto: McClelland & Stewart, 2004), 254.
54 'The Children Stay', in *The Love of a Good Woman*, 182.

55 'Differently', in *Friend of My Youth*, 232.
56 'The Flats Road', in *Lives of Girls and Women*, 25.
57 'What Do You Want to Know For?', in *The View from Castle Rock*, 318–19.
58 Ibid., 321.
59 'Preface', in *Maps as Mediated Seeing: Fundamentals of Cartography*, by Gerald Fremlin with Arthur H. Robinson (Victoria, BC: Trafford Publishing, 2005), xi.
60 'Nine Short Essays About Maps', in *Maps as Mediated Seeing: Fundamentals of Cartography*, 2.
61 'Afterword', in *Maps as Mediated Seeing: Fundamentals of Cartography*, 243.
62 'What Do You Want to Know For?', 339.
63 'Epilogue', in *The View from Castle Rock*, 347.
64 'Introduction to the Vintage Edition', in *Selected Stories, 1968–1994* (New York: Vintage Books, 1996).
65 'The Wilds of Morris Township', in *The View from Castle Rock*, 117.

3

DOUGLAS GLOVER

The style of Alice Munro

We have here to speak of style in a double sense: style as the basket of syntactic moves habitual to an author, but also style as tilt, the characteristic lean or bearing of the author as she represents herself through her writing. Call the latter personality, power, or panache. Alice Munro comes from a part of the world that challenges both eccentricity and ambition (and is not necessarily able to tell the two apart). 'Who do you think you are?' the townspeople of her fictional southwestern Ontario town ask. As if in response to this challenge, Munro forges her style in the furnace of opposition. She plays with expectation and denial of expectation; she insists upon difference. My sense is that she doesn't compose so much by reference (to a notional reality) as by dramatic antithesis. A statement provokes a counter-statement or a counter-construct, subversion, or complication, and the sentences, paragraphs, and stories advance by the accumulation of such contraventions. The initial statement, the facticity of the story, then, by steps and counter-steps, implicates itself in a series of deferrals that render it less unequivocal and more inflected as it progresses. The truth is never the truth but a truth with codicils, conditions, caveats, perorations, and contradictions.

For me the quintessential moment in the contrarian edifice of Alice Munro's oeuvre takes place in her story 'Lives of Girls and Women' (in the book of the same name) when Del Jordan climbs into the car with Chamberlain expecting sex only to find herself enlisted to spy on her mother's boarder, the vegetal Fern. 'I brought my mind back, slowly, from expectations of rape', writes Munro in the voice of Del.[1] My liberal education has armoured me against such thoughts, anathematized men wanting to rape women and men who think that women want to be raped. But in 'Lives of Girls and Women' Munro has written a character, somewhat like herself, who climbs into an older man's car wanting sex. The lovely word 'slowly', the fulcrum of the sentence, indicates the trouble, the reluctance, involved in readjusting to the disappointment of the flesh. Del has already made herself available on a casual basis for illicit caresses, child molesting, in fact. She has admired the brutality of her erstwhile lover's slaps and pinches. When she thinks about 'criminal sensuality' it is her own, not Chamberlain's. Rape in this sense is statutory, not a violent assault against the victim's will. Sex with Chamberlain would be legal rape, would be criminal, but Del is not the unwilling victim.

What interests me is less the thematics of the case than the structural and syntactic aspect of Del's rape reveries, which are purely oppositional. They place her outside conventional cultural norms. She colludes with the bad man to bring about her own sexual degradation. Though in many ways Chamberlain is her notional antagonist, it would be disingenuous to say they are in conflict precisely. More significantly, in terms of the story's syntax, Del's fantasies place her in opposition to her mother. Mrs Jordan is a modern woman of her time, an erstwhile provincial intellectual, a proto-feminist, cultured in a superficial, self-flattering way, slightly comical in the Dickens mode, with her encyclopedia business and her opera books. She creates herself in opposition to her husband (she has left the family house on the Flats Road and moved into town with Del) and to the community of Jubilee, which, to her, is rural, ignorant, petit bourgeois, and philistine. It's enough for the town to be suspicious of someone for Mrs Jordan's allegiance to lean in the opposite direction. She's also ambitious for her daughter, reads the university catalogues, and dreams of courses she would take if she were Del. She's puritanical about sex, despite her liberalism. So much so that when Jerry Storey's mother begins talking to her about diaphragms, Del finds herself offended and, briefly, prefers her mother's silence on sexual matters. But, crucially for Del, her mother is the anvil on which she hammers out her selfhood.

In the last paragraph of 'Lives of Girls and Women', she isn't thinking of the erotic debacle with Chamberlain; she is instead rejecting her mother's advice for young women, the whole earnest speech about the change coming in 'the lives of girls and women', which incidentally ironizes the title of the book.

> I did not quite get the point of this, or if I did get the point I was set up to resist it. I would have had to resist anything she told me with such earnestness, with such stubborn hopefulness. Her concern about my life, which I needed and took for granted, I could not bear to have expressed. Also I felt that it was not so different from all the other advice handed out to women, to girls, advice that assumed being female made you damageable, that a certain amount of carefulness and solemn fuss and self-protection were called for, whereas men were supposed to be able to go out and take on all kinds of experiences and shuck off what they didn't want and come back proud. Without even thinking about it, I decided to do the same. (177)

Lives of Girls and Women, which was published as a novel, is a novel of sorts, a very loosely constructed novel based around a series of stories in the life of a character named Del Jordan in a town called Jubilee in southwestern Ontario. The stories progress chronologically through Del's girlhood (stories about neighbours, ancestors, older relatives, her mother, her early religious enthusiasm) to the summer after she graduates from high school. Each of the chapters functions more like a short story than a chapter. Aside from the progressive chronology and the fact that some characters recur, there isn't a lot of novelistic development (motivational consistency, expanding symbols, tie-backs, and memory rehearsals typical of novels) from one story to the next. This structure alters in the second half of the book, in particular with the run of three stories: 'Changes and Ceremonies', 'Lives of Girls and Women', and 'Baptizing', which all feature Del in an erotic (or romantic) relationship with a male character.

In 'Changes and Ceremonies', Del's erotic attachment amounts to a crush on a boy, Frank Wales, who acts the Pied Piper in her school play, can't spell, and subsequently drops out of school and finds a delivery job for a dry cleaner. Del is only in Grade Seven, and her desire functions at the level of fantasy and girlish banter with her friend Naomi. In 'Lives of Girls and Women', she is about fourteen (it's unclear) – somewhere between Grade Seven and her 'third year of high school', where she is when the next story, 'Baptizing', begins. 'Changes and Ceremonies' is a thematic and structural pre-story to the two long and blazing masterpieces – 'Lives of Girls and Women' and 'Baptizing' – that form the dramatic and thematic core of the book. The three-story sequence is more novel-like (with a consistent motivation throughout) in the conventional sense than the book as a whole, if it really matters what you call it.

'Lives of Girls and Women' is a thirty-page story that relates the details of Del's precocious involvement with Mr Chamberlain, a local radio personality and a familiar presence at the Jordan house where he comes to visit the boarder, Fern. The story advances in a conventional style. In the fifth paragraph, Del states her desire: 'It was glory I was after, walking the streets of Jubilee, like an exile or a spy ...' (144). Later in the story, glory is associated with sex, and later still, in 'Baptizing', the link is made explicit when she connects the blood from her lost virginity with glory. 'When I saw the blood the glory of the whole episode became clear to me' (227). In the first plot step of the story, Chamberlain arouses Del by talking about the teenage prostitutes he had seen in Italy during the war. In the second plot step, she flirts with him in a gaminesque way and he touches her breast (after this she makes herself readily available to his caresses). In the third plot step, she gets into Chamberlain's car (expecting to be raped), but he surprises her by asking her to spy on Fern instead (he is afraid certain letters might implicate him in a breach-of-promise suit). And in the fourth plot step, she climbs into Chamberlain's car, they drive into the country, and he masturbates in front of her.

The structure of the story is elaborated. There is the mother who forms, as I say, an oppositional dipole with Del; also a side plot involving Chamberlain and the boarder Fern; and there is a subplot involving Del's friend Naomi and her family (Munro is always setting up these parallel contrasts: characters, families, ways of speaking, even homes and neighbourhoods). Naomi is similarly fascinated by sex, but she does not find an object of desire. While Del is running after Chamberlain, Naomi falls ill, and, when she revives, she is strangely reticent but exhibits a droll false consciousness in regard to sexual matters – this is enunciated in a sentence marvellous for its series of rhythmic deferrals.

> All the grosser aspects of sex had disappeared from her conversation and apparently from her mind although she talked a good deal about Dr Wallis, and how he had sponged her legs himself, and she had been quite helplessly exposed to him, when she was sick. (173)

'Baptizing' is a mirror story but the opposite (the way the left hand is related to the right hand), a story of consummated desire. It's very long, a novella really, and the action comes three years after 'Lives of Girls and Women'. The two stories form a diptych, a crucial and knowing juxtaposition. Naomi and Del are in high school, but Naomi quickly transfers to the commercial stream, then leaves school for a job in the creamery. What follows is a variation of conventional plot structure. Whereas in the previous story Del dealt only with Chamberlain, in 'Baptizing' there are three large plot steps, each involving a different man: (1) Del goes to the Gay-la Dance Hall with Naomi and ends up drinking in a hotel room with Naomi, Naomi's boyfriend Bert Matthews, and a man named Clive. (2) Del has a hilarious if somewhat clinical sexual encounter with her high school intellectual peer Jerry Storey. (Both these encounters end ignominiously with Del escaping across town in the night on foot.) (3) She has a delicious, all-out love affair with a Baptist mill worker named Garnet French. We should note here that this strategy of varying plot structure by using different antagonists in each plot step is also used in James Joyce's 'The Dead', in which the protagonist Gabriel has dramatic interactions with three successive women, Lily, the maid, Miss Ivors, the fellow journalist, and, finally, his wife.

Each of these major plot events is stepped out, that is, each one is broken up into a series of steps, so that they form a miniature story, a dramatic whole within the larger structure of the entire story. For example, the Gay-la

Dance Hall sequence involves a set-up (Naomi urging Del to accompany her), walking to the dance hall, the entry between rows of men, dancing with Clive, buying drinks (Del is quite happy to drink the whiskey straight), driving to the hotel, hanging about in the hotel room, Del going down the corridor to the bathroom, Del letting herself down the fire escape, Del walking back to Naomi's house and waking her father, Del walking back to her own house and going to bed, Naomi waking Del the next morning, debriefing and aftermath.

The first two plot events (Clive and Jerry Storey) are hilarious, almost slapstick. They are different events but quite parallel in structure. Both involve Del in a kind of dead-pan comic anarchy of desire (drunken Del hanging from the fire escape, clinical Del being bundled naked into the cellar as Jerry Storey's mother arrives through the front door). Both involve comically maladroit erstwhile lovers. Both climax in an escape and a walk home in the night. Both involve a flawed attempt at some form of erotic encounter – here it's fascinating to track the parallels and contrasts between the darker flawed sexual attempt with the ineffable Chamberlain and the farcical escapades with Clive and Jerry. This is a standard Munro structure: inflect by juxtaposition and contrast.

The final plot event in 'Baptizing', the Garnet French episode, is altogether different in that the sexual encounter proposed at the outset is successfully consummated (at night, in the side-garden against the wall of her mother's house). Del and Garnet have a wonderful sex life for the brief weeks that they are together, until the relationship collapses under the weight of internal contradictions that Del has been blissfully ignoring. Garnet wants her to be baptized, join his church (instead of just attending his youth group meetings), and get married, whereas Del has no interest in being subordinated to his mission. She has a secondary desire in the story, to win a scholarship and go to university. But that's not the reason she brings up in the final scene with Garnet, when he tries to force a symbolic baptism in the Wawanash River where they go swimming. What she actually thinks during this scene is highly instructive.

> 'Say you'll do it then!' His dark, amiable but secretive face broken by rage, a helpless sense of insult. I was ashamed of this insult but had to cling to it, because it was only *my differences, my reservations, my life* ... I thought that I was fighting for *my life*. (238–9; my emphasis)

The words 'differences' and 'reservations' are crucial, also the way they are identified with the girl's life, her very self. This scene is a structural duplicate of the masturbation scene in 'Lives of Girls and Women'. In both texts, Del has been playing an erotic game. Both scenes take place outside, in a locale of rural privacy. But, typically for Munro, the scenes present a contrast. Oddly enough, the sleazy encounter with Chamberlain, the semen on her skirt, does not threaten Del's sense of self. She doesn't feel like a victim and doesn't want her encounter to be categorized in a way that portrays her as a victim. In 'Baptizing' she's resisting Garnet, but in 'Lives' she is, in contrast, not resisting Chamberlain; instead she's resisting her mother (and her mother's proto-feminist notion of female self-respect).

In 'Baptizing', dramatic opposition between Del and her mother still exists but in a slightly oblique way. The relationship with Garnet develops quickly in opposition to the desire Del shares with her mother to get good grades and win a scholarship to university. Del loses focus in a fog of erotic bliss the day after she loses her virginity and can barely concentrate in a crucial examination. When the grades come in, her mother's dreams for her are finally defeated. But, as in 'Lives of Girls and Women', Del herself is not defeated or dismayed or, in the least, self-critical; rather she is strengthened, more resolute and determined.

> Now at last without fantasies or self-deception, cut off from the mistakes and confusion of the past, grave and simple, carrying a small suitcase, getting on a bus, like girls in movies leaving home, convents, lovers, I supposed I would get started on my real life. (242)

However, it does not escape the reader that, true to form, Del's final resolve is itself a theatrical (playful) construct of cinematic fantasy.

The stylistic lesson is that though Munro produces a facsimile of a conventional, naturalistic narrative (she pays her dues to verisimilitude, even going so far as to use 'facts' from her own life to tease the reader) that moves forward in a series of plot steps in chronological order, there is another structure imposed on the narrative, a static structure of repetitions, mirrors, and contrasts. 'Baptizing' repeats the theme and plot of Del's sexual desire from 'Lives of Girls and Women', but with the difference that in 'Baptizing' she achieves the sexual glory denied her by Chamberlain. 'Baptizing' also repeats the structure of resistance and separation (individuation) between Del and her mother. Both stories develop internal repetitions as well. In 'Lives of Girls and Women' the second and third plot steps involve Del getting into Chamberlain's car (and being disappointed of her desire both times). In 'Baptizing' the first and second plot events both involve comic erotic catastrophes and Del walking home across town in the dark.

This system of composing by parallel and antithesis extends to Munro's subplots. In a Munro narrative, rarely are characters invented alone (they will normally have a relational other) nor are they static in time; they have their own stories and plots. In both 'Lives of Girls and Women' and

'Baptizing', Naomi serves as a dipole for Del; she is friend, confidante, co-conspirator, and ally (apparently the same but different), and she has her own plot. In both stories, Del and Naomi start together at the Go square, then diverge. In 'Lives of Girls and Women' they are twinned until the moment Del turns secretive about her interaction with Chamberlain. As Del pursues her affair with Chamberlain, her relationship with Naomi fades, Naomi goes underground herself, falling ill and remaining secluded at home except for visits from the doctor. When the two young women start communicating at the end of the story, they are in surprisingly different places: Naomi no longer wants to talk and joke explicitly about sex (though she will dwell on how the doctor washed her) and Del has achieved a dark and secret knowledge of sexuality that she is not willing to divulge.

In 'Baptizing', the girls are co-conspirators in the Gay-la Dance Hall episode, but as in the previous story, they diverge. Naomi is disappointed in Del for making a mess of the hotel drinking scene, and Del isn't interested in repeating that sort of mischief. Naomi disappears from the story through the Jerry Storey episode. We don't know what's been happening to her until the primary plot of the story has nearly reached completion and Del is at the peak of her involvement with Garnet French. Then we learn Naomi's story retrospectively: a series of lovers, accidental pregnancy, projected marriage (without love). Del has been receiving warnings against the disastrous consequences of pregnancy throughout the story, a recurring motif, the steady drumbeat of pragmatic female concern. Yet she enjoys glorious sex and escapes unscathed whereas Naomi's sexual history sounds like a chore and she ends up trapped. Their two plots diverge but balance each other symmetrically as opposing outcomes.

Munro composes Jerry Storey as a subplot as well. He and Del are twinned as male and female star scholars with similar academic ambitions, though (and with Munro there is always a though or a but) Jerry's bent is towards the scientific whereas Del favours the humanities, and Jerry's attitude towards Del's intelligence is condescending and chauvinistic. It's worth mentioning that I think this is the only time in Munro's oeuvre that she mentions the Nobel Prize, and it's Jerry Storey who contemplates winning it. This makes you wonder what Munro was thinking herself, all those years ago.

> After he had said something like this he would always mutter, 'You know I'm kidding.' He meant about the Nobel Prize, not the war. We could not get away from the Jubilee belief that there are great, supernatural dangers attached to boasting, or having high hopes of yourself. Yet what really drew and kept us together were these hopes, both denied and admitted, both ridiculed and respected in each other. (199)

But after their opera bouffe erotic contretemps, their plots diverge as well. Del falls for Garnet French and her studies suffer. When last we hear of Jerry he is sending Del postcards from the road as he tours the American states with his mother, reading Marx in restaurants 'TO ASTONISH NATIVES' (232). In other words, starting from the same ground (teenage scholars living with their mothers), they end up in symmetrically opposed outcomes: Jerry paired with his mother, and Del ultimately alone and free ('I was free and I was not free' [241] is what she thinks, continuing the pattern of inflection by antithesis) having separated from both her mother and Garnet French.

Such structural strategies are everywhere in Alice Munro's fiction. She is very good at concealing her art behind a screen of apparently naturalistic detail that, when read carefully, turns out to be a highly formal elaboration of finite elements.

In addition to the plot repetitions, Munro packs her texts with apparently tangential scenes made to cohere by the technique of thematic forcing. In 'Lives of Girls and Women' the sexual theme is stamped everywhere. When Del visits Naomi's house and Naomi's father makes them read a passage from the Bible (Matthew 25, 1–13), Del thinks:

> I had always supposed this parable, which I did not like, had to do with prudence, preparedness, something like that. But I could see that Naomi's father believed it to be about sex. (156)

Del and Naomi walk through town together (an off-plot interlude) only to end up watching Pork Childs's peacocks. The four paragraphs beginning 'And the peacocks crying ...' lead to a repetition of that word 'glory' – 'Glory in the cold spring, a wonder in Jubilee' – and end with Naomi's exclamation, 'It's sex makes them scream.' In each of these scenes, something non-sexual is stamped with the word sex; while in the same story, Munro inserts the brothel paragraph (Del just pondering the brothel at the edge of town) in which something conventionally sexual is stamped with the domestic and ordinary (the inverse). 'One of them was reading the Star Weekly' (153). And when Del goes to search Fern's bedroom she finds birth control information and pornographic doggerel. '(A big cock in my pussy is all it would take!)' (167) Of all the possible things Del could have found, the author opts for the marker of sexuality.

In the same vein of structural repetition, in 'Baptizing', as mentioned, there are three men – Clive, Jerry Storey, and Garnet French – each in parallel situations with Del but clearly contrasted in personality. Studious Jerry is the near opposite of the shadow-boxing jokester Clive, and Garnet is the Baptist mill worker opposite of the nerd Jerry Storey. (Note also the contrast between Clive and Garnet: Clive shadow-boxes to punctuate his masculine banter, while

Garnet went to jail for nearly beating a man to death; Clive drinks, Garnet does not.) In many cases, Munro supports the contrasts with commentary. We can take the following to represent a typical sort of Alice Munro sentence.

> It was the very opposite of going out with Jerry, and seeing the world dense and complicated but appallingly unsecretive; the world I saw with Garnet was something not far from what I thought animals must see, the world without names. (221)

But also notice the repetition of the dinner scenes: Jerry and Garnet each come to dinner at Del's house; Del has dinner at Jerry's house and also at Garnet's house. Tellingly, the dinner sequence at Garnet's house is amplified and elaborated, a Dickensian, jolly, underclass sprawling family, a set-piece contrast to the other dinners in several ways. Just as in 'Lives of Girls and Women' Naomi's household is contrasted with Del's, in 'Baptizing', the Jordan, Storey, and French households are framed together, an ironic triptych of multiple contrasts and parallels. For example, both Jerry and Del live alone with their mothers; both mothers are 'modern' but in surprisingly different ways. By contrast the rural poverty of the French household is remarkably lively, tolerant, accepting, rambunctious, and, well, healthy. Says Garnet's mother: 'It looks pretty plain to anybody from town, but we always get enough to eat. The air's lovely, in summer anyway, lovely and cool down by the creek. Cool in the summer, protected in the winter. It's the best situated house I know of' (224).

Munro carefully plans these dinner scenes right down to the food. At the Jordan house:

> I was critical of the meal, as I always was before company; the meat seemed underdone, the potatoes slightly hard, the canned beans too cool. (200)

At the Storey house:

> For dessert we had molded Jello pudding in three colours, rather like a mosque, full of canned fruit. (201)

At the French house:

> For supper we had stewed chicken, not too tough, and good gravy to soften it, light dumplings, potatoes ('too bad it's not time for the new!'), flat, round, floury biscuits, home-canned beans and tomatoes, several kinds of pickles, and bowls of green onions and radishes and leaf lettuce, in vinegar, a heavy molasses-flavoured cake, blackberry preserves. (225–6)

And in this case, Del herself nails the moral of the contrast: 'There is no denying I was happy in that house' (226).

Menu lists are not inherently dramatic; they only become dramatic within a system of contrasts wherein they acquire meaning in excess of mere realistic description. These structural repetitions are a matter of style. Munro is not just telling a story but creating a complex pattern of repetition and contrast over and above the mere story. Although she is concerned with what comes next, the chronological thread of narrative, she clearly also composes with an eye to elaborating this system of repetitions, parallels, reflectors, and contrasts. Munro deliberately juxtaposes similar or parallel scenes to add a dimension of meaning not contained in the mere story. Similar things – characters, scenes, locations, families – are contrasted, and different things are stamped with unexpected similarity, creating a complex structure of inter-relation, cross-reference, and identity not, perhaps, reducible to a single simple theme.

In a larger sense, this formal elaboration and pattern-making matches the author's irony, her 'complexity and play-acting', against the conventional expectation of a garden variety well-made story. The first lesson of any Munro story is that the story itself (and in this case the character Del) will resist closure, will resist easy summations and quick definitions; it will reach for complexity and irony over interpretation. Who do you think you are? is exactly the question; and Alice Munro's answer is always, Not who you think I am. Not even who you thought I was in the last sentence.

Resistance, complexity, and difference are the essential characteristics of Munro's style. It should be clear by now that many of the content choices Munro makes are based on a structural demand for contrast. The demand for contrast, in many cases, overrides or subverts the conventional demand story efficiency. In 'Lives of Girls and Women' there is no plot reason for the paragraph about the brothel; in 'Baptizing', we don't need the dinner menus. These textual elements serve the story instead by creating an oscillating grid of similarity and difference. Similar structures are shown to be different; things that appear different at first are shown to be similar. This modus operandi extends from the macro or strategic level of form (the juxtaposition of plots, events, households, neighbourhoods, landscapes, social classes, genders, and character groups) to the micro level, the grammar in the composition of sentences and paragraphs, and thence outward again, to the level of character and theme, psychology and ethics.

Munro creates character by inventing contrast pairs; a person rarely exists alone in a sentence, but instead finds complexity in a contrasting other, a dipole, either another character, or a subversion, or a denial of expectation. She doesn't say, X is Y; she says, X is different from Y, or X is Y but different in relation to Z. You can see this even at the level of the construction of sentences and paragraphs. Here, for example, is a description of Fern and Mrs Jordan:

> All those qualities my mother had developed for her assault on life – sharpness, smartness, determination, selectiveness – seemed to have their opposites in Fern, with her diffuse complaints, lazy movements, indifferent agreeableness. (144)

And here is a straight house-for-house contrast, Del and Naomi:

> Naomi was not popular in my house, nor I in hers. Each of us was suspected of carrying the seeds of contamination – in my case, of atheism, in Naomi's, of sexual preoccupation. (147)

Household attitudes and moral culture are juxtaposed in two sentences using parallel construction.

Often Munro composes a sentence or a paragraph around a but-construction, using the word 'but' or some cognate to create a dramatic shift (contrast) in meaning. In 'Lives of Girls and Women', Del's mother, Mrs Jordan, and Fern listen to opera. Del's mother has a book about opera, but Fern once studied singing and is presumed to have inner knowledge.

> She had questions for Fern, but Fern did not know as much about operas as you would think she might; she would even get mixed up about which one it was they were listening to. But sometimes she would lean forward with her elbows on the table, not now relaxed, but alertly supported, and sing, scorning the foreign words. (145)

The sentences zig-zag, turning at the buts, creating a complex and fundamentally sympathetic picture of Fern, a picture that accretes through a series of rhythmic deferrals until the last phrase. What is deferred is a final meaning as each 'but' contradicts an assumption about Fern, replacing it with a new assumption, which is in turn contradicted.

There is a beautiful thematic passage in 'Baptizing' that further illustrates Munro's use of this grammatical technique. It occurs when Garnet and Del are exploring their sexuality without yet having had intercourse, wild sessions of making out and petting in his parked truck or in the wood by the river. Note how Munro employs the not/but-construction to juxtapose contrasting ideas.

> I would go home from these sessions by the river and not be able to sleep sometimes till dawn, not because of unrelieved sexual tension, as might be expected, but because I had to review, could not let go of, those great gifts I had received, gorgeous bonuses – lips on the wrists, the inside of the elbow, the shoulders, the breasts, hands on the belly, the thighs, between the legs. Gifts. Various kisses, tongue-touchings, suppliant and grateful noises. Audacity and revelation. The mouth closed frankly around the nipple seemed to make an avowal of innocence, defencelessness not because it imitated a baby's but because it was not afraid of absurdity. Sex seemed to me all surrender – not

> the woman's to the man but the person's to the body, an act of pure faith, freedom in humility. (218)

The three not/but-constructions create a complex stepped argument rising to that glorious and complex avowal of the nature of sex, all the more powerful because it is conscious of its opposite.

Sometimes the opposition will be inscribed in the diction. For example, Munro often uses the word 'difference' to ascribe, yes, difference, to make a distinction. In the following extract, difference is registered subjectively (the difference frightens Del) as well as in the diction.

> Well-groomed girls frightened me to death. I didn't like to even go near them, for fear I would be smelly. I felt there was a radical difference, between them and me, as if we were made of different substances. (179)

In a sense, Alice Munro stories are like assemblages of Venn diagrams: each circle defines a separate, autonomous, and different field (she uses the word 'world' often to describe differential subjectivities). But there are areas of coincidence, where the circles overlap, and where people find a solidarity (always tentative and temporary), usually in opposition to someone or something else. It's almost impossible to parse a sentence like the following without the idea of a set of Venn diagrams in mind.

> Her agnosticism and sociability were often in conflict in Jubilee, where social and religious life were apt to be one and the same. (174)

This sentence is constructed with the balanced antithesis of an aphorism ('conflict' vs 'one and the same'; 'agnosticism and sociability' vs 'social and religious life'), and part of the reason for the compositional elegance is Munro's habit of composing in opposed doubles. But the larger point is that much of any Alice Munro text will be taken up with a precise delineation of differences. Her style is to mark the differences.

The structural and syntactic vectors of difference, the various armatures of Munro's oppositional style, converge in the character of Del Jordan, who is after all the one who is telling the story, the putative author. Sorting difference is Del's way of experiencing the world and maintaining her sense of self. It gives her a tilt, an attitude, a personality that is resolutely and sometimes comically contrarian. ('So I felt obliged, out of contrariness, to say ...' (209).) In 'Lives of Girls and Women' she describes herself as 'an exile or a spy'; in 'Baptizing': 'And already I felt my old self – my old devious, ironic, isolated self ...' (240). At crux in both stories she finds herself resisting the definitions of another character (I call them definitions, but equally they could be called judgements or behavioural expectations or forms): her mother's advice in 'Lives of Girls and Women' – 'I did not quite get the point of this, or if I did get the point I was set up to resist it. I would have had to resist anything she told me with such earnestness, with such stubborn hopefulness' (177) – and Garnet French's missionary zeal in 'Baptizing' – 'and I felt amazement, not that I was fighting with Garnet but that anybody could have made such a mistake, to think he had real power over me' (238). Both stories express a universal plot, the drama of individuation, of the child separating from the mother; the mother is both literal and symbolic, acting as a placetaker for the matrix of supportive but ultimately limiting people and/or social structures that dog our lives. Both stories contrive to bring Del to a crisis of resistance, the point at which she encounters/discovers her self as a resisting presence and a clear sense of the difference between the other (the subjective world of the other) and the self she wishes to defend. Del asserts difference and selfhood without moralizing and without trying to create a type or archetype, asserting only individuality as a negative (I am not that) and, as a corollary, the mystery – inaccessibility – of the other. In other words, for Del, and for Munro, there are no essences, only what you might call subjective fields (family, friends, teachers, lovers, social groups), which have a tendency to impinge authoritatively (control, colonize) on the self.

But the fundamental difficulty with individuality (the irreducible difference of self) is in the encounter with another person and the paradoxical discovery that the self is a socially constructed artefact. In the cockpit of relationship, relating becomes an exchange of dimly perceived markers and signs, and the self becomes mysterious. Here is Del dancing with Clive:

> 'Dance me loose,' he said, using one of these phrases, and rolling his eyes at me imploringly. I did not know what he meant; surely I was dancing with him, or he was dancing himself, as loose as anybody could do? Everything he said was like this; I heard the words but could not figure out the meaning; he might have been joking, but his face remained so steadily unsmiling. But he rolled his eyes, this grotesque way, and called me 'baby' in a cold languishing voice, as if I were someone altogether different from myself; all I could think of to do was get some idea of this person he thought he was dancing with and pretend to be her. (188)

And here is Del parsing her relationship with Garnet:

> Perhaps I successfully hid from him what I was like. More likely, he rearranged me, took just what he needed, to suit himself. I did that with him. (220)

At a certain point, it seems, the self itself disappears (except as a point of observation and resistance – I am not this or not that).

> 'You will have to do what you want,' she [Del's mother] said bitterly. But was that so easy to know? I went out to the kitchen, turned on the light, and made

myself a big mixture of fried potatoes and onions and tomatoes and eggs, which I ate greedily and sombrely out of the pan, standing up. I was free and I was not free. I was relieved and I was desolate. (241)

It is out of the tension implied in the paradox, between wanting to be (alone, an exile, or a spy) and the formal imperatives of a social animal (growing up in Jubilee with a mother like Mrs Jordan and needing a boy like Garnet French to achieve the glory of erotic ecstasy) that Alice Munro creates her short stories.

Munro is ultimately ironic in her construction of text, ironic and often quite comic in her delineation of characters driven by competing imperatives. Del wants what she wants (glory/sex), but she is born into a world of myriad conflicting forms (definitions, ethical and social norms, faddish ideas, local wisdom, custom and prejudice, and the complex personalities of other people, who, yes, want what they want). Her style of mind is to think by contrasts (much in the spirit of the form of the aphorism), by setting one person, social group, or idea against another, ultimately by a shifting matrix of difference and analogy.

Inevitably, this has something to do with the nature of language itself, made of words that bear meaning only insofar as they relate to other words, that meaning inscribed in the word 'difference'. Munro gives tantalizing indications of a sophisticated theory of language, even metaphysics, when she plays with the idea of what is beyond language, especially her near-mystical descriptions of sex, conceived here as knowledge beyond language. As she says, in regard to Garnet,

> words were our enemies. What we knew about each other was only going to be confused by them. This was the knowledge that is spoken of as 'only sex,' or 'physical attraction.' I was surprised, when I thought about it – am surprised still – at the light, even disparaging tone that is taken, as if this was something that could be found easily, every day (221)

and

> It was the very opposite of going out with Jerry, and seeing the world dense and complicated but appallingly unsecretive; the world I saw with Garnet was something not far from what I thought animals must see, the world without names. (221)

In 'Lives of Girls and Women', she calls sex – note the paradoxical adjectives – the 'magical, bestial act' (153) and imagines it to be beyond language and responsibility, beyond the 'ambition and anxiety' (154) that characterize existence in the modern age. In the following example, she's thinking about one of the village prostitutes, and in doing so injects a curious line of religious terminology, giving the second sentence an aphoristic quality:

> I was surprised, in a way, that she would read a paper, that the words in it would mean the same things to her, presumably, as they did to the rest of us, that she ate and drank, was human still. I thought of her as having gone right beyond human functioning into a condition of perfect depravity, at the opposite pole from sainthood but similarly isolated, unknowable. (154)

Munro continues the pattern of religious terminology applied to the erotic (as an analogy) when Del begins consorting with Garnet.

> I felt angelic with gratitude, truly as if I had come out on another level of existence. (213)

> Audacity and revelation ... Sex seemed to me all surrender – not the woman's to the man but the person's to the body, an act of pure faith, freedom in humility. (218)

It would be a mistake here to pin a theme of religious belief on to Munro's stories; rather, she is elaborating one last framing opposition, playing with the idea of language and what might be beyond language: non-human, amoral, shed of contradiction and opposition and the need to speak, free of anxiety and ambition, yet revelatory and angelic (as well as bestial – neither angels nor beasts have need of speech). And this sets up the last lines of 'Baptizing' in which Del accepts that 'I would get started on my real life.' Real meaning notionally real, the so-called real, the ironic real, reiterated in the last line in italics: 'Real life.' As if to remind us, as Munro does over and over, that reality is an unstable article, not to be trusted.

Note

[1] *Lives of Girls and Women* (Toronto: McGraw-Hill Ryerson, 1971), 163. All subsequent references will be noted in the text.

4

MARIA LÖSCHNIGG

'Oranges *and* apples'

Alice Munro's undogmatic feminism

Delineating Alice Munro's 'feminism'

'I'm a feminist about certain measures that I would support', Alice Munro told Harold Horwood in an interview published in 1984.[1] Yet, she added, feminism 'as an attitude to life which is imposed on [her] by someone else' was something she rejected.[2] In the same interview, Munro makes it clear that when she writes, she does not 'think of feminist politics' but only of 'what is going on in [her] story'.[3] Munro's work is characterized, above all, by multiplicity, polyphony, digression, and indeterminacy, which indicate the coexistence of equivalent discourses rather than the replacement of one dominant discourse by another. She thus questions predominant patriarchal structures mostly by means of her 'use of the interrogative short story form'.[4] She employs this relativist mode in order to counter fixed ideologies of any kind, including feminism, and 'in order to reveal how these culturally powerful narrational models fall short of the private life stories of women'.[5] It can thus be argued that even though Munro's stories definitely allow for feminist readings, and even though there have been numerous attempts by critics to categorize the author as a 'deeply political writer',[6] Alice Munro's feminism is implicit and non-programmatic.

The unobtrusive and undogmatic nature of Munro's feminism is confirmed not least by her 'confession' after she won the Nobel Prize: 'I guess I am not a political person.' Asked whether she thought it important that a story was told from a woman's perspective, she answers: 'I never thought of it being important, but I never thought of myself as being anything but a woman.' Her stories, as the author further explains, are not explicitly addressed to female readers, but rather she wants to move people, not caring 'if they are men or women or children'.[7] According to Carol L. Beran, we see nothing of Aritha van Herk's 'strident feminist stance' or Margaret Atwood's straightforward 'critique of society's role in victimizing women',[8] which are not only transported by their fiction, but also explicitly articulated in their critical essays. Instead, Beran continues, 'Munro takes us beyond the issue of male power versus female power by presenting images in which forces outside the control of men and women have the ultimate control, levelling the power struggle to an insignificance in the larger scheme of things while attributing great power to artistic creation'.[9] It is indeed mostly through her shaping of her narrative material that her resistance to patriarchal structures and modes of thinking, i.e. her feminist stance, is communicated. Subverting the game played in her story 'Oranges and Apples' (from *Friend of My Youth*), where the rule is that you have to choose, Munro's story writing, especially as far as her depiction of women and feminist issues is concerned, articulates a refusal to follow the rules and instead leads us to accept two (or more) truths, two (or more) options, this *and* the other, instead of an either/or opposition. It is this skilfully transmitted avoidance of falling into the trap of offering yet another master discourse characterized by binary schemes of thought, her setting – in the Cixousian sense – of 'multiple heterogeneous *difference*',[10] which marks the essence of her inherent feminist impact.

Munro's implicit feminism is encoded in various forms on the inextricably connected levels of story and discourse. One of the most striking manifestations of a feminist impact is definitely her foregrounding of 'gender-scripts',[11] a concept referring to culturally acquired characteristics of femininity which are rendered as biologically determined. While Munro exposes the dictate of such scripts and features characters who successfully or unsuccessfully attempt to escape these either/or patterns, this does not mean that the author categorically negates innate differences between male and female behaviour. Rather, her depictions of feminine and masculine behaviour patterns 'demonstrate that the body and its functions are formed in interaction with society and culture',[12] a position shared, in fact, by many post-second wave feminists. Anne Phillips notes in this context: 'Notwithstanding the conceptual difficulties feminists have raised around the distinction between sex and gender, we will continue to need some way of disentangling the differences that are inevitable from those that are chosen, and from those that are simply imposed.'[13] Munro exposes the absurdities of such imposed gender-scripts most radically in her growing-up stories, where concepts of femininity and masculinity are questioned and continually repositioned. However, her implicit feminist stance can also be observed in those stories which focus on motherhood and marriage and accentuate the pressure of these familial factors on women. It will be important to note in this context that although Munro and her protagonists do question and rebel against restrictive concepts of femininity, they 'do not easily, or clearly always want to, divest themselves of their femininity', as Beverly Rasporich aptly observes.[14] Thus Munro can simultaneously and paradoxically be seen as a feminist as well as a feminine author. Like Del Jordan in her processing of her Uncle Craig's town history in *Lives of Girls and Women*, the author does not 'seek to vanquish the masculine narrative (for that would be just another struggle for supremacy on male terms of contest) but allows it alongside and even within her own narrative'.[15] This aim is achieved mostly by her interrogative story mode, her multiple layering of story strands, and her narrative voice which defies fixed discourses and final meanings. Thus, the feminist issues which surface in the text and which include her questioning of gender-scripts, her revision of the fairy-tale pattern, her critical featuring of maternity and gender segregation, and the victimization of women on various levels and in various forms, including the commodification of the female body, must always be seen against the backdrop of her interrogative multivalent writing technique. This narrative mode in fact becomes Munro's major subversive tool for exposing and undermining rigid patriarchal structures without running the risk of proposing yet another totalizing model of thought. Hunter and Mayberry both regard this openness and fluidity of narrative as one of Munro's most effective strategies, precisely because 'they do *not* replicate or even mimic the controlling strategies of those who have controlled them'.[16] Her stories – despite their deceptive realist make-up – may thus be seen as a manifestation of Derrida's idea of the 'free-play of discourse', or Barthes's 'plural text', which also form the basis of Hélène Cixous's idea of *écriture féminine*. This concept of feminine writing, which is defined by Cixous among others as 'ceaseless displacement',[17] does indeed allow for rewarding feminist readings of Munro's stories, but only as long as one remains careful not to lapse, once again, into an essentialist evaluation of the work of a female writer.

'Girls don't slam doors like that'

Among many others, a striking element in Alice Munro's narratives of growing up is her exposure of the constructedness of rigid concepts of femininity and masculinity. Many of Munro's girl characters, especially in her growing-up cycles *Lives of Girls and Women* (1971) and *Who Do You Think You Are?/The Beggar Maid* (1978) but also in individual stories that feature young female characters, are deeply confused by the dictates of gender-scripts. Thus the first-person narrator in 'Boys and Girls' (*Dance of the Happy Shades*) realizes at a certain point that to be a girl means to obey certain rules: 'The word *girl* had formerly seemed to me innocent and unburdened, like the word *child*; now it appeared that it was no such thing. A girl was not, as I had supposed, simply what I was; it was what I had to become.'[18] To be a girl also means to be excluded from 'male' responsibilities, a freedom which comes with implications of an inferior status: 'She's only a girl.'[19] In 'Lying under the Apple Tree' (*The View from Castle Rock*) we find similar 'unstated but far-reaching rules' such as the one concerning bikes: 'All girls who wanted to establish their femininity had to quit riding them.'[20] In Del in *Lives of Girls and Women* in particular, we find a young protagonist who is puzzled by the demands of being a 'real girl'. She longs to be loved and desired as a woman, but feels she cannot put up 'this masquerade'[21] her friend Naomi adopts. She painfully senses her difference from 'well-groomed girls' who frighten her to death and comes to the sarcastic conclusion that '[l]ove is not for the undepilated'.[22] As Kate Millett argues,

> Because of our social circumstances, male and female are really two cultures and their life experiences are utterly different ... Implicit in all the gender identity development which takes place through childhood is the sum total of the parents', the peers', and the culture's notions of what is appropriate to each gender by way of temperament, character, interests, status, worth, gesture and expression.[23]

Del's identity is shaken: confronted with an article in a magazine on the 'difference between male and female habits of thought', she fears that she 'was not thinking as the girl thought'.[24] She is torn between two role models: her mother's repression of her femininity on the one hand, and that of traditional gender-scripts on the other. For the young protagonist, both models prove to be too reductive: 'I did not want to be like my mother, with her virginal brusqueness, her innocence. I wanted men to love me, and I wanted to think of the universe when I looked at the moon. I felt trapped, stranded; it seemed there had to be a choice where there couldn't be a choice.'[25] The fact that she says 'seemed' already indicates that she questions the validity of such a choice – a suspicion which is confirmed by the act of tearing up the magazine. In Munro's girl characters in particular, the painful fascination with 'feminine decorativeness'[26] is textually foregrounded when, for example, the thirteen-year-old first-person narrator in 'Red Dress – 1946' (*Dance of the Happy Shades*) wants the 'protection of all possible female rituals'[27] when she goes to her first dance, or when Rose in 'Privilege' (*The Beggar Maid*) completely falls for Cora's perfect feminine masquerade.[28] This concerns physical codes of femininity as well as behavioural codes, which are featured in an almost comic mode in 'Nettles' (*Hateship, Friendship, Courtship, Loveship, Marriage*). In this story, the narrator recalls her childhood self's 'fanatic feeling of devotion'[29] for nine-year-old Mike with the following words: 'I accepted readily, even devoutly, the roles that did not have to be explained or worked out between us – that I would aid and admire him, he would direct and stand ready to protect me.'[30] As Munro's treatment of stereotypical concepts of male and female identity shows, she does not aim at substituting one for the other, but rather supplements what has been omitted in a process which defies closure. 'For Munro's stories', as Howells aptly remarks, 'undermine the notion of a single identity by showing that the selves of her protagonists are far less stable than the word "identity" suggests.'[31]

The 'damsel in distress'

The fairy-tale pattern which pervades the adolescent fantasies not only of Del in *Lives of Girls and Women* but also of many other Munrovian girl characters, and which is based on the assumption of women being the weaker sex, is turned upside-down in several stories which feature young adult women, who actively decide to reject this power imbalance. 'And as her heroines', as Rasporich pointedly comments, 'pass hopefully through and ironically beyond the traditional passive fantasies of waiting for Prince Charming, for Darcy from *Pride and Prejudice* in "An Ounce of Cure", or the chivalric knight from Tennyson's "silly" poem "Mariana" (*Lives*, 200), they begin to take charge of their own lives and pass into social history.'[32] For that matter, Del in 'Lives of Girls and Women' has by now developed her own opinion of her mother's advice to compensate for this 'feminine weakness' by using her brains and, above all, by avoiding getting distracted by a man. She in fact rejects

> advice that assumed being female made you damageable, that a certain amount of carefulness and solemn fuss and self-protection were called for, whereas men were supposed to be able to go out and take all kinds of experiences and shuck off what they didn't want and come back proud. Without even thinking about it, I had decided to do the same.[33]

As opposed to her mother, Del wants to experience passion and sexuality *and* to participate in the glory that, according to the gender-script, was reserved for men. When she says 'sex seemed to me all surrender – not the woman's to the man but the person's to the body',[34] she indeed offers a rather challenging concept of male–female relationships, a concept which is affirmed by her reaction to Garnet French's forceful attempt to baptize her: 'I felt amazement, not that I was fighting with Garnet but that anybody could have made such a mistake, to think he had real power over me.'[35]

A story in which the 'fairy-tale pattern' receives its most radical and also most comical feminist revision is the epistolary story 'Hateship, Friendship, Courtship, Loveship, Marriage' (*Hateship*). Johanna, who works as a housekeeper for an elderly gentleman and takes care of his granddaughter Sabitha, is tricked into believing that Sabitha's father, Ken, is in love with her by Sabitha's and her friend Edith's interception and forging of letters. The letters trigger romantic fantasies in Johanna and so she travels out to Saskatchewan with the resolution to get married to the unwitting Ken. The situation when she arrives in Gdynia is quite disastrous: nobody picks her up at the train station, and when she finally finds Ken's derelict domicile, she is confronted with a sick and delirious man who does not even seem to recognize her. It is at this point that Munro introduces a comic switch by assigning the role of the brave knight who comes to rescue the beautiful but fragile princess to Johanna herself. She comes, she stays, and she manages to transform Ken's chaotic life into a happy family scenario. Munro, as Coral Ann Howells describes it, 'has deftly turned romance on its head, translating the dynamics of fantasy into real life while subverting the traditional gendered power relationship into celebration of a woman's managerial capacities and a man's gratitude for being rescued'.[36] 'Hateship, Friendship, Courtship, Loveship, Marriage' in fact points to another aspect of implicit feminism in Munro's stories, namely that of the fantasy script, of many female characters' power to live in different dimensions simultaneously 'with the result that her characters are not split subjects but pluralized subjects'.[37] Another story which features this (female) skill to reconcile fantastic and material spaces is 'Carried Away' (*Open Secrets*), where Munro again turns to the letter-form in order to render the building up of such fantasies plausible.

An interesting variant of the 'damsel in distress' motif can be found in 'The Beggar Maid',[38] where it figures as a central subtext in Munro's conveyance and exposure of traditional images of femininity and masculinity. The myth of the beggar maid, rendered concrete in Tennyson's poem of the same name and, above all, in the painting *King Cophetua and the Beggar Maid* by the Pre-Raphaelite artist Edward Burne-Jones, becomes the template for Patrick's courtship of Rose. In her reflections on the painting, the focalizer Rose realizes how Patrick sees her: as a helpless lower-class girl who longs to be saved by the wealthy and chivalrous hero. Rose does not actually identify with the 'Beggar Maid', but she nonetheless flirts with this idea of total submission while simultaneously sensing that Patrick would never fit into the role of Cophetua, with 'his trance of passion, clever and barbaric'.[39] In the end she does marry Patrick, despite her conviction that '[a]ll the time, moving and speaking, she was destroying herself for him'.[40] An essential aspect of Munro's depiction of this courtship and marriage is her 'casting' of Rose as an actress (not only professionally but also as a way of negotiating her private life), who, in contrast to Patrick, is mostly aware of the fact that in order to follow the Cinderella script, she will have to 'act'. As the reader is offered Rose's point of view, following her struggles and inner resistance to Patrick's appropriation of her 'self', the story can be read as a powerful feminist discourse critical of female submission to male thinking which, in the case of Rose, crushes her 'vision of happiness'.[41] Like so many of Munro's protagonists who break out of unhappy marriages, 'leaving husband and house and all the things acquired during marriage ... in the hope of making a life that could be lived without hypocrisy and shame', Rose eventually gives up the role in Patrick's script and moves on to new adventures. However, there is one role she cannot give up, at least not emotionally, which is that of the mother. Munro's oeuvre is rife with stories that take up and transform an Anna Karenina-type plot by featuring women who break out of marriages in their quest for genuine relationships, their longing for true passion, and their insistence on female autonomy. However, it is always the issue of children which poses the severest challenge to their acts of liberation: 'There were miseries I could bear – those connected with men. And other miseries – those connected with children – that I could not', as the first-person narrator in 'Nettles' reveals.[42] Similarly Pauline, the focal character in 'The Children Stay' (*The Love of a Good Woman*), comes to the conclusion that the price women have to pay for walking out on a suffocating marriage is leaving their children: 'This is acute pain. It will become chronic.'[43] Thus, it would be wrong to argue that Munro's female characters all successfully overcome the restrictions of gender-scripts or happily break out of unhappy marriages. Rather, as we usually get the point of view of these afflicted mothers, the reader has ample opportunity to follow these women's histories of (often unfulfilled) desire, agony, disappointment, and humiliation. With regard to their plots, therefore, these stories are rarely about the successful emancipation of powerful women. However, they offer to the reader a whole range of alternatives, often through complex reflections on the part of female characters, and through Munro's multi-layered narrative texture, which urges a questioning of gender norms.

'She *is* the house; there is no separation possible'

Interesting feminist aspects come to the fore in those stories which thematize the family home and the role of the mother. Here, the imprisoning effects of gender segregation are negotiated via mother characters who are trapped in fixed notions of maternity and who are forced to become 'mothering clowns'[44] in their attempts to juggle maternal, marital, and professional interests. In some stories, for example 'Mischief' (*The Beggar Maid*), the idea of the perfect mother is treated in a highly comical manner when the young mothers Rose and Jocelyn 'annoy and mystify' the other women in the maternity ward by disobeying the nurses, by using dirty language, and by reading André Gide instead of engaging in discussions about the arrangement of kitchen cupboards or the use of vacuum cleaners.[45] In this parody of femininity the writer seems to draw from her own experience as a young mother suffering from the 'neighbourhood women who were always dropping by for coffee unannounced ... dispensing unsolicited advice about housekeeping', as Sheila Munro puts it in her memoir, *Lives of Mothers and Daughters*.[46] Here, we also find a statement by the author herself on this matter: 'There used to be these dreadful long domestic conversations about how do you get the diapers whiter or softer, or whatever you're supposed to do with diapers, and I used to think that everybody else really enjoyed them.'[47] For Munro's protagonists to be mothers and to keep up their intellectual identity and personal autonomy, it requires the performance of a 'precarious stunt'.[48] Such a stunt is presented, for instance, at the beginning of the story 'Deep Holes' (*Too Much Happiness*), which features a family picnic at Osler Bluff with the young mother, Sally, juggling her various roles. These comprise breastfeeding her baby daughter, watching her two sons, supervising the picnic, acting like an attentive and admiring wife to her husband – a geologist in whose honour they are having the picnic in the first place – listening to his specialist comments on the unique rock formations, and having a sip of her champagne ('just a sip, because she was still nursing'[49]) while making sure that her sons do not also have a sip behind her back, which the older one manages to do anyway. In addition to all this, there are Sally's private thoughts, which sporadically flow into the narrative. The third-person mode, in fact, with the mother mostly functioning as a focalizer, *shows* rather than *describes* her 'precarious stunt', while in first-person stories such as 'Miles City, Montana' (*The Progress of Love*) the narrator actually seems to reflect on the multi-tasking which is expected of mothers: 'I could be talking to Andrew, talking to the children and looking at whatever they wanted me to look at ... and pouring lemonade into plastic cups, and all the time those bits and pieces would be flying together inside me.'[50] Munro's narratives are also inhabited by a number of mothers who feel the pressure of being inadequate, a pressure exerted either by the family as in 'The Children Stay' and 'My Mother's Dream' (*The Love of a Good Woman*), or by the town community as in 'Soon' (*Runaway*), where this community is metonymically represented by the housekeeper Irene. Pragmatic Irene with her 'competent hands', who is offset against the intellectual Juliet with her illegitimate child, 'watched everything Juliet did, watched her fiddle with the knobs on the stove (not remembering at first which burners they controlled), watched her lifting the egg out of the saucepan and peeling off the shell (which stuck, this time, and came away in little bits rather than in large easy pieces), then watched her choosing the saucer to mash it in'.[51]

Inseparable from the Munrovian mother-figure, who often also struggles to assert her identity as an artist, is the family home, which is depicted as the space against which male and female gender-scripts are pointedly accentuated. The narrator/writer/mother in 'The Office' (*Dance of the Happy Shades*), for example, becomes bitterly aware that while the man can make use of his family home because 'the house rearranges itself as best it can around him',[52] the woman cannot 'practise this place'[53] because 'she *is* the house, there is no separation possible'.[54] Again, the feminist echo is 'heard' only on the extratextual level, while within the world of the story her longing for 'a room of her own' fails in many respects. As far as her family is concerned, they do not see any need for her wish; in fact, to have 'wished for a mink coat' or a 'diamond necklace'[55] would have been met with much more understanding. When she finally does take action and rents an 'office', she is terrorized by the landlord's stereotypical notion of what a 'lady's room' should look like. Even though, meta-fictionally, the narrator takes revenge by using Mr Malley as 'material' for her story, 'The Office' – just like the later story 'Material' – not only foregrounds gender imbalances and the victimization of women, but also problematizes women's ambivalent roles and possible conspiracies in these multi-layered power dynamics. Thus, when she says, 'Bloated, opinionated, untidy men, that is how I see them, cosseted by the academic life, the literary life, by women',[56] the first-person narrator of 'Material' (*Something I've Been Meaning to Tell You*) not only articulates a harsh criticism of the vanities of male academia, but also exposes the women's role as accomplices in this power constellation. Similarly, the narrator in 'The Office' sees how she encourages Mr Malley's impertinences with her 'offerings of courtesy' expressed 'in the hope that [he] will go away and leave [her] alone'. Her 'cold voice' only works in her thoughts and she finds it difficult to get it out of her 'cowardly mouth'.[57] The story refuses to answer the question of whether a more 'masculine' behaviour would have put an end to Mr Malley's intrusions, as the story seems to imply that such a resolute performance would not have been accepted coming from a woman.

'Haven' (*Dear Life*) provides a particularly intriguing example of Munro's continuous deferral of meaning with regard to the complex power relations between men and women. At first sight the story appears to foreground the victimization of two women, the narrator's Aunt Dawn and her Uncle Jasper's 'shunned' sister, Mona, but a closer reading of the story provides access to a multi-layered story structure which impedes a clear judgement of the presented character constellations. As in *Lives of Girls and Women* and, in fact, in many of Munro's other stories, the events are filtered by the consciousness of a girl character and at the same time doubled by that of her mature narrating self. The thirteen-year-old first-person narrator stays with her Aunt Dawn and her Uncle Jasper, the town's doctor, while her parents are in Africa doing missionary work. Soon, the girl notices about her uncle that '[t]he house was his, the choice of menus his, the radio and television programs his', whereas Aunt Dawn's 'most important job is making a haven for her man'.[58] While the narrator does sense the outrageousness of this crude gender segregation, at the same time she records that 'in his office he seemed so easygoing, compared with the way he was at home'.[59] One day his sister Mona Cassel, a violinist, comes to town with her ensemble to give a concert. The girl finds out from her aunt that Mona is *persona non grata* to her brother, who considers art as a 'fraud' and people who go to such concerts as 'a load of horse manure'.[60] When Aunt Dawn, in a rare revolutionary moment, invites the musicians to her house, knowing that her husband would be late as 'it was the night of the County Physicians Annual General Meeting and Dinner',[61] things escalate. The guests stay too long – Uncle Jasper catches them 'in the act' of a private musical performance and is infuriated by Aunt Dawn's deceit. His reaction is, on the one hand, presented in a clearly negative way which is further reinforced by the perspective of the child to whom the glaring uncle 'looks twice his size with his coat unbuttoned and his scarf loose and his boots on'.[62] On the other hand, however, it is also mitigated by the narrator's remark that she was not really surprised by this outburst, knowing 'there was a quantity of things that men hated. Or had no use for, as they said. And that was exactly right. They had no use for it, so they hated it.'[63] However – and here we again find reverberations of the author's art of inclusiveness – she 'didn't go so far as to want it wiped off the face of the earth for that reason'.[64] Duplicity and relativism permeate the story. When Mona, who must have been ill already when she visited, suddenly dies, her brother is surprised to hear that her last wish was to be buried in her old family church. While this issue is not further discussed within the story, it is implicitly revealed to the reader that all the time the violinist must have longed to return to the 'bosom of the family' and that the concert may already have been a step in this direction. Mona's fate inevitably recalls another female 'skeleton in the family closet', namely Alfrida in 'Family Furnishings' (*Hateship, Friendship, Courtship, Loveship, Marriage*), whose 'crime' is not to become an artist as in Mona's case, but to get pregnant by her cousin. Like Mona, however, she is declared an outcast so that the men of the family can go on with their proper lives, and like her she has always craved to be admitted back into this family circle. Whereas in 'Family Furnishings' the focus is more on the narrator coming to terms with appearance and reality as far as her 'material' for her writing is concerned, 'Haven' foregrounds the incessant act of questioning and revising certain attitudes. Thus, we find out about the narrator in 'Haven' that she 'was no longer so uncritical about people like Mona' while, almost paradoxically, concluding this reflection with a piece of feminist critique: 'Devotion to anything, if you were female, could make you ridiculous.'[65] Or is she implying that Mona should have known what price there was to pay for one's eccentricity and passion? It is again left to the reader to play through the whole plethora of options. Not even Uncle Jasper's abominable treatment of Aunt Dawn is exempted from the challenge of Munro's plural text: when the narrator recalls that 'creeping past my aunt and uncle's closed bedroom door early on a Sunday morning ... I had heard sounds such as I had never heard from my parents or from anyone else – a sort of pleasurable growling and squealing in which there was a complicity and an abandonment that disturbed and darkly undermined me',[66] we are inevitably led to assume that the couple's marriage was not such an unhappy one after all. While the story critically foregrounds the existence of gender-scripts in its ironic title, the skilful doubling of voices at the same time defies a simplified correlation of submissive feminine performance with victimization and unhappiness. Of course, the reader is meant to understand Aunt Dawn's claim that 'A man's home is his castle' ironically, but at the same time the fact that it is she who utters this remark suggests that, first, it takes two to make this gender segregation possible and, second, that happiness and female identity can take many forms.

'Women's bodies'

The list of female victims in Munro's stories is long and diverse. While some women, such as Robin in 'Tricks' (*Runaway*), become victims of fate in a way which is reminiscent of Thomas Hardy's characters, others are victimized by male cowardice, male craving for power, and male chauvinism. Thus Vivien in 'Amundsen' (*Dear Life*), who accepts a position as a teacher in a sanatorium for children, is jilted by Dr Alistair Fox right before the wedding ceremony and is given her marching orders with a cowardly excuse: 'I can't do it, he has said. He has said that he can't go through with this. He can't explain it. Only that it's a mistake.'[67] While in Vivien's case the consequences are 'only' the protagonist's utter feelings of mortification and humiliation, Tessa in 'Powers' (*Runaway*) pays a much higher price for her love of Neil, who marries her only in order to use her 'powers', i.e. her gift of second sight, for his own professional success. Having been 'disempowered' and exploited for medical experiments, she is dumped in an asylum where

Nancy, a former friend, visits her and finds out that she underwent dubious therapies in order to wipe out her memory: 'They gave me the needles and the gas too. It was to cure my head. And to make me not remember.'[68] Whereas Tessa is beyond help, there is still hope at the end of 'Dimensions' (*Too Much Happiness*) that Doree will finally free herself from the clutches of the fanatic and power-hungry Lloyd, who in a fit of jealousy and, above all, to teach his young wife a lesson, murders their three children. Lloyd is declared criminally insane and locked up in an institution in London, Ontario, from where he tries to regain his power over Doree via the long and manipulative letters he sends her. Through the narrativization of Doree's reception of the letters, the reader witnesses the persuasive effect Lloyd's words have on the young woman. It is only through a seemingly insignificant incident, namely Doree's reanimation of an injured motorist on her way to see Lloyd, that there are signs denoting her development of an identity disconnected from him. She now senses that to be of use in the world means more than to be of use to Lloyd. Resuscitating the young man mirrors Doree's own revival: both, in some way, have to learn to breathe again. It would not be Munro, however, if the reader were to get off lightly with this prospect of 'healing'. After all, Doree is able to save the young man only because she remembers Lloyd's instructions in case of an accident involving one of their children. Even though the story ends with Doree's resolution not to continue her visits, we cannot be certain if this is really a final decision and liberation from her own prison of submissive dependence. By foregrounding the victimization of women at the hands of male characters, Munro exposes the destructive effects, not only of male chauvinism, but of unbalanced power relations in general.

Of particular interest with regard to feminist considerations are those stories in Munro's oeuvre which deal with the objectification of the female body within a larger context of a female's dependence on male signification of her body. In 'Memorial' (*Something I've Been Meaning to Tell You*), Eileen reflects on male as opposed to female post-coital attitudes after her brief affair with her sister's husband, Ewart. While women, according to her, 'look for clues and store things up in a hurry to be considered later', men like Ewart see it as 'the brief restorative dip': 'A woman's body. Before and during the act they seem to invest this body with certain individual powers, they will say its name in a way that indicates something particular, something unique, that is sought for. Afterwards it appears that they have changed their minds, they wish it understood that such bodies are interchangeable. Women's bodies.'[69] Again, however, a one-dimensional reading of the story is subverted when, for example, Eileen muses about Ewart's body: 'He was not a sexually attractive man. Why not? His large sad butt, his vulnerable priggish look from the rear?'[70] Still, it seems that neither Ewart nor most of the other male characters in Munro's work feel the constant strain of having to adapt to female desires. Generally, it is the female characters in the stories whose bodies are defined by male signification, or rather who have internalized the male gaze and struggle to protect the vulnerability of their (ageing) bodies. In 'Lichen' (*The Progress of Love*), David 'knows that sooner or later, if Dina allows her disguise to crack, as Catherine did, he will have to move on. He will have to do that anyway – move on.'[71] For him, women are disposable commodities which can be substituted as soon as they lose their glimmer of novelty.

In several stories collected in *The Moons of Jupiter* in particular, middle-aged women 'inhabit not just the position of object, but of reject'.[72] In 'Bardon Bus', 'Labour Day Dinner', and 'Dulse', the 'heroines' fail in their pursuit of happiness owing to their dependence on male approval. 'The sexy woman', as psychologist Jessica Benjamin explains, 'is sexy, but as object, not as subject. She expresses not so much *her* desire as her pleasure in being desired; what she enjoys is her capacity to evoke desire in the other, to attract.'[73] This is exactly what happens to Lydia in 'Dulse' when she travels to New Brunswick to 'lick the wounds' inflicted by her ex-lover Duncan, who tried to 'alter those things about her person and her behaviour which he did not like',[74] who drove her to make all these 'gigantic efforts to please' and humiliated her when she failed: '"What have you done to your face?" he said when she came back to the car. "Makeup. I put some makeup on so I'd look more cheerful." "You can see where the line stops, on your neck."' Lydia allows herself to be moulded by Duncan's desires, but in her retrospective analysis of this relationship she not only manages to reflect on her own possible participation in this transfer of power, but also reveals – just like Roberta in 'Labour Day Dinner' – that in her previous marriage it was she who could 'pull the rug out'.[75] 'Vulnerability', according to Eva DeClercq, 'is an ambiguous notion that always involves both the power to wound and the capacity to be wounded.'[76] In Roberta we again find a woman in her mid-forties, in a relationship with George, a man who, as she fears, 'is disgusted by her aging body', including her flabby armpits. Roberta 'applies cream frantically to her wrinkles' and diets 'until her waist was thin enough to please produced a haggard look about her cheeks and throat'.[77] Both Lydia and Roberta, as these stories show, have lost their capacity to be happy because of their futile endeavours to please. Rosalind Coward notes about sexual roles in the 1990s that 'although there may be a much greater variety of female styles, the concern with desirability to men is still uppermost in women's self-representation'.[78] It is therefore one of the great achievements of stories such as 'Labour Day Dinner' that such constellations of domination and submission are presented as dead-ends for both parties. The polyphonic narrative structure of the story, which not only features Roberta's point of view but also gives an insight into the thoughts of George and of Angela, her seventeen-year-old daughter, foregrounds the destructive force of such giving up of any self-sufficiency. By trying to please and becoming 'a person who doesn't ask for anything',[79] Roberta achieves the opposite of what she hoped she would get in return. She is about to lose the respect of Angela and the love of George she so desperately craves. By employing and reconfiguring a multitude of voices, Munro thus manages to provide an illuminating glimpse into the complexities of human suffering, an insight, in fact, which is mostly hidden from her fictional characters, who are denied the super-ordinate vantage-point of the reader of her multiply focalized narratives.

Even though vulnerability is not a female 'privilege', as implied in 'Dulse' and in 'Labour Day Dinner', the fact that women have been and still are more strongly defined by means of an attractive body than are men makes them much more prone to becoming victims of the onslaught of age. The desperate and mostly futile attempts to counter this increasing exclusion from sexual romance are memorably depicted in 'Bardon Bus'. In this story, Munro says, she wanted to have 'a kind of feeling of hysterical eroticism. Very edgy and sad.' She continues: 'This came to me from the feelings I get sometimes in women's dress shops. It's a feeling about the masquerades and attempts to attract love.'[80] 'Bardon Bus, No. 144' stands metonymically for the bliss the narrator experiences with the anthropologist X in Australia. Once back in Canada, her life is dominated by her longing for X, happy memories first, then dreams about letters from him, followed by feelings of inertia: 'I can't ... move my body along the streets unless I exist in his mind and in his eyes.'[81] The humiliation she feels about having been abandoned reaches a climax when she meets up with Dennis, a friend of X's. She not only hopes that this meeting may give her the chance to find out about X's whereabouts, but also strives to make a dashing physical impression on Dennis so that he can tell his friend how charming she is. However, what finally finishes her off are Dennis's remarks on the 'life of women', '[s]pecifically with aging': 'It's in all the novels and it's in life too. Men fall in love with younger women. Men want younger women ... You can't compete with younger women.' Dennis sees his theory as a fact which has to be accepted as '[i]t's probably biologically correct for men to go after younger women'.[82] What Dennis says is ironically confirmed by the almost comic twist at the end of the story, which concludes with the narrator's friend Kay's enthusiastic report about her new lover, Alex, an anthropologist, whom we – and the narrator – recognize as X. Kay, of course, is ten years younger than the narrator. The story radically foregrounds the directly proportional relationship between female vulnerability and ageing. While Dennis sees this as a biological determinant, the story as a whole undermines his dictum through the exposure of sex-role stereotyping which forces women into such masquerades. Or is it the women's (misguided) urge to put on these masquerades which keeps putting them at the mercy of male signification, of reducing them to a passive role as objects of male desire? The story, which brings together, arranges, and rearranges different impressions which the narrator has collected now and then, including the almost picaresque parallel story of her friend Kay and her bizarre adventures with men, ends upon a note of additional insight on the part of the narrator. Not only does she reflect on 'the point at which the splendour collapses into absurdity' when she takes note of all the ridiculously dressed-up (elderly) women, but she also realizes and relates in an almost comical manner – a manner which denotes a good portion of self-reflection and irony – that '[t]here is a limit to the amount of misery and disarray you will put up with, for love, just as there is a limit to the amount of mess you can stand around a house'. The real irony, however, is provided by Kay, who, with her 'new outfit, a dark-green schoolgirl's tunic worn with a blouse or brassiere', is the next one in the line of women who are ready to put on a masquerade for X.[83]

With this, we have come back full circle to the gender-script, which Alice Munro indefatigably exposes for discussion in her work. The implication of 'refusing the either/or in favour of neither/both',[84] as suggested by corporeal feminism and which permeates Munro's stories, becomes the most tangible tableau upon which relations and power structures between men and women can be renegotiated. Stories such as 'Dulse', 'Labour Day Dinner', and 'Bardon Bus' expose a discrimination of women concerning their bodies, and make tangible the stress women undergo when they age: they foreground a persistent prioritizing of physical attractiveness in women as opposed to men, a duty, so to speak, to remain physically attractive which does not exist the other way round. Even though most of these stories offer no solution, they contribute to raising awareness of these manifold inequalities. These issues are rendered by Munro through 'her figuration of the narrative act as participatory, polylogic, and metaphoric'; she thus 'frees the notions of truth and understanding from their association with control and dominance'.[85] Even though, as Mayberry says about Munro's characters, 'only a lucky few succeed, reaching a vision that dismantles binary oppositions like subject and object, victimizer and victimized',[86] the 'vision' is always graspable on the receptive side, i.e. apt to work on readers. By narrativizing the destructive effect of mere subject–object relations, Munro triggers processes of reconsideration without imposing new normative concepts.

'I never thought of myself as being anything but a woman'

Feminist readings of Alice Munro are rewarding because of the mere fact that her stories offer distinctive female perspectives and portray women in different historical, regional, and social contexts. 'As a woman writer', Coral Ann Howells states, 'Munro is always aware of girls and women as thinking, feeling beings located within their female bodies.'[87] If, however, as is the underlying critical position in this chapter, one considers feminism as the subversion and deconstruction of power discourses which have for a long time been controlled by male voices and are based on rationalization, polarization, linearity, and notions of absolute truth, the feminist text will have to do without these prerogatives of absoluteness and power in order to offer convincing alternative models. The concept of *écriture féminine* may serve as a general descriptive model of what Munro achieves in her writing. It is, however, of paramount importance in this context to disentangle the narrative style and the biological sex of the writer, i.e. to avoid monopolizing fluidity and ambiguity for female writers only, as such a narrow definition of feminine writing would again nurture the essentialist dichotomy of femininity vs. masculinity and thus reinforce exactly those dictates of the gender-script which have been an imprisoning corset for so many generations of girls and women. Such one-dimensional feminist notions are misplaced in approaches to an author who claims: 'I never think about being a feminist writer.'[88] Rather, as Hunter puts it, 'Munro uses the interrogative short form in order to open up those dimensions of character and experience that ideological appraisal overlooks or misrepresents. She does not seek the displacement of one version of reality by another, as ideology promises, for that ... is simply to produce another structure of power and law.'[89] Munro's rejection of polarization, which is rendered by the specific make-up of her narrative web, is also visible in many of her female characters' approaches to life. When Denise in 'White Dump' tells her father that she is sick of his 'male definitions and airtight male arguments', she immediately adds, in her thoughts: 'Also, I'm sick of hearing myself say "male" like that.'[90]

By foregrounding and questioning gender-scripts, by offering multiple female perspectives, and by rendering female sensitivities and imaginaries, Munro has mediated female experience in manifold ways. By inscribing these themes into a narrative style which resists the suggestion of prescriptive truths and models, she has managed to develop a mode of literary articulation which does not exchange one system of power for another, but rather deconstructs power as such through her insistently interrogative approach. Thus, Alice Munro is both a feminist and *not* a feminist writer. Regarding the statements she has made in interviews and reading her stories attentively, it turns out that the impossible may be possible after all.

Notes

1. Judith Miller, *The Art of Alice Munro: Saying the Unsayable* (University of Waterloo Press, 1984), 134.
2. Ibid., 133.
3. Ibid., 134.
4. Adrian Hunter, 'Story into History: Alice Munro's Minor Literature', *English* 53 (2004), 222.
5. Ibid.
6. Katherine J. Mayberry, 'Narrative Strategies of Liberation in Alice Munro', *Studies in Canadian Literature/Études en littérature canadienne* 19, 2 (1994), 57.
7. See Lisa Allardice, 'Nobel Prize Winner Alice Munro: It's a Wonderful Thing for the Short Story', available online at www.theguardian.com/books/2013/dec/06/alice-munro-interview-nobel-prize-short-story-literature; accessed 7 December 2014.
8. Carol L. Beran, 'Images of Women's Power in Contemporary Canadian Fiction by Women', *Studies in Canadian Literature/Études en littérature canadienne* 15, 2 (1990), 70.
9. Ibid., 77.
10. Toril Moi, 'Feminist, Female, Feminine', in Catherine Belsey and Janet Moore (eds.), *The Feminist Reader* (Malden, MA: Blackwell, 1989), 111.
11. Laurie Kruk, 'Mothering Sons: Stories by Findley, Hodgins and MacLeod Uncover the Mother's Double Voice', *Atlantis* 32, 1 (2007), 34.
12. Sonya Andermahr, Terry Lovell and Carol Wolkowitz (eds.), *A Glossary of Feminist Theory* (London: Arnold, 2000), 103.
13. Anne Phillips, 'Universal Pretensions in Political Thought', in Michèle Barrett and Anne Phillips (eds.), *Destabilizing Theory: Contemporary Feminist Debates* (Cambridge: Polity Press, 1992), 23.
14. Beverly J. Rasporich, *Dance of the Sexes: Art and Gender in the Fiction of Alice Munro* (Edmonton: University of Alberta Press, 1990), xvii.
15. Hunter, 'Story into History', 224.
16. Mayberry, 'Narrative Strategies of Liberation in Alice Munro', 64.
17. Hélène Cixous, 'Sorties: Out and Out: Attacks/Ways Out/Forays', in Belsey and Moore, *The Feminist Reader*, 102.
18. 'Boys and Girls', in *Dance of the Happy Shades* (London: Vintage, 2000 [1968]), 119.
19. Ibid., 127.
20. 'Lying under the Apple Tree', in *The View from Castle Rock* (London: Chatto & Windus, 2006), 198.
21. *Lives of Girls and Women* (London: Bloomsbury, 1994 [1971]), 198.
22. Ibid., 199.
23. Kate Millett, *Sexual Politics* (London: Rupert Hart-Davis, 1970), 31.
24. *Lives of Girls and Women*, 200.
25. Ibid.
26. Ibid., 96.

27 'Red Dress – 1946', in *Dance of the Happy Shades*, 151.
28 'Privilege', in *The Beggar Maid* (London: Vintage, 2004 [1978]), 33–4.
29 'Nettles', in *Hateship, Friendship, Courtship, Loveship, Marriage* (London: Vintage, 2002 [2001]), 163.
30 Ibid., 165.
31 Coral Ann Howells, *Alice Munro* (Manchester University Press, 1998), 42.
32 Rasporich, *Dance of the Sexes*, xv.
33 *Lives of Girls and Women*, 195–6.
34 Ibid., 242.
35 Ibid., 264.
36 Coral Ann Howells, 'Intimate Dislocations: Alice Munro, *Hateship, Friendship, Courtship, Loveship, Marriage*', in Harold Bloom (ed.), *Alice Munro* (New York: Bloom's Literary Criticism, 2009), 177.
37 Ibid., 170.
38 In *The Beggar Maid*, 77.
39 Ibid., 80.
40 Ibid., 85.
41 Ibid., 99.
42 'Nettles', 178, 170.
43 'The Children Stay', in *The Love of a Good Woman* (London: Vintage, 2000 [1998]), 213.
44 See Magdalene Redekop, *Mothers and Other Clowns: the Stories of Alice Munro* (London and New York: Routledge, 1992).
45 'Mischief', in *The Beggar Maid*, 103–4.
46 Sheila Munro, *Lives of Mothers and Daughters: Growing Up with Alice Munro* (Toronto: McClelland & Stewart, 2001), 30.
47 Ibid., 30.
48 Redekop, *Mothers and Other Clowns*, 5.
49 'Deep Holes', in *Too Much Happiness* (London: Chatto & Windus, 2009), 93.
50 'Miles City, Montana', in *The Progress of Love* (New York: Vintage, 2000 [1986]), 88.
51 'Soon', in *Runaway: Stories* (Toronto: McClelland & Stewart, 2004), 97, 95.
52 'The Office', in *Dance of the Happy Shades*, 60.
53 See Michel De Certeau, *The Practice of Everyday Life*, translated by Steven F. Rendall (Berkeley: University of California Press, 1984 [1980]), 115.
54 'The Office', 60.
55 Ibid., 61.
56 'Material', in *Something I've Been Meaning to Tell You* (New York: Vintage, 2004 [1974]), 24.
57 'The Office', 64, 65.
58 'Haven', in *Dear Life* (London: Chatto & Windus, 2012), 113, 114.
59 Ibid., 115.
60 Ibid., 125.
61 Ibid., 119.
62 Ibid., 123.
63 Ibid., 125.
64 Ibid.
65 Ibid., 128.

66 Ibid., 129.
67 'Amundsen', in *Dear Life*, 62.
68 'Powers', in *Runaway*, 309.
69 'Memorial', in *Something I've Been Meaning to Tell You*, 224, 225.
70 Ibid., 216.
71 'Lichen', in *Progress of Love*, 49–50.
72 Mayberry, 'Narrative Strategies of Liberation in Alice Munro', 64.
73 Jessica Benjamin, *The Bond of Love: Psychoanalysis, Feminism, and the Problem of Domination* (New York: Pantheon Books, 1988), 89.
74 'Dulse', in *The Moons of Jupiter* (London: Vintage, 2007 [1982]), 53.
75 Ibid., 55.
76 Eva DeClercq, *The Seduction of the Female Body: Women's Rights in Need of a New Body Politics* (NewYork: Palgrave MacMillan, 2013), 170.
77 'Labour Day Dinner', in *The Moons of Jupiter*, 137.
78 Rosalind Coward, 'Slim and Sexy: Modern Woman's Holy Grail', in Sandra Kemp and Julia Squires (eds.), *Feminisms* (Oxford University Press, 1997), 360.
79 'Labour Day Dinner', 147.
80 Geoffrey Hancock, 'Alice Munro', in *Canadian Writers at Work: Interviews with G. H.* (Toronto: Oxford University Press, 1987), 222.
81 'Bardon Bus', in *The Moons of Jupiter*, 126.
82 Ibid., 121.
83 Ibid., 125, 127, 128.
84 See Andermahr et al., *A Glossary of Feminist Theory* , 26.
85 Mayberry, 'Narrative Strategies of Liberation in Alice Munro', 64.
86 Ibid., 57.
87 Howells, *Alice Munro*, 5.
88 Deborah Treisman, 'On Dear Life: an Interview with Alice Munro', *The New Yorker* (20 November 2012) , available online at www.newyorker.com/books/page-turner/on-dear-life-an-interview-with-alice-munro; accessed 13 December 2014.
89 Hunter, 'Story into History', 233.
90 'White Dump', in *Progress of Love*, 277.

5

CORAL ANN HOWELLS

Alice Munro and her life writing

Since the early 1970s Alice Munro has occasionally written what she calls 'a special set of stories. These stories were not included in the books of fiction I put together at regular intervals. Why not? I felt they didn't belong.' She is referring to the various versions of her life writing, those autobiographical and memoir stories which come closest to non-fiction. However, any distinction between non-fiction and fiction begins to look decidedly slippery when we consider what else she tells the reader in her Foreword to *The View from Castle Rock*: 'These are *stories*. You could say that such stories pay more attention to the truth of a life than fiction usually does. But not enough to swear on.'[1] Even her later autobiographical narratives in *Dear Life*, which she describes as 'closest' to her own life, retain something of her characteristic elusiveness and complexity: 'They form a separate unit, one that is autobiographical in feeling, though not, sometimes, entirely so in fact.'[2] Munro's attempts to write about herself 'as searchingly as I could' always represent negotiations between factual material and a textual construction where life is mediated and transformed by the writer's imagination and literary skill. In fact, her project bears a striking resemblance to Virginia Woolf's memoir writing (five autobiographical essays collected in *Moments of Being*, which were written over a thirty-three-year span and unpublished during her lifetime) where 'the entire project is posed on the question of self and its relation to language and storytelling strategies'.[3] Bearing in mind that autobiography is a literary artefact, in this chapter I shall analyse Munro's treatment of her own life through her varied modes of self-representation, from her original non-fiction stories published in *New Canadian Stories* (1974) and *Grand Street* (1981) through her memoir writing in *Castle Rock* (2006) to the autobiographical stories in *Dear Life* (2012). Taken together, they trace what Carol Shields has called 'the arc of a human life',[4] and I would suggest that her first non-fiction story, 'Home', and her last story, 'Dear Life', stand as end points in a sustained exploration of self and identity over forty years.

Writing about Munro's literary non-fiction raises interesting questions related to the representation of female subjectivity, to literary technique, and to the tension between the fictional and the autobiographical, where emotional truth is a rhetorical effect. Since the 1980s theoretical and critical studies of life writing have expanded and destabilized traditional generic definitions, so that as two contemporary feminist theorists summarize it, 'We have ... found "auto/biography" to be a flexible term, one that implicates self and other(s) in a context in which a dialectic of relationality is both acknowledged and problematized.'[5] New perspectives and critical tools offer a valuable lens for reading Munro, and my analysis is situated in this context, though as a critic I shall try to heed Virginia Woolf's criticism of memoir writers: 'They leave out the person to whom things happened.'[6] Munro is always seeking to get closer to her own life as she imagines and remembers it, trying as honestly as she can 'to figure out what the story is all about'.[7] Drawing as she does on personal material more than most writers, her stories would seem to be arranged on a spectrum where the intimately personal is gradually transformed through narrative artifice (her 'tricks' as she calls them) to the point where characters and events assume their own fictive reality.

Her life writing has a particularly feminine inflection, for her story as she tells it in fragmentary episodes displays those 'fissures of female discontinuity' which feminist critic Shari Benstock identified as characteristic of women's autobiographical writing.[8] Though she claims to have 'put myself in the center', there is a continual impulse towards decentring within individual stories, and the collected stories give no unified impression of her life. Instead, as Eleanor Wachtel commented on her later fictions, 'There are so many layers of things going on and crosscutting in time and memory.'[9] Beginning with her first memoir, 'Working for a Living', personal history and family history are always embedded within a framework of social history of her small town community in rural southwestern Ontario, though there are scattered references to the impact of wider events like the Second World War in 'Lying Under the Apple Tree' and 'Voices'. Munro is highly sensitive to issues of social class and gender, sometimes directly related to herself as in 'Hired Girl', though often she explores the web of female relationships within her own family – her mother, her grandmother, and her aunts. Through these relations she chronicles her emerging sense of selfhood while subtly recording her increasing resistance to their values and expectations. There are also stories about her father, 'the parent I sorely wanted to please',[10] and Munro returns again and again to the material of her childhood and early adolescence in the 1930s and '40s, as her views of her parents and herself change over time. However, within these apparently frank reminiscences Munro keeps her own secrets. There is remarkably little in her non-fiction about erotic experience and romantic fantasies. 'Lying under the Apple Tree' is the only story which deals with an adolescent girl's sexuality – but is this a truthful autobiography with that duplicitous word 'Lying' in the title? And there are no stories about her marriage and motherhood; 'The Ticket' is really a pre-marriage story dealing with other women's marriages and where her wedding dress becomes an ironic vehicle mocking Happy Ever After endings. Though we are aware of the mature Munro in her continual reassessments of the past, notably in 'Home' and the final story in *Dear Life*, there is only one account of a recent experience in 'What Do You Want to Know For?' and that is about the threat of her own death. Yet, across the gaps and apparent digressions in this life narrative, there is a pervasive sense of organic connections that constitute 'a system ... like a live body network, all coiling and stretching, unpredictable but finally familiar – where you are now, where you've always been'.[11]

Many of these non-fiction stories have been published before and now appear in revised versions with sometimes extensive additions, deletions, and rearrangements. It is with some of those revisions that I am particularly concerned, for not only do they offer an insight into Munro's distinctive writing practice, but they also bring us closest to her ways of making sense of her own life. Beginning with 'Home' as the most spectacular example of autobiographical revision across a span of more than thirty years, I shall then look at her memoir 'Working for a Living', first published 1981 and embedded twenty-five years later in *Castle Rock* as the transition point between her heritage narrative and her immediate family's history. I shall also look at that ambiguously titled story of teenage romance, 'Lying under the Apple Tree', and at the penultimate story in *Castle Rock*, 'What Do You Want to Know For?', whose title best describes the generative principle of Munro's storytelling – her desire to 'find out more, remember more'[12] – in an effort to represent what cannot be seen, what may be deliberately hidden, or simply overlooked. Everything seems to lead to the *summa* of her literary non-fiction in the superb final story (which is also the title story) in *Dear Life*. That is the arc which I shall trace, always remembering that 'it is so difficult to describe any human being'.[13]

'Home'

'Home' is the perfect starting point for any analysis of Munro's autobiographical non-fiction, for nowhere else do we have such a clear insight into her different methods of figuring out her life story from shifting perspectives over time. The two published versions of the same experience of homecoming belong to different forms of life writing: the first version (1974)[14] is presented as a diary written close to the moment, whereas the revised version (2006)[15] adopts a more conventional structure where much of the emotional turbulence is smoothed out, giving the story an aesthetic coherence lacking in the earlier version.

As her first experiment in straight autobiography, 'Home' was written within two months of Munro's return to southwestern Ontario in 1973 from British Columbia after the break-up of her twenty-year marriage and sent, as her biographer Robert Thacker informs us, as a birthday gift to her close friend John Metcalf.[16] Despite its reassuring title, 'Home' is the most unhomely of Munro's stories, pervaded by a sense of emotional disturbance and hints of the uncanny.[17] 'Home' in this first version is a double-voiced narrative written in diary form with paragraphs of metacommentary in italics (the equivalent of marginal notes) at the end of every day's entry. These notes bring us closest to an unedited record of her anxieties about her self-image and her vocation as a writer. If autobiography is engendered by 'a crisis that is not yet resolved',[18] then coming home for a weekend visit precipitates this crisis of self-examination.

'Home' (1) opens with the prospect of a return to familiarity and domestic comfort – 'I come home as I have come several times in the past year, travelling on three buses' (p. 133) – and the first evening sitting in the kitchen chatting with her father and stepmother seems ordinary enough. However, under that everyday surface runs the narrator's sense of unease and affront, for everything about her childhood home so lovingly remembered from far away in Vancouver has been changed. The house has been modernized inside and out by Irlma, her stepmother, apparently with her father's agreement and assistance, for it is he who is putting the new white metal siding over the old red brickwork: 'So it seems now that the whole house is being covered up, lost, changed into something ordinary and comfortable' (p. 135). Kathy Mezei has written about 'the domestic effect' of a house and its furnishings as 'vital to the shaping of our memories, our imagination, and our selves'[19] and here the narrator has to confront her feelings about house and home as a real place and also as a space of memory. For the narrator, the house is haunted by her dead mother's ghost, and her resentment against her stepmother as the usurper of her mother's place and of her father's affections is quite nakedly expressed. Everything about Irlma offends her – her aggressiveness and self-conceit, her vulgar jokes, the way she talks, even her practicality – for, from the narrator's perspective, she is the main source of discomfort and dislocation, the element 'which sort of stirs the ingredients all around, and you've got a whole new world to deal with'.[20] The other profoundly disturbing element here is her father's lassitude and ill health after his serious heart attack the previous year. 'He's not himself', as Irlma announces, which is dramatically confirmed by his terrible fits of vomiting followed by his admission to hospital where the narrator – not Irlma – accompanies him. The scene in the hospital ward, filtered through the lens of his daughter's high anxiety as she sits beside his hospital bed, is presented as a nightmare filled with grotesques and pervaded by a sense of helplessness, a surreal experience epitomized in the song blaring out from the radio of one of his fellow patients: '*Sitting on the ceiling / Looking upside down*' (p. 146). In this crisis, what becomes clear is the central importance of the father–daughter relationship and the adult daughter's need for her father's acknowledgement of their special bond, which excludes Irlma as well.

Coming home has forced the narrator to address her own past, and by the end of the weekend she experiences a profound crisis of identity when, alone on the farm, she is in the barn spreading hay for the sheep. Who is she? Has she become a city woman on vacation, or is she really a countrywoman to whom all these rural activities are familiar? She suddenly feels the erosion of her carefully constructed adult identity: 'It can easily seem to me that I have always stayed here, that all my life away was not plausible' (p. 151). Plunged into an alternative dimension of perception, she confronts her own double, the neurotic middle-aged daughter who never managed to leave home, an image of the unlived life which she has escaped – or has she? 'It is enough to make me scream and run.'

That nightmare vision is where the diary narrative of 'Home' (1) stops, but there is a supplement beginning '*I don't know how to end this*' in the marginal notes which throughout have constituted a subtext, destabilizing the realistic illusion and exposing its narrative artifice. These passages in italics belong to a different register where Munro steps out of the story, speaking personally in her writerly voice to offer a metacommentary on what she has just written. Such interventions reveal her painful self-scrutiny, both in her dissatisfaction with her writing and also in her ambivalence towards the people whose stories she is telling, for as she commented in an early interview, 'I'm looking at real lives, and then I not only have to look at the inadequacy of the way I represent them but my right to represent them at all.'[21] The marginal notes also contain vital information that is omitted from the main text. Functioning like a return of the repressed, they bring to light the complex and contradictory emotions which Munro is negotiating as autobiographical subject. Significantly they all relate to her parents and her stepmother, as she recounts the dream of her mother's ghost repainting the main bedroom at dead of night in defiance of Irlma's renovations, and confesses her scathing rebuke to Irlma for her tactless remark about being her father's preferred choice as a wife.

However, what Carol Shields has called the 'key' to a Munro story is given in the closing paragraphs which are offered almost casually as *'something else I could have worked into an ending'* (p. 152). That is Munro's uncanny realization some time later of the connection between her childhood and adult selves, a connection intimately related to place when, as she stands in the barn spreading the hay, time folds backwards into her first memory of sitting in *'the very same corner of the stable'* watching her father milking a black and white cow which died of pneumonia in the winter of 1935. Like Virginia Woolf, Munro finds that 'scene making is my natural way of marking the past. A scene always comes to the top; arranged; representative'[22] and it is that sudden realignment which spells out her true homecoming. It is, however, a fragile epiphany born out of panic and fraught with dread at the prospect of her father's death. Munro immediately veers away from that subjective revelation to address her reader on points of narrative craft: *'You can see this scene, can't you ... that magic and prosaic safety briefly held for us ... Yes. That is effective'* (p. 153). The story ends with no sense of narrative or emotional resolution, but only with the evidence of struggle within a deeply divided writing subject.

By the time the *Castle Rock* version of 'Home' (2) is published, Munro writes with the assurance of an internationally acclaimed writer with eleven story collections to her credit. Her agonies associated with the autobiographical act have been overlaid, and that early version looks like a first draft of the finished story. There is no double-voicing here, for the diary form has disappeared and the marginal notes have been excised or else incorporated into an apparently seamless textual fabric. Though the same story blocks remain, they are no longer presented as disjunct segments but fused with the missing information into a narrative which is formally and emotionally controlled. The narrator has even made restitution to Irlma for that 'vengeful reporting' about which she felt so guilty in 'Home' (1), though the undercurrents of resentment have not disappeared. ('In describing her to a friend I have said she's a person who would take the boots off a dead body on the street', p. 310). Nevertheless, she is now able to admit her father's admiration and affection for his second wife. That recognition is approached only gradually through apparent digressions, but finally she remembers something he said once in praise of Irlma: *'She restored my faith in women'* (p. 314). And so the matter must be left. The sense of an ending is achieved here in the final narrative block with a return to that brief epiphany in the stable, a memory comparable with Virginia Woolf's 'moments of being' or Wordsworth's 'spots of time', with that image centred on presence – her own and her father's – in a warm enclosed place sheltered from the darkness and cold outside. This is 'home' restored, but the luminous moment is shadowed by another memory of that 'extraordinary winter which killed all the chestnut trees, and many orchards'. 'Home' remains the narrative of a haunted self, a story of loss, longing, and dread.

'Working for a Living'

None of her other non-fictions are as radically revised as 'Home', so I shall focus on the stories in *Castle Rock* and *Dear Life*, while highlighting significant changes from the earlier published versions. Munro's first memoir, 'Working for a Living', was written and published not long after her father's death in 1976.[23] He is the dominating presence here, though we might ask where Munro positions herself in writing about her parents' lives which are so intimately connected with her own.

Unlike a formal biography, this memoir introduces her father as if in an ongoing conversation about him, as a country boy of twelve embarking on his secondary education at a high school in town in 1913. The facts are there but Munro focuses on the boy's confusion in this urban educated world, explaining his state of mind as typical of the social attitudes of those pre-war years, weaving in as if incidentally the social history of his southwestern Ontario farming community together with brief comments on the idiosyncrasies of his Scots-Irish parents, for 'When you write about real people you are always up against contradiction' (p. 136). Reimagining her father's life, she traces how this diffident bookish young man with a 'Fenimore Cooper-cultivated hunger' for the wilderness becomes first a fur trapper and then a fox farmer. (Again Munro gives us the facts: in 1925 he bought his first pair of silver foxes.) Only at this point is a lively young woman schoolteacher introduced: 'She became my mother.'

A remarkable feature of this memoir is Munro's ability to recall particular moments connected with place which at once delineate specific characteristics of her parents and her own affective relationship with them. She records such an oddly Proustian moment when, driving with her husband along the back roads, she sees a deserted country store which seems mysteriously familiar. Suddenly, via her memory of the taste of an ice cream bought at that store years ago, she recalls another car journey made with her father when she was ten years old to a Muskoka hotel where her mother was selling silver fox furs to American tourists. The story winds around as deviously as those unpaved country roads, with an excursion into women's fur fashions in the pre-Depression and pre-war years, the back story of her father's fox farm (including how to kill a fox), and his precarious financial situation in 1941 which was the reason why her mother was away selling furs, ending up at the moment when the girl catches sight of her mother in the hotel. The description of that luxurious place with its lily pond and its 'hushed and splendid rooms' could have come directly out of a Henry James or Scott Fitzgerald novel, though Munro gives it her own inflection as the incongruous figures of father and daughter wander in like a couple of travel-stained tramps. And then this startling encounter with her mother, presented from the child's point of view:

> Across the acre of white tables ... we saw two figures, ladies, seated at a table near the kitchen door, finishing a late supper or having evening tea. My father turned the doorknob and they looked up ...
> The moment in which I did not realize that this was my mother was not long, but there was a moment. I saw a woman in an unfamiliar dress... (p. 150)

That uncanny moment when she sees her mother as Other codes in a complex of emotions which spill out beyond that remembered occasion into her later adolescent feelings of guilt, embarrassment, and estrangement from this woman so unexpectedly stricken with Parkinson's disease in her early forties and who reminisces endlessly about her triumphant Muskoka summer when she saved her family from debt: 'Vindication for her, salvation for us all' (p. 151). In that hotel scene (which remains unchanged from the earlier version) Munro has created a new space in which to think more generously about her mother, with her unfulfilled ambitions and her unappreciated qualities; as she remarked in 1991, 'I sometimes just feel terrible regret about her, what her life must have been like.'[24] Her devastatingly honest charting of contradictions and changes of feeling towards her mother looks like one of those shifts of emphasis which leaves the daughter's narrative painfully open to endless revisitings.

Munro always writes with greater ease about her father, and their feelings of affinity (so beautifully realized in 'Night') produce a more even-tempered sympathetic characterization. Juxtaposed with the mother's story is her account of another visit she made as an eighteen-year-old to the local foundry where her father started working as a night watchman and caretaker after the failure of his fox farm in 1947. Once again the daughter is surprised when she sees her parent in an unfamiliar context, but now there is an immediate acceptance rather than any feeling of shock or estrangement. When he has finished work, her father takes her on a tour of the almost deserted night foundry, where he transforms those unfamiliar dark spaces into a rationally ordered working environment through his easy conversation with its mixture of facts, anecdotes, and jokes. In a parallel movement, the daughter's account moves smoothly from the immediate situation into historical perspectives on changing industrial processes and then back again to her father's storytelling. Remembering his stories later, Munro comes to recognize qualities in him of which as a child she had been unaware – his gregariousness, his gentleness, and his sense of the burdens of family responsibility. The *Grand Street* memoir ends here with the factory visit and with a brief unsentimental assessment of the different ways each of her parents recall their past lives.

The *Castle Rock* version contains significant additions which resituate this narrative in a broader context of her father's later life, of family history, and of her own position within that pattern. Her admiration for her father is made explicit as she recounts how, after his working life, he found another occupation: 'He took up writing' (p. 167). Like his daughter before him, Robert Laidlaw started to write memoir stories published in a local magazine and 'not long before his death he completed a novel about pioneer life, called *The McGregors*'. (It was published posthumously in 1979 by Macmillan.) In her affectionate account of their conversations about writing, we see a fine example of what Egan calls 'mirror talk' when father and daughter become reflections of each other, an impression confirmed when Munro embeds a long extract from one of his stories within her own text. His memoir about his close relationship with his grandfather, the same Thomas Laidlaw mentioned in 'The Wilds of Morris Township', meshes together the lives of those generations of Scottish immigrants from the Ettrick Valley with Munro's own life. Surprisingly for a written narrative, her story begins and ends with voices as her father's voice and her ancestors' voices mingle with her own in an ongoing conversation. That conversation continues in the non-fictional Epilogue ('The Messenger') – another version of homecoming – with the ambiguous murmur of 'a big mother-of-pearl seashell' which she remembers holding close to her ear as a child on a visit to one of her now dead relatives. With its echoes of her own pulse magnified into the sound of the sea, that shell images the blood ties which Munro reconstructs within the subjective spaces of memory and imagination through her composite narrative of identity and origins.

'Lying under the Apple Tree'

'Lying under the Apple Tree' was also published as a memoir,[25] though it looks very different from 'Working for a Living', for unlike that earlier one it highlights the blurred generic boundaries between Munro's fiction and non-fiction. Its equivocal status was summarized by Stephen Scobie: 'It is both an Alice Laidlaw memoir and an Alice Munro short story';[26] Munro herself in the *Castle Rock* Foreword admits that her characters here 'did things they had not done in reality', and we cannot ignore the teasingly intimate relation between this story and 'Baptizing' in *Lives of Girls and Women*. Perhaps it is only in this indeterminate space that Munro, mindful always of her dread of self-exposure, can explore the dawning of her adolescent sexuality in a story which is both an ironic revision of a teenage romance plot and a tissue of deceptions and lies. The factual details are there in the realistic framework of 1940s Ontario small-town social attitudes, which reveal a world not much changed since her parents' youthful lives in the 1920s, and it is against this restrictive background that a thirteen-year-old girl is struggling to define her separate identity. It is, as Scobie suggests, 'the old Alice Munro question, never fully resolved, "Who do you think you are?"'[27] Already she is aware of her difference from her schoolmates in her love of poetry and of nature, of her secret imaginative life to be lived only through books, and where multiple disguises have to be adopted as survival strategies; as she comments, 'A lot of me was under cover.'[28]

Told by an older wiser voice, this narrative is phrased as a youthful discourse of female desire which is at first inexplicitly erotic, though out of this a sexual dimension gradually emerges. Beginning with the girl's secret attempts to worship nature by lying under a blossoming apple tree in someone else's field, Munro subtly constructs her parable of the shift from innocence to experience, where the biblical resonances of apple trees are almost subliminal. Just as the narrative glides with unassuming artistry between the everyday world of conventional social relations and the girl's secret life, so in parallel a not-quite-conventional relationship develops between her and Russell Craik, an eighteen-year-old stable boy who plays trombone in the Salvation Army band. Every Sunday afternoon they go for long bicycle rides together, an activity that on the surface seems almost casual, except that it is kept secret and always concludes with a session of heavy petting – for 'how long? – five or ten minutes'.[29] That comic juxtaposition of the erotic and the mundane is characteristic of the ambiguities of this adolescent romance. In fact it is not a romance at all but a delicately nuanced account of a girl's first experience of powerful sexual attraction and the dawning of erotic desire, which is ironically (and irreverently) foreshadowed in Russell's Salvation Army hymn, 'There is Power, Power, Power, Power, Power in the Blood'.[30] She never thinks that she is in love with Russell, though she is 'half-hypnotized' by the sight of him fully clothed, transfixed by his incessant easy self-centred conversation, and excited by the pressure of his male body against her own. This is sex from a feminine perspective, an adolescent version of writing the female body as the girl makes her first tentative step towards what Cixous has described as 'the emancipation of the marvellous text of herself that she must urgently learn to speak'.[31] But the girl in her innocence and ignorance has no frame of reference from which to speak, and her full sexual initiation in the hayloft never takes place, for she and Russell are interrupted, almost comically, by intransigent reality as Munro replays the trope of sex and violence in a minor key. There is an explosion, for Miriam McAlpin (the woman for whom Russell works and under whose apple tree the girl had lain in order to contemplate nature) comes into the barn and fires off a gun, suspecting an intruder. Suddenly the plot shifts to reveal Russell's male arrogance and his shabby deceptions, for he is already having an affair with Miriam and he shoos the girl away as if she is a dog following him. The final sections of the story shift forward to the future and then back to the narrative present, where the girl in her shock and bewilderment retreats into books, reading almost at random from her parents' selection of popular 1930s and '40s romantic and historical novels, though significantly *Wuthering Heights* is there as well. Books are not only her deliverance from humiliation but they also provide the scripts for her romantic fantasies. Evidently she has not yet moved beyond the conventional plots of popular romance, though the slightly different inflection of the *Castle Rock* ending casts an ironic glance back over this teenage girl's fantasies of desire.

'What Do You Want to Know For?'

'What Do You Want to Know For?' was first published in an anthology of travel stories,[32] and reappears in *Castle Rock*, and though Munro has travelled extensively, she sets her narrative not in Scotland, Australia, or China, but close to home in familiar territory of southwestern Ontario. Surprisingly, the story opens with an unfamiliar sight:

> I saw the crypt before my husband did. It was on the left-hand side, his side of the car, but he was busy driving. We were on a narrow, bumpy road.
> 'What was that?' I said. 'Something strange.'
> A large, unnatural mound blanketed with grass.[33]

The idea of 'something strange', an 'unnatural' lump, and the crypt with its inevitable associations with death hover over the narrative, for in this autobiographical story an ageing Munro is facing the crisis of her own possible death from cancer.

Initially the crypt is nothing more than a curiosity spotted in a country cemetery. Munro describes it in some detail with its plain stone front without names or dates, just a simple cross carved into the arch, and a bank of grass and earth at the back, 'No clues as to who or what might be hidden inside.'[34] Having looked at it, the couple drive on to have lunch with friends. In the anthology there is a black and white photograph accompanying the text which shows the same exterior details that are described in the story, but nothing more – surely an appropriate emblem for a story about buried secrets. What begins as a travel anecdote assumes a more disturbing personal significance when juxtaposed with the information that a lump deep in her left breast has shown up on her most recent mammogram and that the doctor has arranged an appointment for a biopsy. So, the framework is established for this anxious multi-layered story which circles around the image of the crypt, though the reader is made profoundly aware of 'the physical woman as the source of experience and of narrative' (Egan 2005: p. 109)[35] in the shifts between maps and mammograms, bodyspace and landscape, as two different kinds of physical geography.

In her circuitous way Munro diverts her attention and ours by a series of digressions apparently unrelated to her core anxiety, returning first to the travel theme as she charts their car journeys around the countryside using the coloured historical maps of the region in L. J. Chapman and D. F. Putnam's *The Physiography of Southern Ontario* (1951). These depict as if in x-ray the ancient landscape features which underlie present formations, and she shows the reader how to decode those maps: 'Look at just one map … But look at what else … What is all this?'[36] A geography lesson yes, but transformed in this second version into a conversation about drumlins, eskers, and moraines. As she remarks, 'It's the fact you cherish', and a similar desire for facts impels her quest to find out more about that mysterious crypt. Here we see a variant of the process which Douglas Glover calls 'splintering';[37] while he uses it to describe Munro's peculiar technique of image making, I use it here to describe her narrative dislocations, for evidently her wish to learn more about the history of the crypt both hides and reveals her deep desire to know more about the nature of the lump in her own breast, and those parallel quests run throughout the rest of this story.

Munro manages to find out many facts about the crypt, exploring the cemetery, searching for hours in the Regional Reference Room of her old college library, talking to local informants, and even speaking with the woman who was an eyewitness to the last burial there. Historical research becomes a series of personal conversational engagements rendered as direct speech, sometimes incidentally throwing up unexpected connections between herself and her interviewees. She learns that the crypt was built in 1895 by a family named Mannerow in a cemetery for German settlers in the district, and also that they built a second smaller crypt in the same cemetery. She then discovers that on the walls of the local Lutheran church there are texts in German which were whitewashed over in the First World War and only recently rediscovered after a fire when the paint peeled off, revealing a mystery hidden for years in plain sight. But what is hidden in the crypt? Her conversation with the present Mrs Mannerow reveals some details of what she saw inside it – the family coffins and a small table with an open Bible and beside it an old-fashioned coal-oil lamp. Facts may proliferate, but mysteries remain, disguised as normality: 'Nobody knows why they did it. They just did.'[38] One of the German texts in the church was from Psalm 119: 'Thy word is a lamp unto my feet and a light unto my path,' and that biblical allusion might have been expected to shed some light on the question of the lamp in the sealed-up chamber, but all it does is widen the space for speculation, so that the crypt comes to seem like a literalization of the secret life buried underground, hidden in the earth – or inside the body.

Some secrets are destined to remain secret, for there are no revelations but only deferrals of meaning. In the parallel personal narrative the radiologist announces that there is no reason to investigate the breast lump further. Apparently it had been there on earlier mammograms but nobody had noticed it, and 'You could be sure enough' that it was benign. So the threat of breast cancer has been lifted and the mystery of the crypt has been assimilated into 'a pattern of things we know about'.[39] The story ends with a return to ordinariness as Munro and her husband drive home from the hospital through their familiar landscape. We can appreciate Munro's sense of relief, though that feeling is suspended over darker intimations of mortality in the *Castle Rock* version where the final couple of narrative blocks have been shifted around from the earlier version. Instead of ending with a view of pastoral landscape, the resonance has shifted towards the mysterious and the unknowable. With a strange echo effect the story ends as it began, on an unanswerable question which hauls us back to the secrets of the crypt: 'Do you think they put any oil in that lamp?' she asks. Her husband replies that he too has wondered the same thing. They are left in the dark, metaphorically speaking, which is where stories come from, as Margaret Atwood reminds us: 'Where is the story? The story is in the dark ... The Underworld guards the secrets.'[40]

'Dear Life'

With 'Dear Life' Munro seems to have come to the end of the narrative journey through her life story. In her latest volume (possibly her last) she glides from fiction into her autobiographical FINALE, moving from an old married woman's glance 'back through our whole life together'[41] into her last four retrospective narratives. While 'Dear Life' seems to promise a celebration of being alive, it also carries the opposite association of desperate struggle against threatened danger implied in the idiom 'for dear life', a resonance beautifully expressed in the Italian translation of Munro's book, *Uscirne Vivi*, which means 'to escape alive'.

This story winds back over much of the earlier material in the *Castle Rock* non-fictions – her parents' lives with their aspirations and disappointments, her own life at home, their family house, the fox farm, and the landscape of her childhood and adolescence – as Munro's account moves back and forth across time in a haphazard way which mimics the fluidity of memory processes. I am reminded of Douglas Glover's comment that 'Munro seems to realise that the inner life of a man or a woman is also a text, that in our secret hearts we are talking to ourselves.'[42] Munro begins not with her birth but with a vividly recalled fragment of childhood experience, her memory of walking to school, an exercise in locating the self in the world: 'I lived when I was young at the end of a long road, or a road that seemed long to me.'[43] Right from the start we are reminded that this is a subjective representation of a life, tracking back – or rather rambling – down the long road of her personal history.

Loosely structured as a girl's growing-up story, there is one figure who is more distinct than any of the others, and that is her mother. The mother appears in various guises, continually deflecting a self-centred autobiographical narrative into branching lines which plunge back in time into the daughter's imaginative reconstruction of her mother's life story with its drastic break between before and after the early onset of Parkinson's disease. The mother's long illness and death is the central trauma which splits this autobiographical narrative, creating a kind of 'scar tissue' (to use Benstock's word referring to Virginia Woolf's mother's death) 'which knots this narrative and refuses to let the story unwind itself over the years'.[44] Certainly Munro's mother's illness forms the emotional centre in stories such as 'The Peace of Utrecht', 'The Ottawa Valley', and 'Friend of My Youth', though here there is an apparent unwinding through the very strategy of storytelling – telling the story differently. Munro recalls her sick mother's repertoire of oft-repeated stories, though this time she focuses neither on stories of her mother's early life nor on her Muskoka adventure but on one closer to home. She retells her mother's strange story of their crazy old neighbour Mrs Netterfield's unexpected visit to their house when Alice was a baby, and how her mother snatched her up out of her pram in the garden 'for dear life', then rushed inside the house to hide till the trespasser went away. The main event in all its weirdness remains constant, as the old woman searches in the pram and then prowls around the house peering in all the windows. At least this is what happened according to her mother, though thinking back, the adult daughter sceptically notes that these stories of old Mrs Netterfield's 'visitation'[45] got more melodramatic and unlikely in their repeated retellings. Literal truth may seep away, but the story does not disappear, and only years later after her mother is dead is the mystery solved. By sheer accident the daughter, now married and living in Vancouver, comes across a piece of information and a poem in her home-town newspaper by a woman who formerly lived in that town, and more remarkably in 'our house'; her maiden name was Netterfield. With that shock of recognition the mother's story is realigned, and what was mysterious and terrifying appears to have a simple explanation. Perhaps Mrs Netterfield was looking in the windows of what had once been her home, and maybe she was searching in the pram for her own baby daughter, the grown-up woman living in Oregon who had written to the newspaper.

With that image of an old woman peering through the window, past and present swirl together as the story takes a new twist: the young Alice Munro in Vancouver has become an elderly woman who researches her local and family history, and we begin to wonder who is searching for whom? – the mother or the daughter, and which mother and daughter? Munro's mourning for her lost mother is incomplete, no matter how many times in fiction and non-fiction she has confessed her guilt at not returning for her mother's last illness and her funeral. However, this time the story ends differently, for through it Munro has performed a kind of exorcism. Moving from 'I' to 'we' in the two final sentences, she appeals to the reader's sympathetic understanding in a collective acknowledgement of the human condition: 'We say of some things that they can't be forgiven, or that we will never forgive ourselves. But we do – we do it all the time.'[46]

This story – possibly one of the last things Munro has to say about her life – ends with a calmness of mind, but the earlier version had a very different ending. In the *Dear Life* version, Munro has excised the *New Yorker's* final scarifying paragraph which recounts the incident (recorded in 'The Peace of Utrecht') of her dying mother's desperate flight from the hospital in the snow and how kindly strangers took her in. She adds: 'If this were fiction ... it would be too much, but it is true.' Even literary non-fiction, it seems, is selective in the truths its narrator chooses to tell. 'For dear life' – my own life – *uscirne vivi* – this is ultimately a daughter's story of survival.

As an ongoing narrative of discovery, Munro's life writing is as full of gaps, shifting perspectives, fleeting moments of revelation, and as endlessly open to revision as her fictions. Her comment on *Open Secrets* (1994) could just as easily have been made about her non-fiction: 'I wanted to challenge what people want to know. Or expect to know. Or anticipate knowing. And as profoundly what I think I know.'[47]

Notes

1 Alice Munro, *The View from Castle Rock* (Toronto: McClelland & Stewart, 2006), x.
2 Alice Munro, *Dear Life* (Toronto: McClelland & Stewart, 2012), 255.

3 Shari Benstock, 'Authorizing the Autobiographical' (1988), in Robyn R. Warhol and Diane Price Herndl (eds.), *Feminisms: an Anthology of Literary Theory and Criticism* (Basingstoke: Macmillan, 1997), 1147.
4 Carol Shields, *Jane Austen* (Harmondsworth: Viking Penguin, 2001), 10.
5 Marlene Kadar, Linda Warley, Jeanne Perreault, and Susanna Egan (eds.), *Tracing the Autobiographical* (Waterloo, Ont.: Wilfrid Laurier University Press, 2005), 3.
6 Virginia Woolf, 'Sketch of the Past', in *Moments of Being*, edited by Jeanne Schulkind, new edition, introduced and revised by Hermione Lee (London: Pimlico, 2002), 79.
7 Eleanor Wachtel, 'An Interview with Alice Munro', *Brick* 40 (winter 1991), 51.
8 Benstock, 'Authorizing the Autobiographical', 1145.
9 Wachtel, 'An Interview with Alice Munro', 52.
10 Alice Munro, 'Fathers', in *The View from Castle Rock*, 195.
11 Alice Munro, 'Five Points', in *Friend of My Youth* (Toronto: McClelland & Stewart, 1990), 37.
12 Alice Munro, 'The Ottawa Valley', in *Alice Munro: Selected Stories* (London: Vintage, 1997), 80.
13 Woolf, 'Sketch of the Past', 79.
14 Alice Munro, 'Home', in David Helwig and Joan Harcourt (eds.), *New Canadian Stories* (Ottawa: Oberon Press, 1974), 133–53. My thanks to Eva-Marie Kroller for finding and sending me this story in photocopy.
15 Alice Munro, 'Home', in *The View from Castle Rock*, 285–315.
16 Robert Thacker, *Alice Munro: Writing Her Lives* (Toronto: McClelland & Stewart, 2005), 260.
17 For clarity of reference, I shall refer to the first version as 'Home' (1) and to the *Castle Rock* version as 'Home' (2), with page numbers given in the text.
18 Susanna Egan, *Mirror Talk: Genres of Crisis in Contemporary Autobiography* (Chapel Hill, NC: University of North Carolina Press, 1999), 4.
19 Kathy Mezei, 'Domestic Space and the Idea of Home in Auto/biographical Practices', in Kadar *et al.*, *Tracing the Autobiographical*, 82.
20 Wachtel, 'An Interview with Alice Munro', 51.
21 J. R. (Tim) Struthers, 'The Real Material: an Interview with Alice Munro', in Louis MacKendrick (ed.), *Possible Fictions: Alice Munro's Narrative Acts* (Toronto: ECW Press, 1983), 28.
22 Woolf, 'Sketch of the Past', 145.
23 Alice Munro, 'Working for a Living', *Grand Street* 1, 1 (1981), 9–37; page references are given in the text.
24 Wachtel, 'An Interview with Alice Munro', 50.
25 Alice Munro, 'Lying under the Apple Tree', *The New Yorker* (17 and 24 June 2002), 88–114.
26 Stephen Scobie, '"Lying under the Apple Tree": Alice Munro, Secrets, and Autobiography', *Open Letter*, 11th series, 9 (Fall 2003)/12th series, 1 (Winter 2004), 167–75.
27 Ibid., 174.
28 Alice Munro, 'Lying under the Apple Tree', in *Castle Rock*, 210.
29 Ibid., 211.
30 Ibid., 205.

31 Hélène Cixous, 'The Laugh of the Medusa', in Warhol and Price Herndl, *Feminisms*, 351.
32 Alice Munro, 'What Do You Want to Know For?', in Constance Rooke (ed.), *Writing Away: the PEN Canada Travel Anthology* (Toronto: McClelland & Stewart, 1994), 203–20. Page references to quotations are from the revised version in *Castle Rock*, 316–40.
33 Ibid., 316.
34 Ibid.
35 Susanna Egan, 'The Shifting Grounds of Exile and Home in Daphne Marlatt's *Steveston*', in Kadar *et al.*, *Tracing the Autobiographical*, 95–115.
36 'What Do You Want to Know For?', 319.
37 Douglas Glover, *Attack of the Copular Spiders and Other Essays on Writing* (Windsor, Ont.: Biblioasis, 2012), 34.
38 'What Do You Want to Know For?', 339.
39 Ibid., 319.
40 Margaret Atwood, *Negotiating with the Dead: a Writer on Writing* (Cambridge University Press, 2002), 176–7.
41 'Dolly', in *Dear Life*, 254.
42 Glover, *Attack of the Copular Spiders*, 94.
43 *Dear Life*, 299.
44 Benstock, 'Authorizing the Autobiographical', 1150.
45 This is the source for the subtitle 'A Childhood Visitation' in *The New Yorker* (19 September 2011) where the story was first published: www.newyorker.com/magazine/2011/09/19/dear-life.
46 *Dear Life*, 319.
47 Pleuke Boyce and Ron Smith, 'A National Treasure: Interview with Alice Munro', *Meanjin* 54, 2 (1995), 227.

6

MARGARET ATWOOD

Lives of Girls and Women
A portrait of the artist as a young woman

Alice Munro's *Lives of Girls and Women* is a *Bildungsroman*, a novel tracing the youth and education – both formal and informal, both spiritual and carnal – of its central character, Del Jordan. It is also a *Kunstlerroman*, a novel depicting the formation of an artist. In this novel Munro maps out her core territory – the town of Wingham, under various names – if not for the first time, much more thoroughly and with greater assurance than in the Wingham-related stories in her first book, the 1968 *Dance of the Happy Shades*.

She also hones her method of synthesizing opposites, analogous to the thesis–antithesis–synthesis of rhetoric proposed to us in high school in the 1950s as the proper way to structure an essay. In *Dance*, this tripartite arrangement of Munro's had not yet been fully developed; instead, the book presents somewhat raw chunks of 'material' – the small-town mother-lode that Munro would later revisit from various angles. These stories are remarkable for their detail and excellent of their kind, but they do not yet have the conclusive Munro signature: an effect produced by the forced linkage of radically different adjectives or anecdotes representing mutually exclusive realities, both of which are then affirmed. Instead the stories tend to end with a distancing rather than a melding together. 'I am a grown-up woman now', the narrator says at the end of 'An Ounce of Cure'. 'Let him unbury his own catastrophes.'[1]

In her interview with Graeme Gibson in *Eleven Canadian Novelists* (1973) – the first long interview she ever gave – Munro credits the second-to-last story in *Dance*, 'The Peace of Utrecht', with being 'the most autobiographical story I've ever written ... and from then on this was the only kind of story I wrote, and then I began writing the book [*Lives of Girls and Women*].'[2] In 'The Peace of Utrecht', two sisters confront the past, most especially their memories of their ill, incoherent, and finally dead mother, a mother closely modelled on Munro's own. The narrator has escaped town, but the other sister has been trapped by the past and is living in a kind of stasis. 'Take your life', the narrator urges her sister. 'Why can't I?' is the devastating reply.³ No melding of opposites there.

In the stories in *Dance*, *either* and *or* are kept apart, but the title story is an exception. In it you can almost see the authorial light bulb going on: 'It doesn't have to be one or the other! It can be, "But also!"' This story concerns a piano recital at which a child from an institution for the mentally damaged plays angelically, much better than the 'normal' children. But 'the moment she is finished it is plain that she is just the same as before, a girl from Greenhill School. Yet the music was not imaginary. The facts are not to be reconciled.'⁴ However, the old piano teacher – an otherworldly creature herself – is not astonished by the child's performance, for she has received a communiqué from 'the other country where she lives'.⁵

In this story, the saving second realm is art. The facts are not to be reconciled in *this* country, the country of the mundane; but they can be reconciled in 'the other country', where miracles are acceptable and, indeed, expected. In religion, this intersection of the transcendent with the mundane would be called 'grace' – a redemptive quality that comes from elsewhere and is bestowed on you, despite the fact that you haven't caused it and don't deserve it. Grace of this kind occurs often in Munro's work, and though it isn't always connected with art, its root model is religious. To quote my 2006 introduction to the collection *Carried Away*:

> in Canada ... prayers and Bible readings were daily fare in publicly funded schools. This cultural Christianity has not only provided material for Munro: it's connected with one of the most distinctive patterns in her image-making and story-telling.
>
> The central Christian tenet is that two disparate and mutually exclusive elements – divinity and humanity – got jammed together in Christ, neither annihilating the other ... God became totally a human being while remaining at the same time totally divine ... Christianity thus depends on a denial of either/or classifying logic, and an acceptance of both-at-once mystery. Logic says that A cannot be both itself and non-A at the same time, Christianity says it can. The formulation 'A but also non-A' is indispensable to it.
>
> Many of Munro's stories resolve themselves ... in precisely this way.⁶

In *Lives of Girls and Women*, Munro combines the deep dive through layers of surface detail into hidden secret depths – the close-to-the-bone semi-autobiographical 'material' she first explored in 'The Peace of Utretcht' – with the reconciliation of opposites she first discovered in 'Dance of the Happy Shades', and makes both of them essential to the insights experienced by her growing writer-protagonist.

Lives of Girls and Women has seven chapters and a short Epilogue. In each of these eight sections, Del Jordan, the burgeoning writer, encounters one or more ways of arranging words, either on the page or in speech, either informally or rhetorically. Newspapers, scandal sheets, women's magazines, spoken anecdotes, overheard conversations, letters, sermons, operetta librettos, novels read in the library, poems by Tennyson and others, local histories, and more – each is fed into Del's word-hoard. In each chapter, these different verbal arrangements are presented to the reader and greeted with avidity and curiosity by Del herself – is this how life is? – then rejected as not reflecting 'reality'. But subsequently they are incorporated into Del's view of 'reality' in a new way that has to do with stories and storytelling, and that melds 'reality' and 'unreality' so that both are validated. 'Reality' is not single, she repeatedly realizes: it is double. Or double at the very least.

Woven into these word-hoard variations are four other patterns, lightly sketched at first, but culminating later in the book in bravura scenes that foreground them. I'll call these patterns the Drowning Maiden, the Crazy Person, The Failure, and The Storyteller. (There's a fifth one, Performance, that I'll deal with briefly when we come to the Epilogue.) Here are my interpretations of these patterns.

The Drowning Maiden stands for what happens to you if things become too much for you, often in connection with men and sex, and if the forces of society thus win the fight – for a fight is going on all the time in this book, between the artist-soul in Del and the expectations and demands of others. If society's view wins, you will be submerged, and the spirit in you will die. Why is it that drowning is the form of spiritual (and indeed suicidal) literary death so frequently chosen for women before the advent of pill overdoses? It is somehow more romantic and feminine than, for instance, hanging (what with the swollen tongue) or blowing your head off (think of the mess), both of which are methods chosen by the male suicides mentioned by Del's mother in the Epilogue.

The Drowning Maiden pattern is informed, not only by real suicides and drownings, such as that of Virginia Woolf, but especially by ones in books: ever since Ophelia was rejected by Hamlet, and went mad, took to singing, and drowned herself, girls who've lost the sexual struggle and been overcome by their failure to fulfil society's expectations have been sinking to their dooms. Exit Maggie Tulliver, of *The Mill on the Floss*, but especially 'The Lady of Shalott', the Tennyson poem – so popular in high school curricula of the 1940s and '50s – that juxtaposes Art and Life in a way that shows them as mutually exclusive. Though she doesn't exactly drown, the Lady carries the full load of the dying swan/warbling/drowning Ophelia connections. There's a comic riff on the Drowning Maiden motif in *Anne of Green Gables*, in which Anne, playing at being the Lady, finds her barge sinking under her and is reduced to a bedraggled waif who has to be rescued by

Gilbert Blythe; for this motif, in its origins tragic or pathetic, can also be played as farce, and is, by Munro herself.

The Crazy Person stands for what you risk becoming if you reject the Drowning Maiden, defy the forces of conformity rather than failing to tick their boxes, and follow the other path, that of individual rebellion. If you assert your wilful 'self' too much and stop caring what other people think, you might go right off the edge, which is what happens to the nineteenth-century female poet in Munro's later, magnificent story, 'Meneseteung'. On the other hand, the Crazy Person can stand for exemption: if you're crazy, you can hardly be expected to adopt the behaviour expected of sane and responsible people. You'll be granted a kind of freedom from them, though at a price.

The Failure represents perhaps the biggest fear of all: if you are seen to visibly try for something, but fail in your attempt, the result will be not only dejection on your part, but also ridicule: people, especially the townspeople and your relatives, will laugh at you, and you will be shamed.

I can think of no other writer who returns to the emotion of shame so frequently and meticulously as Munro. Shame is different from guilt, guilt being a matter of private conscience. Munro's characters are not much interested in guilt; on the whole, they revel in their secret transgressions. It's being found out, or caught at a disadvantage, or having things private to you looked at and then talked about and laughed at, that obsesses them. Margaret Laurence is more interested in guilt than shame, whereas Alice Munro has staked a major claim to shame – especially to female shame, very often connected with bodies and sex, but also with grandiose ambitions considered unsuitable for girls.

The best way to avoid shame is not to tell: secrets loom large in *Lives*. The best way to avoid failure is not to try. However, people in *Lives of Girls and Women* do try, and fail, and tell, and are found out and shamed. What to do? Re-purpose the failure and shame. Turn it to use as a writer. We can watch young Del Jordan figuring this out right before our eyes in episode after episode of *Lives of Girls and Women.*

Over coffee and a muffin, in Toronto, some time in the 1980s, Alice Munro was telling me about a horrific string of events that had happened to her. 'That's terrible', I said.

'It's all material', she replied.

In her own later story, 'Material', she questioned the right to use this sort of material – especially when drawn from other people – for art. When writing *Lives*, however, she was not yet having any such qualms about 'material'. Reality is there, somewhere in the jumble of life. It must be explored, figured out, then incorporated. To do so is, in part, says Munro in her interview with Gibson, 'the fight against death, the feeling that we lose everything every day ... the sights and sounds and smells – I can't stand to let go without some effort at this, at capturing them in words ...'[7]

On the one hand, writing is an activity with no practical use as understood by the town described in *Lives*. On the other hand, it's a way of turning observed into observer, so that reader and writer alike can look at the once-feared but now-captured townspeople, described in all their peculiarity. Munro also says: 'what I really like, I like when it's funny and I love it when someone laughs ... I think when you have made something funny, you've achieved some kind of reality. That's what I'm trying to get.'[8]

So, rescuing what-is from death: a serious quest. Achieving 'reality' through funniness: also, it seems, a serious quest.

Enter the fourth recurring pattern, the Storyteller, who can preserve reality, redeem it, and evoke from the reader the laughter of recognition. The Storytellers in this book can be liars and failures, illusionists and self-deceivers, or malicious self-servers, but all of them are models for young Del because they can do the desired thing: rescue the flotsam of life from oblivion and transform it into something both funny and serious at the same time. That these effects are often temporary does not make them any the less real.

Before looking at these four patterns – Drowning Maiden, Crazy Person, Failure, Storyteller – as they are woven throughout the book, I'd like to mention two key names. First, there's the town's name, 'Jubilee'. We think of a jubilee as a celebration, but there isn't much of the celebratory about the dour, judgemental place depicted: the nearest we come to a formal celebration is Uncle Craig's funeral. However, in the Bible the jubilee year was one in which debts were to be erased and slaves released. It gave you freedom and a blessing, and that is what Del Jordan is handed at the end of the book.

Echoing that theme is Del's last name, 'Jordan'. The Jordan is the river that the Israelites crossed to get to the Promised Land, and also the river in which Jesus was baptized by John the Baptist. Del will have symbolic rivers to ford on her way to the promised land of writerhood; she will also undergo baptism, though not in the regular way. The baptismal river of *Lives*, the river of ordeal that one must get through or else be drowned in, is called the Wawanash. This river winds throughout the book, flooding, receding, carrying things away, always available for the drowning of girls who might give up, and binding the chapters together.

'We spent days along the Wawanash River ...' the book begins.[9] Drowning is lightly threatened on the second page by Uncle Benny, Del's red-necked, childlike neighbour: there are deep holes in the Wawanash, he tells Del, and you could fall into them. He is prone to exaggerated, unbelievable tales, with poltergeists and amazing fortunes in them, and it is he who is the source of Del's first engrossing reading material: a lurid scandal tabloid in the style of 'Midnight' and 'Hush'. It has shock headlines such as 'FATHER FEEDS TWIN DAUGHTERS TO HOGS' and 'SENDS HUSBAND'S TORSO BY MAIL' (5).

Young Del gobbles this up; then, she tells us, 'I ... reeled out into the sun, onto the path that led to our place, across the fields. I was bloated and giddy with revelations of evil, of its versatility and grand invention and horrific playfulness' (5). However, this Gothic vision is undermined by the mundane features of Del's own house. Both can't be true: the torso wrapped in Christmas paper, the washtubs hanging on nails. Benny's 'world unlike the one my parents read about in the paper' is compelling, but 'doubtful' (5).

Benny is the first collector of junk in the book, and his attitude towards it is that of Del the writer, much later: 'He valued debris for its own sake and only pretended, to himself as well as to others, that he meant to get some practical use out of it' (4). Del's mother predicts that Benny's prospective housekeeper will be defeated by the trash in his house, and will either walk away from it or be overwhelmed by it and 'throw herself in the river' (13).

But this does not happen, because the housekeeper, Madeleine, whom Benny has been tricked into marrying, turns out to be the first Crazy Person in the book; crazy not with despair – that might lead to drowning – but instead with rebellious anger. There are two 'idiots' in the vicinity, but they seem to have no choice in the matter, whereas Madeleine seems to be wilfully acting, and what she enacts is over-the-top transgressive rage. 'Her violence seemed calculated, theatrical' (17). In other words, it's remarkably like the headlines in the lurid tabloids. Despite this theatricality, Madeleine – a child-beater – teeters on the edge of real, lethal violence.

The marriage is a failure, Benny's attempts to protect Madeleine's abused child are a failure, and his journey into the city to rescue this child is also a failure. But out of that humiliating string of failures comes a success:

> So lying alongside our world was Uncle Benny's world like a troubling distorted reflection, the same but never at all the same. In that world people could go down in quicksand, be vanquished by ghosts or terrible ordinary cities; luck and wickedness were gigantic and unpredictable; nothing was deserved, anything might happen; defeats were met with crazy satisfaction. It was his triumph, that he couldn't know about, to make us see. (25)

Benny as creator of a 'world', with 'us' at some remove, seeing his vision, but unknown to him – could it be that Benny is Del's first model for authorship? The author is always distanced from his or her readership by time, and can never 'know' whether the vision has been grasped by the reader or not. In addition to this model, what Del gains from Benny is an insight into the duality of the real. The 'other' world is not that of angelic art, as in 'Dance of the Happy Shades'; instead it is nightmarish, infernal. But it exists, as real as the mundane one.

As for Madeleine, she's eventually transformed by Del's family into another sort of story, a funny one at which, after a while, they would all 'just laugh'.

> We remembered her like a story, and having nothing else to give we gave her our strange, belated, heartless applause.
> 'Madeleine! That madwoman!' (27)

Madeleine, both deadly serious and a joke. And Madeleine, that crazy example of womanhood run amok, who gets away with it.

The Drowning Maiden is hinted at a little more strongly in the second chapter of the book, 'Heirs of the Living Body', when Del goes paddling in the Wawanash River against parental orders, and her not-mentally-normal cousin, Mary Agnes, yells at her, 'You're going to drown, you're going to drown' (43). Mary Agnes is the second Crazy Person we encounter, and, like Madeleine, she exhibits outrageous behaviour, though, having been damaged at birth and also being family, she is petted and excused for it. Del herself briefly enacts craziness when she bites Mary Agnes in the arm for trying to force her to view her uncle's dead body. 'Mad dogs bite like that! Your parents ought to have you locked up!' scolds Mary Agnes's mother (56). But Del gets what she wants, an exemption from corpse-viewing duty, and realizes two things: first of all, she herself has now become a story:

> they would remember that I was highly strung, erratic, or badly brought up, or a *borderline case*. But they would not put me outside. No. I would be the highly strung, erratic, badly brought up *member of the family* ... (57)

The position of Crazy Person, then, does not in itself expel you. Transgression might be something you can pull off while still remaining a part of your society.

The Storytellers in this chapter are the two delicately malicious elderly aunts, making fun of others behind their backs and relating tales of pranks they once played while dressed up as other people, and their brother, Uncle Craig, who is writing an exhaustive and plodding history of Wawanash County. Del inherits something from each – the making fun and the obsession with the historical junk-collection of daily detail – though she does not know that yet.

There is a third kind of verbal structure in the chapter that is placed more obviously in the foreground. Del's progress-minded mother tries to explain death and bodies to Del by telling her about a magazine article titled 'Heirs of the Living Body', which describes a future in which parts of dead people will be transplanted into the living. She concludes, fatuously, that thereby 'Death as we know it now would be done away with!' (49)

Counterpointed against this future-oriented verbal structure is the one conveyed by the hymn singers at the funeral; the quoted verse is from 'O God Our Help in Ages Past'. It is sung with 'longing and conviction'. The poor bewildered mother doesn't understand why the past-oriented hymn singers would be upset by her transplantation notions, which she finds 'beautiful'. 'Do they think your Uncle Craig is wearing some kind of white nightshirt and floating around Eternity this very minute? Or do they think they put him in the ground and he decays?' she wails (49).

Del's father replies, 'They think both.' A score for Del: transcendent ecstasy and the insulting, outrageous decaying of the body can both be real. Or at least, both can be believed at once. 'They think both' might be a motto for the entire book.

The next chapter is called 'Princess Ida', which readers in 1971 might have recognized as a Gilbert and Sullivan comic operetta satirizing higher education for women. Del's idealistic mother uses this name as her *nom de plume* when writing letters to the newspaper that advise improvements – such as giving out prophylactics – and that everyone in town secretly laughs at; but she has taken this name from the original, a narrative poem by Tennyson called 'The Princess'.[10] Tennyson's Ida is admirable though wrong-headed, whereas Gilbert's – as so often with his women, especially those with pretensions – is a joke.

Tennyson's poem has a nineteenth-century frame enclosing a medieval mock epic romance, both of which contain dialogues between men and women that argue the pros and cons of the case for female equality as these were seen in 1847. Princess Ida – named after a mountain mother-goddess – feels equality can be achieved only through a segregated university for girls, who will otherwise be subjected, violated, enslaved, and tortured by men, in various ways listed in the poem. Thus she has refused to honour her betrothal in infancy to Prince Hilarion, whose father declares that women ought to be subjected by men, as that is the natural order of things.

It's an either/or that's resolved by Tennyson in a truly Victorian manner, via the Mr Rochester/*Aurora Leigh*/*North and South* gambit: Hilarion must be seriously wounded and nursed back to health by Ida. Once he is helpless, Ida's tender womanly nature is aroused and she can love him; and once she loves him, she dejectedly assents to marriage, to the accompaniment of a moving speech by Hilarion that proposes not either/or, but both: they will be each other's complements, and work together for the improvement of woman's lot. (Fat chance of that happening in Jubilee, we can almost hear young Del snorting.)

As Ida tends the sick-bed and falls in love, she reads the erotic song, 'Now sleeps the crimson petal, now the white', followed by 'Come down, oh maid, from yonder mountain height', in which her segregated idealism is seen as barren, because love is of the fertile, baby-making valley.[11] And what should be in a valley but a river? And what should a river be equated with but sexual passion so strong it can sweep you away? And Prince Hilarion has already plunged into a river to rescue Ida from drowning, which on the symbolic level implies that sexual passion can be safely contained only within true love and marriage. (Keep this bundle of river imagery in mind, because it will come in handy soon.)

On the surface of it, the 'Princess Ida' chapter is about Del's mother going on the road as an encyclopedia salesperson, partly to supplement the family income, but partly because she believes people can be improved with the acquisition of knowledge, such as 'the wives of Henry VIII in order ... the social system of ants, the methods of sacrificial butchery used by the Aztecs ...',[12] lists of bric à brac no more useful than Uncle Benny's junk or Uncle Craig's local details, in the eyes of the town. Del is at first fascinated by the encyclopedia, and because she has a freak memory, can easily lap up the written verbiage and then regurgitate it, a facility the mother exploits in selling the books. But then Del becomes self-conscious, and threatens real regurgitation if made to perform.

The formal verbal pattern in this chapter is the dry, factual mode of the encyclopedia. The Storyteller here is Del's mother, who counterparts this dryness by relating intense tales of her own early hardships and heroic strivings. (Like Tennyson's Princess, she is noble and suffering, but at the same time preposterous.) The Crazy Person is Del's grandmother, her mother's mother, a 'religious fanatic' (75), with an assist from Del's uncle, who as a boy was 'evil, bloated, cruel', and who has tied up Del's mother in the barn and '*tortured* her ...' (77). 'Nothing really accounted for her darkened face at this point in the story, for her way of saying *tortured*. I had not yet learned to recognize the gloom that overcame her in the vicinity of sex' (77).

But what came next in the mother's epic story? Marriage to Del's father. It was an anticlimax, as the Hilarion arrangement was for Tennyson's Princess Ida, who experienced falling in love as a capitulation, a failure. 'Had all her stories, after all,' thinks Del of her mother, 'to end up with just her, the way she was now, just my mother in Jubilee?' (80) Worse, the mother's letters to the newspapers contain overwritten, saccharine references to Del herself: she is being made into a story, she is being used as material, and in awful prose too! How shaming! This is a table that is being turned before our very eyes, because the mother herself, along with her story-making and her

A portrait of the artist as a young woman

letter-writing, has just been made into a story by Del. As Del says, she and her mother are not so different; but Del has learned to conceal her striving desires, 'knowing what dangers there were' (81).

Then the wicked brother comes to visit, a sagging rich man dying of cancer and filled with sentimental reminiscences about his saintly mother and the simple, good life back on the farm. No hint from him of crazed religious fanaticism or of wicked violence done to the mother in the barn: their two versions of the past do not in any way accord.

Can we rely on stories? Do they contain the truth, or just the storyteller? Munro resolves this doubt indirectly, in three ways. First, the mother, whatever her failings, does not deliberately lie; like Del, she is intent on the truth. Second, after the mother reveals that the brother is leaving her three hundred dollars in his will, 'there was something in the room like the downflash of a wing or knife, a sense of hurt so strong, but quick and isolated, vanishing' (91). It is usual in a Munro story for the truth of intuition to trump any statement of supposed fact.

Third, the mother, doing a crossword, tries to remember the name of an Egyptian god with four letters. Del, despite her encyclopedia knowledge, gets it wrong by supplying a goddess: wrong gender. So who is the four-letter god? Munro would not have given us this puzzle without having an answer in mind. There aren't many choices. I vote for Apep, god of evil, danger, and destruction. He best fits this dark chapter, with its central tale of the sexual torture of a child.

The Drowning Maiden is hidden within this chapter, just as the Wawanash River is described as 'hidden'. She's hidden within the poem within the poem behind the pen name within the story: the princess who almost drowns, who is rescued, and who then must do what women are supposed to do, and capitulate to love and marriage. Even Del's strong-willed, eccentric, high-minded mother has done that.

The next chapter is called 'The Age of Faith'. The verbal pattern presented is the Anglican religious liturgy, which Del takes a shine to because it is so lush and mysterious. The two worlds colliding are those of faith and unfaith – God, and the way things appear in daily life, where prayers are mostly not granted. The Crazy Person is old Mrs Sheriff – accepted as mildly nutty by everyone in town – who has a strange turban-like hat, and

> had had bizarre troubles in her family which either resulted from, or had resulted in, a certain amount of eccentricity and craziness in herself. Her oldest son had died of drink, her second son was in and out of the Asylum (this was what the Mental Hospital was always called, in Jubilee), and her daughter had committed suicide, drowning herself in fact, in the Wawanash River. (102)

This daughter is a Drowning Maiden; we don't hear much about her in this chapter, but we will later.

Del resolves the 'unavoidable collision ... of religion and life' by posing herself a question: '*Could there be God not contained in the churches' net at all ... God real, and really in the world, and alien and unacceptable as death? Could there be God amazing, indifferent, beyond faith?*' (115). Questions that expect the answer yes. Or possibly: questions that expect a story to be written that incorporates such qualities, such ruthlessness, such contradictions, such dualities.

In the fifth chapter, 'Changes and Ceremonies', Del has become an adolescent, and sex and gender have entered a more urgent phase. The chapter begins, 'Boys' hate was dangerous, it was keen and bright, a miraculous birthright, like Arthur's sword snatched out of the stone, in the Grade Seven Reader' (117). (There's the 'sword' of sex-related hurt again, as in 'Princess Ida'.) How to negotiate this hatred, except by overcoming it through yielding charm, as women are advised to do in 'The Princess'?

On the surface, this chapter treats of Del's first tenderly romantic crush – on a boy called Frank Wales – and the humiliations and betrayals involved. But this darker thread is counterbalanced by the bright, artificial operettas put on at the high school every year by Miss Farris and the possibly gay music teacher, Mr Boyce. ('Farris', perhaps, as in Ferris wheel, as in up in the air, as in carnivalesque; which would account for the odd simile of the operetta 'belly[ing] out like a circus balloon' (123).)

There are six operettas performed at the high school, in sequence, year after year: '*The Pied Piper. The Gypsy Princess. The Stolen Crown. The Arabian Knight. The Kerry Dancers. The Woodcutter's Daughter*' (130). Though they seem real, these names were invented by Munro – I checked with her – so they are the author's version of the wish/dream operetta landscape suitable for her book as a whole. A magical artist figure whose gifts are scorned by the townspeople, and who gets back at them through art, like Del; a low-born outsider – like Del – who's really a princess; theft and trickery, which Del will shortly engage in; an outlandish lover, like Del's, upcoming; gaiety and dancing, shortly to be presented ironically through the Gay-La Dance Hall; the importance of daughters, especially the daughters of outlier fathers such as those who run fox farms at some distance from town, like Del's. Needless to say, the operettas would all have happy endings: such operettas did.

These made-up operettas, along with the Jeffrey Farnol and Marie Corelli romances Del mentions as having been read earlier in the library, supply the verbal-pattern background appropriate to Del's wistful romantic daydreaming about Frank Wales, though her longed-for role as a dancer in the show is played as comedy: her headdress starts slipping off, she has to go through the whole dance routine with her head tilted at a ridiculous angle, and, as her best friend Naomi spitefully informs her, everyone in the audience was laughing at her.

Del says of Miss Farris, 'She sent those operettas up like bubbles, shaped with quivering, exhausting effort, then almost casually set free, to fade and fade but hold trapped forever our transformed childish selves, her undefeated, unrequited love' (141). Miss Farris, as well as being highly strung like the earlier, cousin-biting Del, is an artist, then; another of those who is able to redeem, transform, and preserve reality, in however minor a way. And Miss Farris – like Uncle Benny and Uncle Craig – is a collector of worn-out items and a recycler of them: every year, she pulls down from the school's attic and refashions the stored-away, dusty old costumes from years before. But the 'undefeated, unrequited love' – who or what is it for? Possibly Mr Boyce – that's what the town thinks – though Del doesn't agree. 'Whatever she was after, it could not be Mr Boyce', she says (123). It must be art: an art Miss Farris can express only through the imperfect medium of an amateur, flawed, evanescent high school production.

But Miss Farris is also a Drowning Maiden: she is found drowned in the Wawanash River. Something has been too much for her, something has overcome her. We never learn what, although theories abound – accident, foul play, suicide? However, there is really no explanation. Is it God in the world, alien and unacceptable, who's at work here, leaving Del with two pictures of Miss Farris – the excited painter of students' faces before the operetta, the corpse floating for six days in the river? 'Though there is no plausible way of hanging those pictures together', says Del, 'they are going to have to stay together now' (141). It is clear that Del herself has now stepped forward to assume the position of Storyteller, with its alchemical power and the authority to meld and validate two contradictory worlds that come with it.

Towards the end of 'Changes and Ceremonies' there's a suggestive paragraph: 'winter was the time for love, not spring ... spring revealed the ordinary geography of the place; the long brown roads, the old cracked sidewalks ... Spring revealed distances, exactly as they were' (140). Gritty realism, in other words. And that's what we get a dose of in the next chapter, 'Lives of Girls and Women'.

This chapter replays the romance and tragedy of the preceding chapter as irony and farce. In place of dedicated, doomed, musical Miss Farris, there's another female singer – easy-going, lazy Fern Dougherty, who has the gift of a beautiful voice but not the ambition to develop it, and who pays no attention to the 'grand, inflated emotions' of the serious music she sings (145).

Fern, as her name hints, is of the vegetable world. The first metaphor we see applied to her is 'watermelon' (144). She's had a baby out of wedlock, according to Del's friend Naomi's mother, a district nurse, but this event – which in a more highly strung person might have inspired a fling into the river – seems to have made no dent in Fern; nor has she opted for marriage, saying she always preferred 'having a good time', which means, it seems, drinks in road-houses and trips to the dubious Gay-La Dance Hall (145). Thus she is also an upside-down, vulgar version of the marriage-avoiding Princess Ida.

The Crazy Person is represented by best friend Naomi's nutty, undignified old father, who wanders around the town uttering prophecies without putting his false teeth in – nothing special to admire there – and by Del and Naomi themselves, who mime being crazy – or at least damaged – to astonish passing townspeople. 'Making fun of poor helpless afflicted people. The bad taste, the heartlessness, the joy of it,' Del comments (158).

'What is this performance?' says old Dr Comber. Not a dance performance, then, as in *The Pied Piper*: instead, a performance that is a malicious imitation (158).

That's not the only performance. The place of Frank Wales, the young operetta star wistfully mooned over in the previous chapter, is taken by Art Chamberlain, Fern's beau and secret lover. He's back from the war, reading nose-product commercials on the local radio station, inherently lightminded, and now the subject of Del's erotic sexual fantasies. These fantasies are no longer about tender love, but about being more or less raped: hard sex without the responsibility of choosing. Sex will somehow just happen to Del in a shadowy, lurid, overblown way, simply and suddenly and violently, and she can hardly wait.

Art's name is of interest. First, it's a riff on 'art', for Art, as we shall see, is a performer of sorts; then it's a reminder of King Arthur with his sword, which in Del's transmutation has become the sword of sexual hurt and hatred, for Art is strongly although casually misogynist, and treats young Del with considerable callousness. But perhaps it's also a nod to Dickens's Artful Dodger of *Oliver Twist*, because Art is also a corrupter of innocence, a teacher of the art of pilfering, and an escape artist who ends by skipping out on Fern.

The verbal patterns in this chapter are a big step down from romantic operettas and Marie Corelli, consisting as they do of Naomi's nutty father's reading from the Bible of the parable of the foolish virgins, which he thinks is dirtily about sex, and also of the filthy cock-and-pussy doggerel verses and disgustingly graphic birth control information Del finds in Fern's bureau drawers. She's been spying on Fern at the instigation of Art, who's been whipping her up with secret, brusque, vicious pinchings and squeezings, and who wants to use Del to recover his earlier love-letters to Fern in order to avoid marriage.

This is the one chapter in which the Wawanash River does not appear at all. Its place is taken by a nasty little creek, its banks littered with trash. To this place Art drives Del, who is burning with excitement: are her depraved fantasies about to come true? From what we know about Tennyson's river imagery, we can predict they are not: it's entirely the wrong body of water. Instead, Del gets a sort of burlesque show: after Art reaches in 'to part some inner curtains', and says 'Boo!' he displays his penis and then jerks off, making noises that are 'theatrical, unlikely' (169–70). This performance, though quite interesting to Del, is a complete failure as a sexual escapade. All Art has to say to her on the way back in the car is, 'Quite a sight, eh?' (171). Which is deflationary, to say the least.

Del doesn't yet know how to make this episode into a 'funny, though horrifying, story' (173–4). (Though Munro has just done that in the book for us, the readers.) Instead, Del has learned the difference between the glamorous lechers of daydreams and shoddy daily-life real ones, who cannot be satisfyingly simple, but retain 'all the stubborn puzzle and dark turns of themselves' (174).

Del's mother, reflecting sadly on the unsatisfactory choices open to women, predicts, Ida-like, 'There is a change coming I think in the lives of girls and women ... All women have had up till now is their connection with men ... No more lives of our own, really, than domestic animals' (176). But she is always predicting the future with unlikely features in it, so this blows past Del, as does even the need for caution and 'self-respect'. Del resents this sermonizing, because it is like 'all the other advice ... that assumed being female made you damageable ... whereas men were supposed to be able to go out and take on all kinds of experiences and shuck off what they didn't want and come back proud. Without even thinking about it', she concludes, 'I had decided to do the same' (177). A plan she then tries out in the next chapter, with mixed results.

The seventh chapter is called 'Baptizing'. Here the Wawanash River has its most important scene in the book.

The key word of the chapter is 'surrender'. There are a number of variations on it. Naomi, the once-rebellious best friend, quits school, gets a job, becomes well-groomed, takes to collecting objects for her hope chest, and tells Del she too will have to do this sooner or later. Del is frightened by the verbal patterns on offer: songs that imply she will have to be soft and pink as a nursery for a man to love her, and women's magazine articles that tell her women are incapable of abstract thought but have to make everything personal. They have titles like 'Femininity – It's Making a Comeback!' and 'Is Your Problem That You're Trying To Be A Boy?' (181). Everything around Del is telling her that she has to squeeze herself into the prevailing mode, not one she favours. Yet she does not want to be a boy. She does not want either the nursery pink girl or the boy manqué; neither the either nor the or of gendered life as lived in Jubilee is acceptable to her. She will not surrender to them.

She still indulges in fantasies, but they are of a different sort of surrender. She gets them from the operas she listens to on the radio, operas like *Carmen* and *Lucia di Lammermoor*: 'Voluptuous surrender. Not to a man but to fate, really, to darkness, to death ... I was shaken, imagining the other surrender ... Carmen's surrender to the final importance of gesture, image, self-created self' (184).

She takes three cracks at surrendering to sex. First, she goes to the grubby Gay-La Dance Hall, here seen up close in all its tawdriness, where she and Naomi get picked up by two older losers. Del gets hideously drunk and mistakes her direction when coming back from the washroom, and wanders off into the night, thus escaping them. Second, she has a try with her study partner from school, the super-bright but not at all appealing Jerry Storey. However, just as he's got her clothes off, to the accompaniment of awkward dialogue from the Southern-accent comic strip, *Pogo*, his vigilant mother comes back to the house and Jerry shoves Del into the cellar, stark naked, so she won't be seen. After a time her clothes arrive down the laundry chute, and she makes her way home through the snow, furious. 'I would never get a real lover', she worries (206). After failing twice, she gives up on love and sex and throws herself into studying for the final exams that will get her out of Jubilee and into university, because that is the form her long-felt need for 'glory' is now taking.

Then, when she isn't even looking for it, along comes the 'real lover'. Del goes to a revival meeting out of contrariness, and a different form of 'glory' and different kind of 'surrender' are proposed to her: the 'Glory' of revival singing, the 'surrender' to 'The Lord's Grace' that will save sinners from 'the river of fire', in which you'd be 'drowning, but never drowned' (212). In the midst of this, Del is approached by a stranger, and they end up electrically holding hands. Finally, the real thing, and with it, transportation to an 'other' world: 'I felt angelic with gratitude, truly as if I had come out on another level of existence' (213).

This boy's name is Garnet French. It's a bad-boy good-girl affair of intense physical attraction, though Garnet has been 'saved' after a stint in jail, and is the leader of a small group of socially obscure Baptists. Del neglects her studies and gets caught up in sexual exploration: here is grace, gift, faith, surrender. 'Sex seemed to me all surrender – not the woman's to the man but the person's to the body, an act of pure faith, freedom in humility. I would lie washed in these implications, discoveries, like somebody suspended in clear and warm and irresistibly moving water' (218–19). That is one of the baptisms of the title. There follows a period of sexual ecstasy that, in an opera, would be a soaring duet.

The second baptismal event is not so happy. The Wawanash River has gone down: 'The river was still as a pond; you couldn't tell to look at it which way the current was going. It held the reflection of the opposite banks ...' (237). The affair has reached a moment of stasis, in other words. Opposites and reflections are about to assert themselves.

While they are swimming in the Wawanash, Garnet French proposes marriage, and then babies – love is of the valley – but first, he says, Del must be baptized. Del is in peril here: she's feeling lazy, picturing herself as a huge floating cabbage. One more step and she'll be a Fern, stuck in the vegetating world, the garden of earthly delights.

But though she has unthinkingly assented to the babies – 'Where would such a lie come from? It was not a lie.' (237) – Del resists the baptism. She and Garnet begin to fight, first in play, then in earnest; Garnet says he will hold her underwater until she agrees to be baptized. It's at this pivotal moment that Del almost becomes a Drowning Maiden, figuratively and almost literally speaking. 'I thought that he might drown me', she says. 'I really thought that. I thought that I was fighting for my life' (239). What she is fighting for is 'my difference, my reservations, my life'; that is, her life as an artist, the artist that 'meant to keep him sewed up in his golden lover's skin forever' (238). She doesn't want the real person; she wants only the version she has made of him, and that we have witnessed her making during the story about him that she's been telling us.

She refuses to surrender, and that's the end of the affair. They both know it. The scene has the force of a spell being broken: Del speaks of sleepwalking, of waking up. Not that this is simple. There follows a series of yes/no opposites – 'I was free and I was not free'; 'I was relieved and I was desolate'; 'I was watching. I was suffering' – culminating in the final pairing: '*Garnet French, Garnet French, Garnet French. Real Life*' (241–2).

But we readers know by now that one does not exclude the other. Both are equally real, and therefore both are equally unreal: the 'real life' Del has in mind is one she's learned about from movies, ones in which girls leaving 'home, convents, lovers' get on buses with small suitcases (242).

This artificiality is enforced by Del's own theatricality, her performance of suffering, which she watches in the mirror, backing it up with a line from Tennyson's 'Mariana', 'one of the silliest poems I had ever read', which she says out loud 'with absolute sincerity, absolute irony' (241–2). Nowhere in the book do the two self-excluding realms collide and meld with such force.

But where did Del get the strength to break the exceedingly strong enchantment of her first real love? In the Epilogue, Munro does something else that she will do again and again in later stories: she time-jumps.

We've learned in 'Baptizing' that although Del passed the final exams, she did not get the scholarship, sabotaged as she was by love. But in 'Epilogue: The Photographer', it's only July, not August – when exam marks used to be posted, and when Del breaks up with Garnet – and Del does not yet know where she stands academically. It's in the Epilogue that she receives the power that will allow her, later, to withstand that other magic gift, her love-and-sex life with Garnet. So when she enters the Wawanash for that significant swim, she's already armoured, already fortified; she already has the counter-charm.

The power she is given in the Epilogue is two-fold: a realization about the true nature of her artistic calling, and a blessing that has the force of an initiation.

First, the true artistic calling. We've been told earlier that Del has been writing scraps of this and that, including a poem with peacocks in it, but here we are told that she's composed a whole novel, albeit in her head. She has erected this novel on top of a small base of 'real life' – the Sheriff family, with its 'crazy' mother, its younger brother who's been in and out of 'the Asylum', and the sister, Marion, who had walked into the Wawanash River – pregnant, many thought – thus becoming another Drowning Maiden.

Del's novel is Gothic to a delicious extreme: exactly the kind of novel a talented adolescent might have come up with at that time. It's a compendium of bad Faulkner, perhaps, with some Carson McCullers thrown in, and maybe a Ray Bradbury overlay for the town. ('[T]he writers who first excited me were the writers of the American South', Munro says in her interview with Gibson, 'because I felt there a country being depicted that was like my own ... the part of the country I came from is absolutely Gothic. You can't get it all down.'[13]) Marion, in Del's novel, is not lumpy and withdrawn, as in the photo of her that hangs in the high school. Instead she's been turned into a slender nymphomaniac called Caroline, who drowns herself after the mysterious demon-lover of a Photographer whom she's been chasing after disappears. As for Bobby Sheriff, he's somewhat like the idiot in *The Sound and the Fury*.

Del has cherished this unwritten novel, holding it close: 'The main thing was that it seemed true to me, not real but true, as if ... that town was lying close behind the one I walked through every day.' Shades of Uncle Benny in the first chapter and his 'other world' that is 'a troubling distorted reflection' of this one.[14]

But to Del's surprise, Bobby Sheriff – on whom her crazed fictional son is based – is home from the asylum, and looks just like other people, and asks her into his house – 'Said the spider to the fly, eh?' – for a piece of the cake he has baked. Del 'did not know how to get out of it' (249). So she sits on the porch and eats the cake, while Bobby drones away about brain nutrition. While this is going on, Del starts thinking about such things as the hall carpet and the wallpaper and the doorway through which Marion had gone on her way to drown herself. She throws 'Caroline' away, and asks herself, '*What happened to Marion?*' (251).

'Reality', though it can be 'dealt [with] so cunningly, powerfully' in novels, persists (251). From now on, her work will be to find out how to combine the creation of fiction with the solidity of 'reality' in a way that does justice to both. (As we readers have just witnessed Munro doing.) Two pages later, Del completes the thought: 'People's lives, in Jubilee as elsewhere, were dull, simple, amazing and unfathomable – deep caves paved with kitchen linoleum' (253). Another time-jump: Del tells us that in the future – her future as a writer – she would, like Uncle Craig writing his formerly disparaged history, try to make lists of everything in the town.

'The hope of accuracy we bring to such tasks is crazy, heartbreaking', she says; 'what I wanted was every last thing ... held still and held together – radiant, everlasting' (253). She wants the full powers of the Storyteller – powers we recognize by now.

But Del wants something else from this encounter with Bobby Sheriff. She wants a 'clue ... to madness ... There must be some secret to madness, some *gift* about it, something I didn't know' (251–2).

What follows might seem puzzling, unless the reader knows something about the wisdom of accepting gifts from otherworldly beings who offer them to you. Del has been kind to Bobby by accepting his invitation and eating his cake, so now, like any demi-god or magic creature in a fairy tale, he blesses her. 'I wish you luck in your life', he tells her (253). She's been told, earlier, that she's been lucky – lucky not to get raped by Art, lucky not to get pregnant by Garnet – but nobody in the book has ever *wished* her luck before.

Then Bobby Sheriff rises on his toes 'like a plump ballerina'. 'This action, accompanied by his delicate smile, appeared to be a joke not shared with me so much as displayed for me, and it seemed also to have a concise meaning, a stylized meaning – to be a letter, or a whole word, in an alphabet I did not know' (253–4). Bobby's action is the culminating performance in a long string of performances that began with Madeleine, 'that madwoman', and continued through the aunts' dress-ups, Del's encyclopedia recitals, the liturgies and prayers, the operettas, Art's one-handed sexual display, and Del's recital to her mirror. It is the least 'theatrical'. It is the least artificial. It is the most mysterious, the only such performance whose meaning Del cannot fully grasp.

Del says, 'Yes.' But what is she saying yes to? To the luck; but also to the joke that is also an unknown word. I'd say this word is a protective charm, a gift to her from one of the Crazy People – a charm that confers upon her some, but not too much, of their difference and apartness and exemption. With the help of this charm, she will resist becoming a Drowning Maiden, and she will be able to undertake the 'crazy' task of writing a book containing Jubilee, with every 'smell, pothole, pain, crack, delusion' (253).

In her interview with Gibson, Munro said, 'I feel that the last section of *Lives of Girls and Women* is a failure, and I did the best I could with it.'[15] But this reader doesn't find it a failure at all. In the space of a mere eleven pages, Munro subtly draws together all the motifs – all of the clues – that we have been tracing in the novel, and makes them pay off brilliantly. The narrative does not finish with either marriage or death, both of which used to be thought of as providing closure, at least for female characters. Instead, it leaves its protagonist at the same point that James Joyce leaves his hero in *A Portrait of the Artist as a Young Man*: at the threshold. The door is open, and the young writer is about to step through it; but the success of this venture is implied rather than described, the proof of it being the book the reader is reading as the story ends.

Notes

1. Alice Munro, 'An Ounce of Cure', in *Dance of the Happy Shades* (Toronto: The Ryerson Press, 1968), 88.
2. Alice Munro, interview by Graeme Gibson in *Eleven Canadian Novelists* (Toronto: House of Anansi Press, 1973), 258.
3. Alice Munro, 'The Peace of Utrecht', in *Dance of the Happy Shades*, 210.
4. Alice Munro, 'Dance of the Happy Shades', in *Dance of the Happy Shades*, 223.
5. Ibid., 224.
6. Margaret Atwood, introduction to *Carried Away: a Selection of Stories*, by Alice Munro (New York: Alfred A. Knopf, 2006), xix.
7. Munro in Gibson, *Eleven Canadian Novelists*, 243–4.

8 Ibid., 252.
9 Alice Munro, *Lives of Girls and Women* (Toronto: McGraw-Hill Ryerson, 1971), 1. Text references are to page numbers in this edition.
10 Alfred Tennyson, *The Princess: a Medley* (London: Edward Moxon, 1860).
11 Tennyson, *Princess*, 166–7.
12 Munro, *Lives of Girls and Women*, 65.
13 Munro in Gibson, *Eleven Canadian Novelists*, 248.
14 Munro, *Lives of Girls and Women*, 248.
15 Munro in Gibson, *Eleven Canadian Novelists*, 253.

7

W. H. NEW

Re-reading *The Moons of Jupiter*

Re: beginnings

In 'What Is Real?' (1982), Alice Munro sketches the strategies she follows when she reads stories written by others. 'I can start reading them anywhere; from beginning to end, from end to beginning, from any point in between in either direction' (332).[1] This procedure, she goes on to explain, relates to her sense of how a story unfolds: a story is less like a road, leading to some defined destination, than like a house, a structure whose enclosed spaces connect with each other in such a way that the space outside is also shaped anew. It's an effect she says she wants to achieve for readers of her own stories as well, noting a proviso about the composition of good stories: they're not driven by blueprint; they can begin with an image (observed or invented), an overheard conversation, a fragment of memory, or in some other way; but the structure for each 'house' has to be separately built, allowing the reader to enter creatively through different doors.

Some of Munro's stories reveal a trace of plot. Some hinge on mystery. Several foreground travel. Several more emphasize the values of a community in place. Taken together, most highlight dimension – the lineaments rather than the linearity of time, and the strata of narrative, the interconnecting seams of story that lead a primary character from one understanding to another. Munro's characters, moreover, live in complex time. They test the compass of empathy; they dispute both antipathy and esteem; and rather than acquire uniform identities – within families and without – they keep *rediscovering* their connection with the world, repeatedly probing the caves of self-knowledge that shelter why they act as they do. Revelation reads as a *process* here rather than as a *moment*, for insight seldom appears as an epiphany, a flash of total comprehension, but more often as a slow recognition that knowledge is ambiguous, certainty an illusion, and fixity a false goal. 'Story' unfolds cumulatively, from wherever it 'begins' – the structural arrangement directing the narrative effect.

Re-reading *The Moons of Jupiter*

The structure of Munro's books does not, however, oblige the reader to follow a single path in order to share in this discovery; it offers readers alternative (and interconnecting) paths instead. Re-reading *The Moons of Jupiter* (1982) from several vantage points, for example, reveals how strategies of literary structure affect the reading process. Specifically, overlapping readings that follow from alternative starting points (opening, ending, mid-point, and process) demonstrate how the plurality of rhetorical patterns in a single book underpins the complex architecture of understanding in Munro's narrative world.

Beginning with process: the shaping of the text

The history of the composition of Alice Munro's fifth book, *The Moons of Jupiter* (first published by Macmillan in Toronto in the autumn of 1982, and by Knopf in New York, and Allen Lane in London, in the spring of 1983), tracks a process of revision, selection, and arrangement. Ten of the twelve stories in the collection (counting the two parts of 'Chaddeleys and Flemings' separately) had appeared previously in journals. Five of the ten appeared over five years in *The New Yorker*: 'The Moons of Jupiter' in May 1978, 'Dulse' in July 1980, 'The Turkey Season' in December 1980, 'Prue' in March 1981, and 'Labor Day Dinner' in September 1981. 'Connection' and 'The Stone in the Field' (the separable parts of 'Chaddeleys and Flemings', which William Shawn, editor of *The New Yorker*, had rejected as 'reminiscence') appeared respectively in *Chatelaine* in November 1979 and *Saturday Night* in April 1979. *Toronto Life* published 'Accident' in November 1977; *Tamarack Review* published 'Mrs Cross and Mrs Kidd' in its winter 1982 issue; and *Atlantic Monthly* published 'Visitors' in April 1982. 'Bardon Bus' and 'Hard-Luck Stories' appeared for the first time in book form.

In their initial publication, the stories appeared as stand-alone narratives; the texts all changed when they reappeared in the book version, sometimes only slightly altered, sometimes revealing extensive further editing, including complete shifts in point of view. Early on, three other stories were considered for inclusion in *The Moons of Jupiter* but excluded because they 'fit' less well in what Munro was planning.[2] 'Working for a Living' (*Grand Street*, 1981) and 'Wood' (*The New Yorker*, November 1980) were later collected in *The View from Castle Rock* (2006) and *Too Much Happiness* (2009) respectively. 'The Ferguson Girls Must Never Marry' (*Grand Street*, 1982), has attracted little subsequent critical notice. In its final twelve-story format, however, *The Moons of Jupiter* drew almost uniform high praise from reviewers around the world, who singled out the book's style, its depiction of women, its arrangement, and especially its demonstration of Munro's increasingly dexterous formal practice.

Reading this history of composition provides one way to access the book; it emphasizes the degree to which each separate story appealed to a journal editor as a complete and satisfying narrative. It positions the book at its time of composition, throwing incidental light on the growing importance in Munro's life of her agent (Virginia Barber) and of her editors (Douglas Gibson in Canada and Ann Close in the United States), who challenged her to revise, even if (as was often true) she was already providing them with alternative versions of many of the stories, sometimes after they had been accepted. (Charles McGrath, an editor at *The New Yorker*, received two successive versions of 'The Turkey Season', for example; preferring elements from each, he combined the two, with Munro's agreement, in the version that was finally published.[3]) Barber, Gibson, and Close reaffirmed that the stories William Shawn had dismissed as non-fiction memoir were in fact fictional narratives, inventions written with rhetorical care. They also helped Munro decide on the final arrangement. The history of selecting, rewriting, and arranging the stories into book form tells of a further editorial desire for a satisfying sequence and cumulative effect. In the last instance, the book was designed to be read as a *collection*, a coherent and interactive, formally adventurous inquiry into such issues as family, love, separation, gender, death, time, and storytelling itself.

The ordering of the twelve stories took several weeks of planning on Munro's part, working with her two editors. The final book version places 'Chaddeleys and Flemings' and 'The Moons of Jupiter' at the beginning and end respectively, constituting a frame, within which the remaining stories are sequenced. Two architectural strategies are thus immediately in play. Framing focuses on a perspective of containment – the window or door through which the reader enters and exits the story house, as it were. Sequencing focuses on the distribution of narrative rooms or spaces within. Neither process excludes the other, but each sets in motion a separate rhetoric. Together (along with other modes of discovery) these narrative tactics comment on the world outside the fiction, the strange and familiar territory that individual readers call 'real'.

Beginning with the frame: the paradox of connecting

The framing stories – 'Chaddeleys and Flemings' and 'The Moons of Jupiter' – are those that critical writings have most commented on.[4] The stories hint at allusions to the Chamney and Laidlaw branches of Munro's own family (though as she wrote in an introduction to the 1986 reprint of *The Moons of Jupiter*, which Robert Thacker quotes as an epigraph to his biography, 'Some stories are closer to my own life than others, but not one of them is as close as people seem to think'). More importantly, the stories shape an entrance and exit for those who read the book from beginning to end, or (more loosely) they shape the 'house' that such a reader is likely to inhabit. They tell stories of inheritance, resistance, acceptance, and survival: stories about values (those that construct convention) and about value (whatever persists to support a creative life).

On the surface, the frame stories tell a straightforward narrative. An unidentified woman recalls meeting the older generation on both sides of her family; she contrasts family behaviour with that of her husband and others; she mentions her father's illness and she comes to terms both with his dying and with her own grown daughters' independence. But more is happening in the rhetoric than a simple précis of a family plot. Family references in the framing stories do make clear that the narrator of both 'Chaddeleys and Flemings' and 'The Moons of Jupiter' is conceptualized as the same character. The name 'Janet', however, is used once only, in the father's voice and in an internal memoir of childhood within 'The Moons of Jupiter' (218). It seems peripheral. But in a book so full of names, and so clearly using names and dress and other details to distinguish individuals, for the book to move from an absent name to a specific name, even once, suggests a growth in self-awareness on the narrator's part: from her opening quest to identify a place in her family (and in relationships with men) to a closing acceptance of her equivocal place in time.

The frame stories enclose what comes between: a set of stories that examines what happens in families, read through the filter of the one family that Janet claims as her own. Textual details tell a more complex story, teasing out the nuances of gesture, the ambiguity of such terms as *likeness* or *dissimilarity*, the power of choice to set alternative actions in motion, and the capacity of people nevertheless to repeat patterns of behaviour and suffer the same positive and negative consequences as those they thought they'd be able to avoid. The structure suggests that this is a contemplative book, not an unrealistic family romance: one that portrays hunger as well as happiness, anger as well as dissatisfaction, worry as well as desire, confidence as well as shame. By resisting the fixedness of distinctions, by recognizing alternatives as arbitrary and sometimes illusory, *The Moons of Jupiter* refuses judgement.

In the first half of 'Chaddeleys and Flemings', the narrator remembers her mother's ebullient four cousins (called 'maiden ladies' – 'old maids' being 'too thin a term ... to cover them' [1][5]); in the second half she recalls her father's six living sisters, 'lean' (25), stiff, and reserved. The particular language she uses to portray these differences articulates the mix that represents her apparent inheritance. The rhetorical dance of opposites that Munro sets in motion is, however, more complex than a simple distinction implies. The first four lines of 'Connection' declare difference in a series of separate names and discrete fragments: 'Cousin Iris from Philadelphia. She was a nurse. Cousin Isabel from Des Moines. She owned a florist shop. Cousin Flora from Winnipeg, a teacher. Cousin Winifred from Edmonton, a lady accountant.' (1) Yet the phonological progress in this list already dissolves difference and declares connection: *Iris/nurse, Philadel/Isabel, florist/Flora, Winnipeg/Winifred*. These names and occupations cross national and provincial boundaries, distinguishing them from *Dalgleish* – a town the cousins don't consider 'real' (4) and a name that the narrator's stockbroker husband Richard later uses as an epithet of contempt and dismissal (11); he prefers the oxymoronic exactitude of 'Point *Grey*' (15) to the display of Iris's 'iridescent' (16) dress and character. But Dalgleish is pivotal. What Richard misses, and what subsequently leads the narrator to separate from him, is not that Iris and the other cousins are *from* Dalgleish (they are not), but that the narrator is. Dalgleish brought the cousins together, with each other and in the narrator's mind and home; and the mix is part of who she is. The rhetoric of separateness paradoxically expresses connection; and relatedly, Richard's desire for uniformity, convention, and class – he makes self-serving distinctions between vulgar and decent – leads to separation. Richard reads ebullience as lack of control, adornment as excess, story as untruth, and play as immaturity. The cousins, by contrast, accept play as the cause and consequence of joy, and consider flourish to be its natural expression, whether in dress and food ('a five-pound box of chocolates' (3)) or in fanciful tales of danger and heritage and prodigality (6).

Munro's double-edged use of the children's round, 'Row, row, row your boat', further shapes the arc of 'Connection'. When first mentioned, it's one of the cousins' many games of 'audience and performers' (4) – berry-picking, dressing up in old clothes, fishing, singing: everything from 'The Yellow Rose of Texas' to the Doxology. When the round returns, after the argument between the narrator and her husband, after he's hit by a flying lemon meringue pie and 'his speech stopped' (18), the round echoes only in the narrator's head, recording how childhood voices diminish into one, 'an unexpected note of entreaty, of warning, as it hangs the five separate words on the air. *Life is*. Wait. *But a*. Now, wait. *Dream*' (18). When the two halves of 'Chaddeleys and Flemings' first appeared in *Chatelaine*, this last sentence of 'Connection' appeared at the end of 'The Stone in the Field'. Revising the text for book publication, Munro moved the sentence to the end of 'Connection'[6] where it carries still more resonance. The word 'row', meaning *propel forward* when children sing it, mutates within the story into 'row', meaning *quarrel* when the narrator remembers it. The mutation disrupts both the sentence that ostensibly promises a fairy-tale dream and the conventional dream itself.

In 'Connection', a multiple reversal takes place – separation leads to connection, connection breaks into fragments. Categories and divisions alike prove too easy to accept as guides to living. 'The Stone in the Field', for example, functioning as the second half of 'Chaddeleys and Flemings' (the 'and' in the conjoined two-story title declaring a balance, if not necessarily an equivalence), might be expected to restore connection or further complicate the contrast and separation established in 'Connection', the first half. Rhetorically, it does both. By its title, '*The* Stone in *the* Field' promises a focus on singularity, which it fulfils; but the story also opens an inquiry into the capriciousness of communal alternatives. It tells about the narrator's apparently unchanging Fleming aunts, and also about her parents' separate refusals to be governed by social convention; about a gay man (Poppy Cullender) whose sexuality is largely ignored in Dalgleish but whose life there is not made easier by actions deemed unrealistic (21); and about a foreign hermit innominately called Mr Black who meets over time with a surprising measure of kindness.

Poppy Cullender's sexuality is implied rather than specified, though the narrator leaves little doubt as to her own reading of the man and his actions (21); Herb Abbott's homosexuality, in 'The Turkey Season', is also represented indirectly, through the eyes of an adolescent just coming to terms with her own sexuality. Yet in both stories the judgemental attitudes of Huron County are clear, and such community attitudes (and those expressed during subsequent decades of sexual liberation) provide another context for reading the sexual lives of Munro's characters.[7]

'The Stone in the Field' opens in what initially seems an arbitrary set of distinctions: 'My mother was not a person who ...' 'Our house was full of things that had not been paid for with ...' 'He did not have a shop ...' (19). The rhetorical commonality is negation, the apparent denial of the usual, the socially expected. As the narrator's mother observes, negation is the underside of familiarity. 'Some people can't survive in a place like this. It's not permitted. No' (21). She herself is unusual – she was a 'trader and dealer' (19) in a town where house pride was more the norm for married women – but these general assertions of difference together function as prelude to the narrator's presentation of the seven Fleming aunts. The passage is noteworthy for its lack of detail:

> 'Susan. Clara. Lizzie. Maggie. Jennet was the one who died.'
> 'Annie,' said my father. 'Don't forget Annie.'
> 'Annie. Lizzie. I said her. Who else?'
> 'Dorothy,' said my mother, shifting gears ... (24)

The list here conveys the aunts' difference from community norms: their deference to their father, their largely unvoiced selves, their lifelong isolation on the lye-polished family farm. But the repetitive trochaic rhythm of their names (including 'DOR-thy': the middle *o* is elided in standard Canadian speech) affirms similarity rather than distinctiveness. It is the narrator's mother who 'shifts gears'.

Three main scenes follow this moment: a surprise visit to see the aunts; a hospital scene, during which the narrator's father tells of how and why he ran away from home; and an extended scene recording the life of the hermit. The first of these continues the negative rhetoric with which the story has begun: the paint on the house was 'not white ... but yellow' (24). There were 'No embraces, no touch of hands' (25). 'It was no use I could never get them straight' (25). 'There was no sign of frivolity, no indication that the people who live here ever sought entertainment. No radio; no newspapers or magazines; certainly no books' (26). 'They offered no refreshments' (27). Human contact is painful; 'they could not ... They could no more understand ... they had no understanding of ... Nobody came into ... None of them would look at...' (28). Even the one exception is expressed through inversion: 'My father' looked like them 'though he did not stop, and his face had opened up in a way that theirs had not' (25). The intensity of the negation that 'perfectly' (29) encases the aunts, stopping them from even imagining 'otherwise' (29) – the 'though' that reshapes their brother – makes even the narrator's mother's attempts to open up alternative possibilities nugatory. In this context, her question – 'Why not?' (29) – functions both as a casual conversational gambit and as a resonant question about social attitude and responsibility (*What is the value of refusal?*), one that the rest of the story contemplates further.

The final scenes, in the hospital and back on the farm after commercial language has erased its earlier identity, anticipate 'The Moons of Jupiter'. The scene involving Mr Black, his anonymity and the disappearance of any stone (or conventional literary marker) that would memorialize him, engages the narrator in thoughts of writing a story. The arc of this story, however, like that of the first half of 'Chaddeleys and Flemings', rules out conventional romance and desperate acts of derring-do. All that can be asserted is *what is* and *what must have been*, leading to the ambiguous final phrase: 'the life buried here is one you have to think twice about regretting' (35). Ambiguous because it permits regret and turns away from it. Because it asks 'Why not' – what happens when you negate the past, and what might happen if only you do.

In 'The Moons of Jupiter', the closing story of the frame, the narrator, Janet, talks further with her dying father and at the same time frets about her own daughters and their lives (with and/or without men). Revised to first-person narration before its *New Yorker* publication but written in the third person when submitted and accepted in 1977 (possibly under the title 'Taking Chances'[8]), this story repeatedly distinguishes between what's said and what's sure. Words like 'seem' and 'ought' and 'try' abound (217). The characters tell anecdotes; they recite fragments from poems (225); they recall details (or 'blur', 222); they seek exactitude, confidence, 'connection' (225, 231) – but they end up recognizing the artifice of names and truths; they value choice instead, the 'innumerable' repetitions and variations of galaxies (231) and the plural 'forms of love', even those 'measured and disciplined' (230). Janet ends up concerned not so much with loss or dying as with time itself, the processes of life that transform perspective. Even a mundane event outside a Bloor Street shop instructs her 'how a transformation might be made' (229). And after her father tells her that 'Ganymede', one of the moons of Jupiter, was not a shepherd but a cupbearer (233), Janet begins to read differently her own role in time. The mundane is part of physical human experience, not to be ignored, not necessarily superseded by some pastoral abstraction. So when at the end of the story she turns away from visiting museum tombs and goes off 'to eat' (233) before returning to the hospital, the shift in perspective from the past to the present, from what's gone before to what's happening now, closes the frame (and the book) in a pragmatic acceptance of living.

It is possible to read the frame stories, then, as a narrative of family over time, in which each of the figures performs a variety of roles. The narrator (who herself changes from child to young adult to mature woman) casts her father as ironic chorus, young rebel, knowing brother, reliable helpmeet (an image that her husband and lovers cannot live up to), and dying wise old man. She portrays her mother as odd person out, as questioner and challenger, and as lost figure being grieved over. Her aunts and children and distant cousins appear as mirrors of the main action. Intrinsically this is a happy family, in which love and loss coincide: a form of readable contrast or acceptable contradiction that 'Chaddeleys and Flemings' initially proposes. But does the family frame therefore contain everything else and structure how to read the entire book? Or does it not enclose the other nine stories so much as it filters them, not impose an interpretation upon them so much as provide a glass through which to read the significance of sequence?

Beginning with sequence: casting alternatives

The sequence of nine stories between the opening and closing frames shapes another way to read the book. *Sequence* seems the more apposite term than *series* here, for two particular reasons: (1) the nine stories are arranged with an approximate reference to stages in the characters' lives (youth, maturity, age); and (2), whereas the term 'series' suggests a set of items (not as random as a *miscellany*, but not necessarily closely related), the term 'sequence' implies a set of items that is deliberately arranged according to a successive pattern, such as chronology or spatial sweep (e.g. west-to-east). The reader's attention in these stories is drawn to changes in time and perspective. Their preoccupation with age-related episodes (and differing degrees of maturity and independence) can also be read as a slanted mirror to the action in the frame stories and an inquiry into alternatives to the experiences the frame-narrator undergoes. The placing of the nine stories between the framing stories also performs an effective narrative function. A sequence postpones a consequence, conclusion, action, or realization; here it *delays* the need or willingness to address the issue that the concluding frame must return to: the death of the father and the shift in the narrator's role from daughter to mother.

The shaping of this sequence (after Munro had rewritten most of the stories and selected the final twelve) was a matter of some discussion between Munro and her editors, Douglas Gibson and Ann Close. Gibson wanted to space out the 'really strong stories' and follow a 'life flow pattern' from childhood to old age; he also suggested grouping the first-person stories together and the third-person stories together. Ann Close pushed for 'Accident' to appear before 'Bardon Bus'. The final order was agreed upon in May 1982, four months before publication.[9]

As published, the sequenced stories fasten on the satisfaction or failure of social and sexual partnerships:

> 'Dulse': *third person* (converted from the first-person version published in the *New Yorker*); Lydia (editor, poet) withdraws from a liaison with a man (Duncan) to live temporarily on an island off the East Coast, where a gift of dulse (for which she has not yet acquired a taste) renews her sense of self, and where an old man (Mr Stanley) is sheltered by his love of Willa Cather (whose imperiousness and sexuality he self-protectively ignores);

'The Turkey Season': *first person*; an adolescent girl's experience as a turkey gutter at Christmas introduces her to the speech, character, and sexual aspirations of her fellow workers (the story is dedicated to Joe Radford, Munro's sister's husband, whose work experience in the turkey barns supplied her with narrative details);

'Accident': *third person*; an affair between Frances and Ted goes awry when an accident kills a child and acid-tongued family members claim a superior morality; but after separation comes reunion;

'Bardon Bus': *first person*: the narrator recalls an affair with a man she calls X and also recounts the sexual behaviour of her friend Kay, realizing over time that Kay is now being seduced by X;

'Prue': *third person*; Prue, who lives on and off with Gordon, 'tells her life in anecdotes' (129) whose bizarre twists are never explained; taking something from each encounter, she then puts it away and forgets about it;

'Labor Day Dinner': *third person*; competing attractions in a foursome nearly disrupt a family; a near-accident adjusts priorities, silences the adults, and gives voice to a daughter, who asks about home;

'Mrs Cross and Mrs Kidd': *third person*; two dissimilar octogenarians who have known each other for decades end up in the same care home, where friendship dissolves into competition for a different companion and sense of self-importance, only to meet comeuppance and later retrieve a small share of dignity;

'Hard-Luck Stories': *first person*; the narrator meets up with an old friend, Julie; over time they talk about marriage and different kinds of love, and (with Douglas) talk giddily about running away to Nova Scotia;

'Visitors': *third person*; an ageing married couple, Mildred and Wilfred, of indeterminate faith, host his brother, Albert, and sister-in-law, Grace, whose Pentecostal beliefs limit ease of conversation and appreciation of narrative; despite tensions, a family bond persists.

This order scarcely suggests a family arc, so any 'mirroring' of the frame is inexact. The irregular alternation of first- and third-person perspectives also comments more on the integrity of each story than it directs how to read the book. More telling, as a marker of a collective unity, are the nuances of relationship that the separate narratives reveal. They read as a set of permutations on a thematics of connection: love and discord, disaster and recovery, whether drawn against a backdrop of family or structured to disclose some other community model. While settings vary from Australia to Nova Scotia (with places in between), the mores of Huron County, Ontario are repeatedly implied.[10] Certain motifs recur: family structure, marriage, love, liaison, flight, bonding, self-esteem (lost or regained), self-importance, and competition. Accidents disrupt or bring together; sex fulfils or dissatisfies; slippages in time allow the past to impinge upon the present or be set aside. Never far away from any of these motifs is the narrative awareness that words tell these stories, and that words fabricate answers as much as they pose questions, invent complications as much as they ease into cliché.

Several phrases in the frame stories emphasize the importance of lines: those that include (such as family), those that exclude (such as community mores), those that configure narrative itself. All delineate the character of connection and disconnection, coupled together in the scene in the hospital, for instance, when Janet thinks of her ex-husband, Richard. She turns to her father to say something but sees the monitor instead, 'the line his heart was writing' (228). A lifeline, of course, is metaphorically what narrators repeatedly compose when telling their own or others' lives (with similar cautions, for literary conventions can include and exclude as fiercely as social conventions do). The end of 'The Stone in the Field' illustrates this. Here the narrator reflects on the untold narrative of Mr Black and then on story-making codes: 'If I had been younger, I would have figured out a story. I would have insisted on Mr Black's being in love ... I would have wished him to confide ... his secret ... I would have made a horrible, plausible connection ... Now I no longer believe that people's secrets are defined and communicable' (35). In other words, a life told in the conditional is one thing; a life lived in the conditional is another. The sequence of stories that makes up *The Moons of Jupiter* dramatizes this distinction. The stories between the opening and closing frames might even be read hypothetically as 'Janet's stories', her writerly attempts to recast the exigencies of her family connections into other forms of narrative, and to delay her own need to act.

These stories present behaviour; they trace moments that suggest why changes occur; but always they leave final explanations of behaviour alone. Sometimes one story will echo another diffusely, as when Mr Black and his stone marker semantically reappear in 'Visitors' (207) with the character incongruously named Blanche Black and the apparently offhand remark that conservation people 'don't leave one stone' behind (212). Cumulatively, the sequence probes how the telling of stories constructs explanations and alternatives, the set of variations leading not to a finite conclusion but to an acceptance that knowing is perpetually uncertain – which sets up a reading of 'The Moons of Jupiter' that focuses on the tales that people tell each other: fictions, adventures, confessions, encounters, histories, contracts, promises, lies.

Reading *The Moons of Jupiter* in this way highlights the instability of words and requires the reader to accept a paradox: that this book, even while demonstrating the writer's artistic achievement, her skill *with words*, is also challenging the neutrality of language and the acceptability of passive listening. One of the features of the book that early reviewers applauded[11] – Munro's growing willingness to experiment with form (shifting time and point of view, fragmenting scene, refusing a single, consistent, normative identity, resisting closure) – exemplifies this nascent challenge to easy linguistic order. When Munro writes that a reader can begin at the beginning of a story, the end, or at any place between, she is underlining not just the potential arbitrariness of meaning, but also the possibility that when conventions are ignored, a surprise can startle one into insight.

Beginning in the middle: the flexibility of order

Start reading, then, arbitrarily, in the middle: halfway down page 117 of a 233-page book, eight pages into 'Bardon Bus', eleven pages before the beginning of 'Prue'. A passage begins with the narrator reflecting on her friend Kay's love life: 'She is getting over someone now; the husband, the estranged husband, of another woman at the farm.' The sentence looks casual – it has the flavour of an aside – but the rhetoric is deliberate; it declares identity, then modifies identity, then reveals how identity is further modified by connection and, in the next sentence, can be codified by name and occupation: 'His name is Roy; he too is an anthropologist.' Short, blunt, information announced by 'is', as though the labels conveyed the whole. A brief conversation follows, alluding to 'Somebody you know all about', their words dancing between confession and misdirection. Then the narrator shifts into indirect speech, which alters what has just been observed, for it redirects the focus to herself: 'I tell her I'm getting over somebody I met in Australia, and that I plan to be over him just about when I get the book done.' The tone is wry. But serious. The narrator analyses what she has just said: 'I think about the words "getting over." They have an encouraging, crisp, everyday sound' (117). Given the context, this observation asks to be read for its artifice, its effect, not as a fixed truth. The following story, 'Prue', might also be read from this vantage point, as an exploration of the casual brittleness of serially 'letting go'.

A page before this passage, the narrator has been describing Kay's apartment and drawing conclusions about behaviour from the articles she itemizes: books on prisons, riots, caves, anatomy, architecture, revolution – a series of subjects that overtly declares variety but collectively speaks about (and against) structural containment. Indirectly, the list also underscores the limitations generally imposed on women's lives (or in Kay's world, accepted as though they were her only option). Munro's phrasing then openly connects *how words work* with *how women live*. Referring to Kay (but revealing herself), the narrator declares that she 'takes up a man and his story wholeheartedly. She learns his language, figuratively or literally' (116). Her comments then trace a series of stages from initial attraction to some place beyond regret: irony, apology, infatuation, anguish, cold common sense, wit, and survival. Reading backwards and forwards from this point in 'Bardon Bus' is to enter into a carefully orchestrated dance with words. (Relatedly, *The Moons of Jupiter* also recognizes the language of touch and silence, relating both powers of awareness to women's sense of self when Janet, towards the end of the book, silently watches and interprets her daughter Judith's gesture towards Don (223).)

The conversation about 'getting over somebody' and 'self-love' displays the casual density of Munro's style. On the surface talking about love, but also thinking about words and the book she is writing, the narrator throughout the story is the articulate voice of insight and strangled action. Details about friends and lovers and the 'row on row' (119) of X's women (the phrase echoing the round that's sung in 'Connection') carry the plotline forward. Details about time (the verbs shifting from past and perfect forms into the present progressive) undercut any notion of perfect duration. Details about dress and language emphasize the instability of what is taken for granted.

The narrator, for instance, mentions the Toronto Reference Library (118) and Pliny's description of soap (120), but she finds that sources of 'fact' are unreliable. She talks of the journals of Victor Hugo's daughter Adèle,[12] especially the passage that records Adèle's inability to connect the real man she sees on the street with the man in her head she once loved (117). The narrator also mentions the plotlines of conventional novels (12) and poems that run through her head that usually have 'some relation to what is going on in my life', but then she distances them: 'that may not be what seems to be going on' (122).

Lines from poems, hymns, and Christmas songs are quoted throughout *The Moons of Jupiter*. In 'Bardon Bus', for example, the line 'Even such is time' is the title and first line of a poem by Sir Walter Ralegh, concerning youth, age, and possible immortality. 'Back and sides lay bare' ('Hard-Luck Stories', 191) alludes to William Stevenson's drinking song about coping with life's difficulties, 'Jolly Good Ale and Old'. When Janet's father, in 'The Moons of Jupiter', 'can't see the connection my mind is making' (225), he quotes from Joaquin Miller's 'Columbus', in which the Admiral sustains his crew through darkness (to 'Time's burst of dawn') by insistently shouting 'Sail on!' Mrs Kidd's recitations (160–1) come from Robert Browning's 'An Incident of the French Camp', Bliss Carman's 'The Ships of Saint John', and 'Old Brass Wagon', an American folk tune. Many of the allusions also convey a sense of time, in that they suggest the often heroic contents of early twentieth-century school readers and the forms of performance poem characteristic of late nineteenth-century salon recitation. None of these particular poems, however, is to be found in the authorized reader for Ontario high schools in the 1920s and '30s, *Shorter Poems*, ed. W. J. Alexander (Toronto: T. Eaton Co., 1924), although other poems by Browning and Carman do appear.

As with standard language, so with standard fashion. Seeking to change her mood with a change in season, the narrator of 'Bardon Bus' goes looking for colour and jewellery, but the result is not what conventional fashion might promise, for she ends up watching the primping that goes on in the shop and realizing that she has misinterpreted what she has seen: one of the makeovers is happening not to a woman but to a 'pretty boy' (125). Her friend Kay, meanwhile, never stops equating surfaces with depths. Even at the end of the story she dons a new 'outfit' for a new beau – *outfit*: a word associated with surface appearance and expeditions. The outfit, moreover, turns out to be a schoolgirl tunic, an arbitrarily 'kinky' (128) display that emphasizes the transience of the only relationships she knows.

The narrator herself goes on to lie, to read, then to despair at the monotonous 'language, of pornography and romance alike' (123), a sample of which she then writes out, vacuous and quick ('You see the sort of thing I mean' (124)). While she acknowledges the emptiness of the words, the passage nevertheless constructs an implied context for her old, superficial, faithless, empty lover, the one she's called X, paradoxically filling 'X' with identity and at the same time emptying the connection of difference and desire.

Reading the book by starting with 'Bardon Bus' thus opens up a conversation with the rest of the book, especially a conversation about women and words. Writers and writing are not casual allusions here – not accident, though 'accident' is the subject of more than one story – but invitations to choose to speak. 'I'-narrators throughout the collection are writing books, notes, journal entries, stories. They're also gathering words, as moments, as details. Details acquire cumulative power. Perhaps perceived initially in isolation, they gather resonance and force, as a passage in 'The Stone in the Field' establishes. The narrator records her father telling her about Mr Black and his burial site, adding that when his own grandmother and two uncles died, they were buried in shrouds made of lace curtains. She records her immediate puzzlement. But then he says, 'that's the kind of a detail I thought might be interesting to you' (32). Implicitly he recognizes the role that she has already chosen: to be a writer. Inside the story that's written, the link between lace and shroud turns into a resonant comment on the link between one kind of domesticity and death.[13]

Storytelling – read as an evasion of reality or as reality told inferentially and cumulatively by details: images, nuances, occasions of exchange – informs the whole of *The Moons of Jupiter*, sometimes by what characters say and sometimes by what they leave to be inferred. Throughout, characters (writers and others) are tantalized by what words can and cannot do, and cumulatively their comments constitute a book-long conversation about authorship. In 'Labor Day Dinner', Roberta recalls playing a game of 'toothpick' words with some man on a cruise (153), but she tires of it; and later on, when she and George are on the verge of an accident, 'There isn't time to say a word' (159): silence proving more powerful than cliché. When Mrs Cross and Mrs Kidd are both trying to claim precedence in the games room of their care home, Jack, the man who has had a stroke and is without language, hits the scrabble board in a fury and sends the letters flying, silencing even the most articulate person present (177).

The stories also comment on the form and function of storytelling. When Julie, in 'Hard-Luck Stories', asks why 'ironical twist-at-the-end stories' went out of fashion, the narrator replies, 'They got to seem too predictable' (181–2), but then she immediately proffers an alternative answer: 'Or people thought ... who cares the way things happen?' Other stories counter this conclusion by alluding to the popularity of vapid romance (in 'Bardon Bus') and the power of gossip (in 'Accident'), despite its emptiness and inaccuracy. Surfaces can have wide appeal. Prue, declares the narrator, 'presents her life in anecdotes' (129) that entertain her listeners because she invests so little in them; she makes no demands and sounds no complaints, though the point of her stories appears to foreground the strangeness of life and its inconclusiveness.

But sometimes the surface is all there is, and the desire to see or convey more leads a listener/reader to desire difference – which, if it's only for the sake of difference, can paradoxically mean the satisfaction that comes from narrative familiarity. In 'Visitors', Albert's mundane story of a man named Lloyd Sallows, who went into a swamp and never came out, does not satisfy Mildred because she wants the closure of the conventional mystery, western, fantasy, romance. 'If Wilfred had been telling that story, Mildred thought, it would have gone someplace, there would have been some kind of ending to it' (215). Her mind creates several possibilities involving bets, nakedness, gangsters, and money, but when she asks Albert why he told the story, he remains bound by physical detail: he picks up 'a cold piece of hamburger' and puts it down, saying, 'It's not a story. It's something that happened' (215). Which calls into question yet again the reality of fiction and the fictionality of the real.[14]

Beginning with endings: cycling with words

Starting with the frame reads the book through a family filter; starting with the sequence probes perspective and arranges issues by gender, time, and disorder; starting in the middle purls outward to the edges in a running conversation about silencing and saying. So what happens at the ends of stories? What story do endings tell, and do they offer another approach to the book? *Endings*, writes the short story writer Clark Blaise, can be interrogative, stoic, rhetorical, judgemental; they can reach out, reassure, accuse; they can turn metafictionally back on a story or scamper playfully away from it. 'All I would leave a good reader with', he ends his own essay, 'is the injunction to look at endings as urgent, final communications. They are the cords we have bitten (sometimes only raggedly chewed) in the act of giving birth.'[15] Ending in this way, Blaise clearly embraces metaphor as a resonant cap to what has come before. The stories in Munro's first collection, *Dance of the Happy Shades*, also characteristically push towards a closing flourish. But in *The Moons of Jupiter*, Munro resists the conclusive impulses of closure and engages instead with the seemingly plain rhetoric of the everyday.

Although 'Chaddeleys and Flemings' opens in flamboyance, the rest of the book – through the sometimes sardonic voices of narration, most obviously in 'Visitors', and in the wry asides that punctuate many of the stories[16] – repeatedly invites the reader to recognize the limitations and possibilities of what is seen, heard, read, touched, sniffed, tasted, felt, and acted on. The subversive power of the ordinary might not seem immediately resonant (Munro's character Mildred finds no excitement in it; her character Julie reminisces about stories with an O. Henry-type twist), but as 'Bardon Bus' makes clear, even though superficiality can deceive, reactions to surface realities can at least encourage caution if not guarantee informed choice.

Recurrent references to food further exemplify how sensory experience constitutes a leitmotif in the book, associated with pleasure, guilt, display, or sometimes with contradictory attitudes. Each of the stories mentions food. 'Connection' contrasts the display of the cousins' exotic 'American' food (oysters, olives, chocolates) with the fancy dinner the narrator later prepares in North Vancouver, where a lemon pie, designed to be elegant, turns into a weapon. 'The Stone in the Field' contrasts the presence of animal feed with the absence of refreshments. Contrast occurs elsewhere too: the cooking of dinner vs the taste of dulse in 'Dulse'; pork chops vs blood at the accident scene in 'Accident'; consuming vs wasting in 'Hard-Luck Stories'; the two sides of the dining room in 'Mrs Cross and Mrs Kidd'. Several stories ('Dulse', 'Prue', 'Stone', 'Turkey', 'Labor Day Dinner') address the *work* that is associated with food (cook, waitress, farmer, gutter, plucker) and the gendering of these roles. Hamburger features in 'The Turkey Season', 'Mrs Cross', and 'Visitors', where the cutting up of a hamburger patty is linked with interrupted storytelling. Preparing and eating dinner in 'Labor Day Dinner' serves as an architecture of the marriages in the story; the contrast between duration and the moment (of dinner being finished) questions the distinction between avoidance and collapse. Many other food phrases appear in the collection, in simile (some women being 'wobbly as custard' (1)), as a way to epitomize character (Greta's preoccupation with pie, in 'Accident' (88)), or simply to range across alternatives, from soup to drinks to a picture of the Lord's supper ('Mrs Cross and Mrs Kidd' (164)).'[17]

Over the course of the book, the power of the apparently plain becomes even more evident as details accumulate and interact, to the point where a list of the twelve story endings tells a quasi-story in its own right:

> Now, wait. *Dream.* (18)
> think twice about regretting. (35)
> from a distance. (39)
> So we sang. (76)
> a way to go yet. (109)
> never had anybody do that before. (128)
> more or less forgets about it. (133)
> Aren't we home? (139)
> get started on the trip back. (180)
> We could all be happy. (197)
> Not next week. (216)
> I went back to the hospital. (233)

Admittedly, un-threading the final phrases this way, ripping them out of their particular stories, creates an artificial text, but this list of endings can nevertheless be read as an arc, one that perhaps indirectly suggested how finally to arrange the stories for publication. The list certainly articulates a cyclical course of action comprising departure and return (*Now wait, find distance, sing all the way, forget where you are, start back, not yet, here again, now*). The assembled endings thus harmonically echo the cyclical metaphor in the book's title: planetary satellites circling a centre, or (less tangibly) circling a constant of some indeterminate sort, whose reality is both fixed and in transit – like love, itself a contradiction, of a sort that Munro's next book (in 1986) would call a 'progress'.

Recast yet again – *in search of, in possession of, ready to let go, ready to move on* – the words of the story endings in *The Moons of Jupiter* house the paradoxes that the connected lives of child/parent, friend/former friend, wife/husband, lover/lover cumulatively reveal: contradictions that openly declare *but*, yet repeatedly imply *and* as well. Underpinning the book's rhetorical design and dramatized most directly as the double heritage of Chaddeleys and Flemings, paradox resonates in the silences among the characters and in all the dialogues: between past and future, home and away, distance and nearness, memory and forgetting, assertion and denial.[18] Text = process, and process = a way of structuring the reader's response within narrative and informing behaviour outside it, in the spaces of lives being lived.

For all its forays into disillusion and dissolution, that is, *The Moons of Jupiter* as a whole accepts the minutiae of experience and affirms a continuing testament to living actively amongst them. This commitment – to both choice and continuity, both independence and connection – shapes the dilemmas that the characters face. It also sustains most of the characters – family, mother, lover, father, neighbour, co-worker, child, partner, friend – whether seeking renewal or refusing to despair, across time. Concurrently aware of the presence of the past and the problems of the present, Janet especially, in the critical title story, also learns to accept the promise of future, which is to say, the possibility of calmly becoming past. *The Moons of Jupiter* does not end with unilateral closure; it calls for a different kind of recognition: to realize that going back – re-reading – means beginning again.

Notes

1 Alice Munro, 'What Is Real?', in John Metcalf and J. R. (Tim) Struthers (eds.), *How Stories Mean* (Erin, Ont.: Porcupine's Quill, 1993), 331–4 at 332. First published in John Metcalf (ed.), *Making It New: Contemporary Canadian Stories* (Toronto: Methuen, 1982).

2 Quoted in Robert Thacker, *Alice Munro: Writing her Lives* 2nd edn (Toronto: McClelland & Stewart, 2011; first published 2001), 390. Thacker also quotes a 1980 letter to Douglas Gibson in which Munro referred to her current project as 'a more held-together piece of work'; while she might be referring to the *Moons* stories, Thacker suggests (367) that she is more likely alluding to the stories that were later collected in *The Progress of Love* (1986).

3 Details on publishing history are drawn from Thacker, especially chapter 7: 'Feeling Like Rilke's Editor', 367–441, and 385–8; and from Allan Weiss (comp.), *A Comprehensive Bibliography of English-Canadian Short Stories 1950–1983* (Toronto: ECW, 1988), 472–6. See also JoAnn McCaig, *Reading in Alice Munro's Archives* (Waterloo, Ont.: Wilfrid Laurier University Press, 2002).

4 See, for example, E. D. Blodgett, who in *Alice Munro* (Boston: Twayne, 1998) adapts Barthes and Jakobsen to a reading of metaphor, paradox, and the syntax of absence (7–9); Coral Ann Howells, who in *Alice Munro* (Manchester University Press, 1998) discusses 'constructions of provisional order' (84) and emphasizes pluralities of perspective and meaning (67–84); and Isla Duncan, who in *Alice*

Munro's Narrative Art (New York: Palgrave Macmillan, 2011) adapts the theories of Genette to a study of focalization and free indirect discourse.
5 All quotations from *The Moons of Jupiter* refer to the first Canadian edition (Toronto: Macmillan, 1982). The jacket design by Ivan Holmes features a detail of a Christopher Pratt painting of a woman looking in a mirror. Munro dedicated the book to her friend Bob Weaver, the influential editor and radio producer with the CBC, whose programme *Anthology* broadcast a reading of 'The Turkey Season' (6 October 1982).
6 Possibly at the suggestion of Doug Gibson (Thacker, *Alice Munro*, 371).
7 As Margaret Atwood has suggested in 'Alice Munro: an Appreciation', *The Guardian* (11 October 2008); accessed online 14 October 2014.
8 Thacker, *Alice Munro*, 390.
9 Thacker provides further detail regarding sequence order (*Alice Munro*, 390).
10 Huron County, Ontario, is of course real, adjoining the eastern shore of Lake Huron, though the towns of Dalgleish, Hanratty, and Jubilee are created within Munro's fictions. For more extended commentary on topology and the competing realities of knowledge and 'strangeness' in Munro's stories, especially regarding urban–rural contrasts, illusions of authenticity, and the conventions of 'tourist' freedom and 'native' knowledge in 'Bardon Bus', see Robert McGill, 'Somewhere I've Been Meaning to Tell You: Alice Munro's Fiction of Distance', *Journal of Commonwealth Literature* 37, 1 (2002), 9–29, esp. 14–15, 18–21.
11 Thacker ably summarizes the reviews (*Alice Munro*, 391–4), one of the most insightful being 'A Sentence to Life' by Tom Crerar (*Brick* 18, (spring 1983), 2), which argues that time is the 'real subject' in the book: 'time as a condition, a sentence to life'. The effect of the word 'sentence' here is to further suggest how *The Moons of Jupiter* crafts a flexible narrative grammar to convey the experience of time from her characters' shifting points of view.
12 Adèle Hugo's diaries (*Journal d'exil* (Paris: Lettres modernes, 1971)) had been adapted in 1975 into the film *L'histoire d' Adèle H.*, directed by François Truffaut and starring Isabelle Adjani.
13 An extensive body of feminist scholarship theorizes and addresses in greater detail the language and circumstances of Munro's female characters. See, for example, Judith Miller (ed.), *The Art of Alice Munro: Saying the Unsayable* (Waterloo, Ont.: Wilfrid Laurier University Press, 1984); Beverly J. Rasporich, *Dance of the Sexes: Art and Gender in the Fiction of Alice Munro* (Edmonton: University of Alberta Press, 1990); Magdalene Redekop, *Mothers and Other Clowns: the Stories of Alice Munro* (London and New York: Routledge, 1992); Katherine J. Mayberry, 'Every Last Thing: Alice Munro and the Limits of Narrative', *Studies in Short Fiction* 29, 4 (fall 1992), 531–41.
14 It might also be taken as an authorial comment on the way some of her fiction was rejected or received (i.e. as 'reminiscence' rather than story).
15 'On Ending Stories', reprinted in Metcalf and Struthers, *How Stories Mean*, 166–9. First published in John Metcalf (ed.), *Making It New: Contemporary Canadian Stories* (Toronto: Methuen, 1982).
16 Cf. Mark Levene '"It Was about Vanishing": a Glimpse of Alice Munro's Stories' (*University of Toronto Quarterly* 69, 4 (fall 1999), 805–60), who reads the collection as an acutely sombre elegy marked by excruciating loneliness (8–9).

The importance of humour in Alice Munro's stories remains a largely unexamined critical topic.

17 For an extended account of the importance of food in 'Labor Day Dinner' and the importance of this story to a reading of 'The Moons of Jupiter', see Ryan Melsom, 'Roberta's Raspberry Bombe and Critical Indifference in Alice Munro's "Labor Day Dinner"', *Studies in Canadian Literature* 34, 1 (2009); accessed online 14 October 2014.

18 For further reading on silence, time, paradox, and patterns of imagery, see, e.g., Blodgett, *Alice Munro*; Howells, *Alice Munro*; James Carscallen, *The Other Country: Patterns in the Writing of Alice Munro* (Toronto: ECW Press, 1993); A. J. Heble, *The Tumble of Reason: Alice Munro's Discourse of Absence* (University of Toronto Press, 1994); Helen Hoy, '"Dull, Simple, Amazing, and Unfathomable": Paradox and Double Vision in Alice Munro's Fiction', *Studies in Canadian Literature* 5 (spring 1980), 100–15; Louis K. MacKendrick (ed.), *Probable Fictions: Alice Munro's Narrative Acts* (Toronto: ECW Press, 1983); W. R. Martin, *Alice Munro: Paradox and Parallel* (University of Alberta Press, 1987). On Munro's 'complex rhythms and aesthetic effects', see Douglas Glover, 'The Mind of Alice Munro' (2010), reprinted in *Attack of the Copula Spiders and Other Essays on Writing* (Windsor, Ont.: Biblioasis, 2012) 83–104.

8

ROBERT MCGILL

Alice Munro and personal development

Train lines

Alice Munro's fiction challenges any inclination her readers may have to attribute development to individuals, regions, or humanity as a whole. Repeatedly, her stories question the notion that a person who grows older necessarily grows wiser or more mature, just as they throw into doubt the idea that technological and social change has led to demonstrable progress in particular places or for the species. Thus, the stories reflect Munro's observation in a 1982 interview that she was drawn to writing short stories rather than novels because, she said, 'I don't see that people develop and arrive somewhere. I just see people living in flashes.'[1]

In this respect, a key figure in Munro's writing is the train.[2] Especially in her stories set in rural southwestern Ontario during the middle decades of the twentieth century – the place and period that Munro has most often documented – the train features as a prominent mode of transportation, particularly for the working-class and female characters who are often her protagonists. From 'The Ottawa Valley' in *Something I've Been Meaning to Tell You* (1974) to several stories in Munro's most recent collection, *Dear Life* (2012), Munro makes train journeys central to her narratives. As she does so, she reminds her readers that trains no longer run through southwestern Ontario as they did during her childhood in the 1930s and '40s. In 'Carried Away', the opening story of *Open Secrets* (1994), we are told that the passenger train taking people to the town of Carstairs 'had stopped running during the Second World War and even the rails were taken up'.[3] In 'Save the Reaper', a story in *The Love of a Good Woman* (1998) set in the same region, the local train station is gone, replaced by a 'fake-old-fashioned mall'.[4] Through the provision of such details, Munro tracks the rise and decline of industrialization in Ontario, along with industry's replacement by a consumer economy. As she does so, it is less than clear that this development has been a wholly positive one.

The railway's status as a manner of relic in Munro's stories also brings to the fore the train's metafictional role in them. In that regard, it is notable that in several of her stories – from 'Wild Swans' in *Who Do You Think You Are?* (1978) and 'Save the Reaper' in *The Love of a Good Woman* to 'Chance' in *Runaway* (2004) – trains are the locations of fleeting sexual encounters between strangers. As such, trains gain a striking affinity with the short story as a form, which is a site for similarly fleeting, desire-laden encounters between readers and authors. Moreover, a train's cars, separate yet joined, resonate in terms of the short-story collection with its separate texts bound in one volume. And while a train journey moves from beginning to end, guided by rails just as the reading of a story happens unidirectionally on the page, one can often move more or less freely within and between a train's cars, enacting the same movements that Munro has described undertaking when reading a story, saying that she likes to 'go into it, and move back and forth and settle here and there, and stay in it for a while'.[5] Munro's implicit resistance to following the short story's conventional arc of rising action, climax and denouement has been echoed in critical appreciations of her own stories, which have celebrated her avoidance of traditional plot development.

Munro's resistance both to conventional plots and to sanguine notions of regional development suggests the usefulness of considering her fiction with respect to other kinds of development as well. In what ways, for instance, might it be fair to say that Munro has developed as an artist? And what views of human development does Munro's fiction promote? These questions are related, in that Munro's fiction is often self-reflexive, commenting on itself even as it explores its characters' lives. Meanwhile, critics have offered their own views on Munro's artistic development. Surveying those views below, I focus on critics of the past decade who have identified phases in Munro's writing and who have sometimes drawn on the concept of 'late style' to describe her most recent collections. Recognizing the validity of these critics' observations, I wish to confirm and elaborate on the view that Munro's career has been marked more by continuity and recursion than by transformation. In that respect, her career's trajectory mirrors an approach to life and art that her stories recurrently, if implicitly, advocate: namely, one of return and revision. At the same time, Munro's stories caution readers against assuming that such return and revision will necessarily bring improvement. A story from Munro's 2012 collection, *Dear Life*, merits especially close consideration in this respect. As hinted by the story's title, 'Train', the narrative is one in which the railway once more proves to be a fertile figure for Munro, a figure with ramifications in terms of how we might imagine the course of a human life, of a writer's career, and of short stories themselves.

Munro's progress

A myth of artistic development substantially overturned by Munro's career is that writing short fiction is only a stepping-stone for authors on the way to writing novels. Munro has said that early in her career, she was repeatedly asked when she was going to write a novel, and that only after selling her first story to *The New Yorker* in 1977 did she stop thinking of herself 'as a writer who had halted at some, you know, intermediate stage of development'.[6] Following Munro's lead, critics of her work have been at pains to insist that the short story is hardly an inferior form. Still, a certain ambivalence remains evident whenever critics insist that Munro's short fiction has the richness of a novel, as though the novel were the benchmark of literary quality, or when they chafe against the word 'short', insisting that Munro simply writes 'stories'. In that regard, critics invariably notice the increasing length of her stories beginning in the 1980s, a trend that appeared to culminate in 1997 with the novella-sized 'The Love of a Good Woman'. As early as 1990, Beverly J. Rasporich observed that Munro's stories had also come to involve broader time-frames, larger casts of characters, and more complex narrative structures; in other words, they increasingly resembled novels.[7] A common critical response to these changes has been to herald them as signs of Munro's increasing prowess. Accordingly, although her career has deterred critics from perpetuating a developmental narrative of the short story as an apprentice form, it has not kept them from constructing narratives of her artistic development that rely on evaluative criteria which privilege the novel.

Another developmental narrative circulating implicitly in Munro criticism emerges from the fact that while many of her early stories resemble autobiography, she later turned more often to writing tales that appear less personal. If the predominant type of narrator in Munro's first two books, *Dance of the Happy Shades* (1968) and *Lives of Girls and Women* (1971), is a woman telling stories about her youth in southwestern Ontario, Munro thereafter adopted third-person narration with greater frequency, and she also ventured farther afield in time and space: for instance, 'Meneseteung' in *Friend of My Youth* (1990) is set in nineteenth-century Ontario, while 'The Albanian Virgin' and 'The Jack Randa Hotel' in *Open Secrets* have international settings. These shifts might seem to corroborate a popular apprehension that writers often begin by writing autobiographically before graduating to other material. However, such a shift's commonness does not, in itself, license the conclusion that autobiographical writing is immature writing. Munro herself has challenged that conclusion by turning to explicitly autobiographical work late in her career, publishing stories of family history in *The View from Castle Rock* (2006) and concluding *Dear Life* with a 'suite' of texts that she calls 'the first and last – and the closest – things I have to say about my own life'.[8] The prefaces that Munro has written to accompany these stories do mark the texts out as different from her other writing and, perhaps, as works not to be evaluated in the same manner. However, Munro's refusal to identify the texts straightforwardly as memoir suggests a resistance to the very distinction between fiction and non-fiction that facilitates a derogatory view of autobiography as a less imaginative, less mature mode of writing.

The critical inclination to identify an arc of artistic development in Munro's career is further evident in attempts to ascribe phases to it. For instance, although Munro was a critical success from the start, winning a Governor General's Award for *Dance of the Happy Shades*, certain critics have noted the relatively conventional nature of her early stories. Munro herself has dismissed some of these as imitative 'exercises',[9] while Christian Lorentzen has asserted that 'Munro started out as an epiphany-monger':[10] that is, her early protagonists tend to experience climactic, revelatory glimpses of some truth in a way that, by the 1960s, was virtually generic in short fiction. Other critics have suggested that Munro's career has reflected a shift often associated with Canadian fiction in general through the latter half of the twentieth century: namely, from realism to postmodernism. There is a consensus that Munro's particular version of postmodernism entails an emphasis on what Coral Ann Howells calls 'indeterminacy and multiple meanings', along with the use of formal techniques underscoring that emphasis.[11] If there is disagreement among critics on this point, it is principally as to when, exactly, the new emphasis became conspicuous in Munro's work. Rasporich identifies 'a new depth' in *The Moons of Jupiter* (1982), 'not only philosophically, but technically'.[12] For Ajay Heble, *The Progress of Love* (1986) is the point of departure, the book in which Munro began to present 'tales that turn on what has been left out, or what cannot be told or written'.[13] Lorentzen takes Munro's true innovations to be first apparent in *Friend of My Youth*, observing, 'In it the endings of stories call into question the whole manner of their telling.'[14] In 2006, Munro's editor at *The New Yorker*, Charles McGrath, claimed that her real innovations had begun in the stories that were collected in *Open Secrets*, asserting: 'in the last fifteen years she has been doing radically experimental things with form and with time and has been quietly demolishing our perceptions of what is and isn't possible in the short story'.[15] But if there is disagreement about when the key shift began, there is a consensus that 'The Love of a Good Woman' stands as the culmination of this period of Munro's career, not only in terms of that story's prodigious length but also in terms of its return to various situations and themes that had distinguished her earlier writing, making the story what Dennis Duffy calls a 'keystone text'.[16] Such a view of the story implicitly characterizes the 1980s and '90s as the time of a peak phase for Munro, one in which she was at the height of her powers.

This characterization is further evident in assessments of Munro's subsequent collection, *Hateship, Friendship, Courtship, Loveship, Marriage* (2001), beginning with Munro's own observation that the ideas in the book's stories seemed to have become 'simpler' and 'more scaled down' than those in her previous work.[17] The comment encouraged a critical view of Munro's post-1998 work as manifesting a 'late style', the term being one that has gained currency in literary scholarship largely thanks to Edward Said's book *On Late Style* (2006).[18] For Said, late style becomes manifest in the work of artists who are both late in their careers and approaching the end of relatively long lives. Regarding Munro, critics have considered her twenty-first-century work to be 'late' in various respects. For instance, they have observed her increased attention to older age. Reviewing *Hateship, Friendship, Courtship, Loveship, Marriage,* Howells noted a new concern on Munro's part 'with the lives and deaths of elderly people as their stories scroll out over many decades'.[19] Critics have also followed Munro in attending to her 'scaled down' approach – an approach seeming to confirm Robert Kastenbaum's claim that late works by older artists often feature 'an economy of means, a conciseness of expression'.[20] For example, James Grainger has observed a shift in Munro's work, beginning 'roughly' with *Runaway*, 'from the complex, oblique narratives and intricately layered portraiture of her mid-career work toward a pared-down, almost expressionist form of storytelling'. Grainger attributes this shift to the fact that 'Munro had just about exhausted, in the best way possible, the naturalist long-story format'; he also attributes to her a desire not to 'try to repeat past successes'.[21]

A poetics of recursion

But what is most remarkable about Munro's career is the way in which it has followed a gradualist arc marked by continuities more than by ruptures. Joyce Carol Oates has claimed, 'Of writers who have made the short story their metier ... Munro is the most consistent in style, manner, content, vision',[22] while Ailsa Cox asserts that Munro remains in 'many respects ... not only the same person but also the same writer that she was at thirty-nine.' Even Munro's late style is something that Cox sees as 'a development of earlier forms and techniques rather than a startling new departure'.[23] To use the terminology employed by David Galenson in his study of artists' careers, Munro is an 'experimentalist', a term Galenson uses to identify not artists who are avant-garde, as the term might suggest, but ones who are scientific in their approach. According to Galenson, experimental writers each confront a particular challenge in writing by testing various techniques and possible solutions, with each text building on past efforts.[24] John Van Rys implicitly recognizes just such an experimental quality in Munro's career when he observes that for decades, she has been 'developing, testing, elaborating, and stretching' the idea that 'life can one moment deal us a blow and the next release us through a surprise'.[25] As for the signature stress on indeterminacy that critics see in Munro's mid-career writing, it is actually evident as early as the penultimate sentence of 'Walker Brothers Cowboy', the opening story in *Dance of the Happy Shades*, in which the narrator remarks:

> I feel my father's life flowing back from our car in the last of the afternoon, darkening and turning strange, like a landscape that has an enchantment on it, making it kindly, ordinary and familiar while you are looking at it, but changing it, once your back is turned, into something you will never know, with all kinds of weathers, and distances you cannot imagine.[26]

The moment involves a manner of epiphany on the narrator's part, but it is an anti-epiphany, one foregrounding the unknown and unknowable in the everyday, something that Munro's writing has continued to emphasize throughout her career.

In a 1983 interview, Munro implied a belief in her own artistic development when she spoke of writing 'turning-point' stories that broke new ground for her and 'discovery' stories in which she found herself 'trying to find out how to *do* it, how to *tell*' a certain kind of narrative. In the same interview, though, Munro spoke out against the notion that she might be 'developing' as an artist, declaring: 'I disagree with this picture of writing that you progress from one book to the next and that you do different things, you open up new areas of your own consciousness and for your readers, and that it's supposed to be a kind of step-ladder. It seems to me just an enormously chancy thing every time.' She accepted that there had been 'changes in technique' for her, but she insisted that such changes were often motivated simply by a desire to stay 'interested in working'. It is not the case, she said, 'that there's necessarily a development'.[27] With these words, Munro advocated a notion of a writer's career as something marked not by progress so much as by paradigm shifts. To be sure, she has demonstrated in other ways an investment in the idea of improvement – not least, in her incessant revisions of her stories. Not only did she undertake a last-minute overhaul of *Who Do You Think You Are?* just as it was going to press, for example, but many stories in her collections differ significantly from the versions previously published in magazines. However, readers might disagree as to whether the changes are always improvements; the revisions might be taken as representing only shifts in Munro's perspective over time. That possibility is compelling in the case of one recent story, 'Corrie', that Munro published in three different versions: first in *The New Yorker*, then in the 2012 PEN/O. Henry Prize anthology, then in *Dear Life*. In each version, the ending has Corrie reacting differently to a significant revelation. While readers might argue the merits of each ending, they might equally observe that the differing versions work together to suggest the radical contingency of life, the ways in which slight shifts in perspective – in this case, Munro's along with Corrie's – can dramatically alter a life's direction. As Munro herself said in 1982 of her tendency to revise: 'it's not even that you are necessarily improving the story. You are telling it the way you see it now.'[28]

Such comments bespeak a poetics of review that repudiates the presumption of amelioration. This poetics is also evident in Munro's penchant for revisiting certain scenes and situations in different stories. Evidently, this penchant has been a source of concern for Munro: during a 2001 interview, she admitted to worrying that readers would say of her recent work, 'More of the same, more of the same.' But Munro also claimed to have told herself, 'I don't care if they say that, I'm just going to do it.'[29] It is a striking comment, insofar as it anticipates contradictory views of her work: one in which her recursive poetics is a liability, one in which it is a strength. A reader of her work espousing the latter view has been Jonathan Franzen, who, recognizing that Munro repeatedly creates characters with biographical details echoing her own, pronounces: 'Look what she can do with nothing but her own small story; the more she returns to it, the more she finds.'[30] One might further observe that Munro's emphasis on return is one that models for readers a way of apprehending her fiction and, moreover, the world. In her stories, the implicit imperative to herself, to her characters, and to her audience is not simply 'Look!' but, rather, 'Look again!' Some years ago I pointed out that 'excursion' has been an important word in Munro's writing, a term used to identify her stories as figurative tours of her fictional territories in which she, her characters, and her readers set out on journeys together.[31] Looking again at her writing, I see that recursion is an equally important concept in it. Even when her characters strike out on travels that, from their perspectives, come without precedent, Munro inevitably hints that the characters – together with Munro and her audience – are following in the footsteps of those who have similarly set out before them. Each time, we are invited to notice something about these journeys that we may not have previously observed. Each time, we are encouraged to appreciate that history does not simply progress but, rather, repeats itself, if with significant modulations of detail.

Character non-development

While Munro has rejected a characterization of her work as improving over the years, she has also resisted the idea of personal development when it comes to describing adult life. In a 2001 interview, she remarked: 'You're the same person at nineteen that you are at thirty that you are at sixty that you go on being.' Munro went on to insist that 'there is some root in your nature that doesn't change'.[32] In this comment, she echoed the protagonist of her story 'Accident', collected in *The Moons of Jupiter*, who thinks: 'She's had her love, her scandal, her man, her children. But inside she's ticking away, all by herself, the same Frances who was there before any of it.'[33] Insofar as Frances does not accept that significant life events have been transformative for her, she is a typically Munrovian character. If the titular phrase of *Hateship, Friendship, Courtship, Loveship, Marriage* echoes a social expectation that a person's life will progress through certain stages, much of Munro's fiction dramatizes characters' non-conformity in that regard, as well as the complications – sometimes comic, often tragic – of conformity.

Munro's scepticism about narratives of human development is perhaps most obviously forefront in *Lives of Girls and Women* and *Who Do You Think You Are?*, both of which follow their protagonists from childhood through to adulthood – and, in the case of *Who Do You Think You Are?*, through a marriage, parenthood, and a career. But as a *Künstlerroman* – the novel of an artist's development – *Lives of Girls and Women* notably refuses to show its protagonist-narrator, Del, explicitly as someone whose writing improves over time. There is only an implicit contrast between Del's self-reportedly failed novel about her home town and her subsequent achievement in having written about the town in the memoir that constitutes *Lives of Girls and Women* itself. As for *Who Do You Think You Are?*, one of its many remarkable aspects is the suggestion in the story 'Mischief' that when the protagonist, Rose, becomes a mother – achieving what a reductively evolutionist mindset might call the developmental endpoint of a woman's existence – she returns to a virtual second childhood. In the maternity ward, Rose befriends another new mother, Jocelyn, and they soon become 'hysterical as schoolgirls', such that a nurse tells them it is 'time for them to grow up'. For Rose, motherhood is evidently less a sign of maturation than a kind of regression. Later in the story, Jocelyn expresses her belief that 'going to a psychiatrist was something that everybody should do at developing or adjusting stages of life', thus corroborating a normative model of development that would, indeed, construe her and Rose's behaviour in the maternity ward as regressive.[34] However, as Sara Jamieson has noted, *Who Do You Think You Are?* works to identify Jocelyn's view with a 'particularly middle-class narrative of development as the human norm', one that treats the subject position of the bourgeoisie as though it were a universal.[35]

Who Do You Think You Are? ends with a qualified epiphany, as Rose, having read about the death of a man named Ralph Gillespie from her home town, thinks: 'What could she say about herself and Ralph Gillespie, except that she felt his life, close, closer than the lives of men she'd loved, one slot over from her own?'[36] The ending is quintessentially Munrovian insofar as it models self-questioning without providing definite answers or marking a clear shift into a more mature level of insight. 'The Ottawa Valley' features a similar ending, as the narrator-writer looks back on the story itself as her attempt to represent her mother, asserting, 'it is to reach her that this whole journey has been undertaken'. In doing so, the narrator neatly conflates the literal train journey described earlier in the story with the journey through the narrative. The story ends with the narrator's statement that her mother

> looms too close, just as she always did. She is heavy as always, she weighs everything down, and yet she is indistinct, her edges melt and flow. Which means she has stuck to me as close as ever and refused to fall away, and I could go on, and on, applying what skills I have, using what tricks I know, and it would always be the same.[37]

The narrator's epiphany is another anti-epiphany, a denial of development, an assertion of continuity over change. Her realization suggests that although recursion and review encourage one to see things that one has not seen before, they do not necessarily transform one into somebody new and improved.

Munro's skill in presenting such anti-epiphanies is one of the reasons critics have noted the significance of the momentary in her work. Todd VanDerWerff, for instance, claims that 'her true strengths lie in boiling human lives down to singular moments and revelations'.[38] However, insofar as 'singular moments' are commonplace in the modern short story, such a description of Munro's stories recognizes only what is most conventional in them while failing to acknowledge what is least conventional: namely, her increasingly strong tendency over the course of her career to tell stories covering years, even decades. The presentation of such broad temporal scopes has allowed her to represent life in terms of longer paths of development than that suggested by the short story's generic emphasis on epiphanic transformations. As Munro has done so, she has explored ways in which people develop over lengthy stretches of their lives – and, more conspicuously, ways in which they fail to develop.

Throughout her career, Munro has depicted characters who are, to use David Peck's phrase, 'developmentally stunted':[39] figures with apparent mental disabilities. They include Mary Agnes Oliphant in *Lives of Girls and Women*, Milton Homer in *Who Do You Think You Are?*, and Verna in 'Child's Play', which was collected in *Too Much Happiness* (2009). These characters would seem to serve as foils for the texts' protagonists, standing in contrast with the latter's developmental possibilities. Certainly, such protagonists are liable to express a wish to change. In *Who Do You Think You Are?*, for instance, Rose makes clear her desire to 'manage a transformation' (79). Yet as Munro tracks her protagonists across their lifetimes – with several later stories following characters who retire, become grandparents, or face dementia – there is an emphasis on failures to transform in conventionally positive ways.

Myths of maturation in 'Train'

Perhaps more than in any of Munro's previous collections, it is in *Dear Life* that trains are conspicuous as figures of human development. The volume opens with two stories, 'To Reach Japan' and 'Amundsen', in which train journeys are prominent, and its longest story, 'Train', begins and ends with such journeys. At the beginning of 'Train', a soldier named Jackson is on his way home to a town in southwestern Ontario after having served in the Second World War. He ends up at the farm of a woman, Belle, with whom he spends the next eighteen years in a platonic relationship. This arrangement seems to suit both of them because, as he puts it, 'She was a certain kind of woman, he a certain kind of man' (188). In 1962, Belle develops a cancerous lump and has an operation in Toronto to remove it. Afterwards, still in the hospital, she tells Jackson that when she was a young woman, her father once came to stare at her naked while she sat in the bath, and she believes that his subsequent death upon being hit by a train was a suicide catalysed by the encounter. Faced with Belle's revelation, Jackson abandons her without even saying goodbye and becomes the superintendent at an apartment building in the city. Years later, a woman appears at the building looking for her adult child, and Jackson recognizes the woman as someone from his home town. Her name is Ileane, and, we discover, it was to avoid marrying her that Jackson jumped off the train all those years before. Seeing her again in Toronto, he anticipates being confronted by her and promptly abandons his life once more, boarding a train to look for work in the northern town of Kapuskasing. Before he does so, though, for the first time in the story he recalls his stepmother's 'fooling, what she called her fooling or her teasing', when he was six or seven, which had stopped after he attempted to run away (215). Accordingly, the title of Munro's story, 'Train', evokes not only mass transportation but also a train of episodes. In doing so, the title suggests two divergent possibilities: first, that Jackson's life involves preparation for something, 'training'; second, that it involves mere juxtaposition, not development. As the story progresses, it confirms the second possibility: there is no clear line of improvement for Jackson in his life, and his experiences over the course of the story leave him no more prepared to face unexpected challenges or confront his past than he is at the outset.

Early in 'Train', as Jackson is approaching Belle's farm for the first time, he encounters a snake 'slithering between the rails' of the train tracks; late in the story, Jackson's last name, Adams, is mentioned in passing (177, 208). Together with the fact that Jackson leaves his seemingly idyllic life of pastoral labour with Belle after she introduces a discourse about sexuality to their relationship, these details encourage us to consider 'Train' in relation to the story of the biblical Fall. One might notice, for instance, that if Jackson's life with Belle evokes Eden, it is remarkable that Belle lives on the farm first, while her Adam arrives afterward. A shift in the power balance from that of the biblical couple is thus implied, with 'Train' positioning the man as the woman's helpmate rather than vice versa. Munro's versions of Adam and Eve also differ from their biblical antecedents in bringing personal sexual histories to their garden. In Belle's case, her memory of her father's apparent shame at looking upon her in the bath ironically echoes Adam and Eve's shame at the thought of standing naked before God; in Jackson's case, his respective flights from his stepmother, Ileane, and Belle mean that he is an Adam who, rather than being expelled from the garden along with Eve, abandons her and Eden of his own accord. These alterations to the Genesis narrative transform the story of human development that the biblical narrative has popularized. In Genesis, the fate of Adam and Eve allegorizes human life as one in which childhood innocence gives way to an adulthood of sexuality. In contrast, Munro's story echoes psychoanalytic theory by identifying how such a line of development is complicated by childhood irruptions of sexuality in relation to parental figures. At the same time, 'Train' troubles notions of historical progress in terms of gender relations by gesturing to other intertexts in such a way as to suggest that a pattern of men abandoning women is a transhistorical one. The first such intertext is the *Odyssey*. As a narrative about a soldier's return from war, 'Train' alludes to Odysseus' long voyage back from the Trojan War to Ithaca and his wife, Penelope. In that regard, Jackson's stay with Belle echoes Odysseus' seven-year stay with Calypso on her island. The names of Belle's mother, Helena, and of Ileane, whose name means 'Trojan', further nod to the Homeric intertext. Insofar as Jackson decides not to return home on the brink of reaching it, though, he is less Homer's Odysseus than Dante's: in the *Inferno*, Odysseus never returns to Ithaca but, instead, overcomes his feelings of attachment to his wife and family in order to explore the world. However, if Dante's Odysseus is a model for Jackson, he is an ironic one, for in the *Inferno*, Odysseus urges his compatriots to join him in exploration by telling them, 'You were not born to live as a mere brute does, / But for the pursuit of knowledge and the good.'[40] In 'Train', Jackson manifests no such goals. Rather, he pursues a life of unselfconscious labour that is not so different from that of the 'mere brute' whom Odysseus derides. In this regard, Jackson upends a common developmental narrative in which ageing involves the acquisition of knowledge. At the same time, his first name recalls that of a similar figure in Munro's 'Carried Away'. In that story, a man named Jack Agnew abandons a woman upon returning to a southwestern Ontario town from the First World War. By doing a similar thing a generation later, Jackson figuratively lives up to his nominal status as 'Jack's son'. Connecting the two characters across time and across her collections via their names, Munro both gestures to her recursive poetics and insists on the transhistorical obduracy of male abandonment. In doing so, she demonstrates a scepticism about narratives of historical progress that one finds elsewhere in her work as well. Munro's stories set during the 1960s and '70s, in particular, suggest that for all that was accomplished by the Women's Liberation Movement with regard to things such as divorce laws, abortion rights, and the availability of contraception, society has remained fundamentally sexist in important ways. To cite just one example: in 'The Bear Came Over the Mountain', collected in *Hateship, Friendship, Courtship, Loveship, Marriage,* Munro characterizes the era of 'free love' principally as a time in which husbands became freer to cheat on and leave their wives. However, as 'Train' suggests, Munro's attention to the complications of progress with regard to gender relations is hardly accompanied by a nostalgia for the past. Rather, she reminds us that patriarchy has long granted men the prerogative to pick up and leave at times of their choosing.

As Belle's name suggests, another key intertext in 'Train' is the fairy tale 'Beauty and the Beast'. In certain respects, Belle and Jackson resemble their fairy-tale precursors: in the original version of the fairy tale, for example, the prince's transformation into a beast happens after he rejects a marriage proposal from the fairy who raised him, a version of the archetypal 'wicked stepmother' whom Jackson's stepmother also evokes.[41] However, several echoes of 'Beauty and the Beast' in Munro's story are pointedly ironic. For example, Beauty's close relationship to her father in the fairy tale leads her to sacrifice herself to a life with the Beast, not unlike the way in which Belle ends up with Jackson, but the father–daughter bond in the fairy tale is not freighted with sexuality in the same literal way that the one in Munro's story is. Meanwhile, Jackson is a Beast who never falls in love with Belle and never transforms back into an earlier, ideal state. It has been claimed that 'Beauty and the Beast' is a story foregrounding its protagonists' 'developmental trajectories';[42] in contrast, 'Train' emphasizes Jackson's lack of development. No relationship frees him from the thrall of his apparently primal trauma. Consequently, while nods to 'Beauty and the Beast' in 'Train' serve as reminders of how fairy tales have contributed to common notions of human development, Munro's story insists that happy-ending transformations are less than inevitable. Likewise, by presenting a protagonist who does not change, 'Train' refuses to let plot development and character development go hand in hand. The story does not venture so far as to assert that people are unable to change, but it does intimate that they change less often and less completely than popular narratives would suggest.

Arrested development, hidden drives

For the most part, 'Train' depicts Jackson and Belle as figures suffering from a version of arrested development. Even in adulthood, Belle refers to her father as 'daddy', and she has 'childish bangs' (179). Also, she continues to live in her parents' house after both have died, and she seems to be caught in a state of arrested technological development, too, still using a horse and buggy when Jackson meets her, even though, as he notes, other people in the area were getting rid of horses '[e]ven before the war' (180). She turns out to be wary of development in other senses as well: for instance, on the way to Toronto in 1962, she is 'alarmed' by the new multi-lane highway (190). She is even sceptical about the advent of socialized healthcare in Canada, claiming that since its inauguration, 'nobody did anything but run to the doctor'. Jackson thinks of Belle as someone who 'was stopped at some point in life where she remained a grown-up child' (189).

For those who want to see it, there are hints of an eventual developmental arc for Belle. First, her post-surgical memory of her bathroom encounter with her father stands as a typically cathartic moment in trauma narratives, one in which revelation promises change. The notion that recounting a traumatic experience can be a positive breakthrough is corroborated by Belle's declaration after recalling her experience: 'Now I see. Now I have got a real understanding of it and it was nobody's fault' (198). Later in 'Train', there are further suggestions that Belle's life has changed in positive ways after her surgery and revelation, even as Jackson discovers that she died only a few years later. Reading her obituary, he surmises that she ended up living with her friend Robin, identified earlier in the story as someone who once challenged Belle's desire not to 'uproot her mother' by moving back to the city. We are told that Robin responded to Belle's statement of this desire by saying 'it was [Belle] herself she was talking about, scared of uproot. She – Robin – went away and joined whatever they called the women's army' (185). Robin's candour, androgynous name, and challenging of conservative desires confer a certain queerness upon her, one further suggested when she is named in Belle's obituary as her 'lifelong friend' (203). There is no other evidence that Belle and Robin entered a romantic relationship with each other, but the possibility hinted at by the obituary's inclusion of Robin's name suggests a new trajectory for Belle that she has earlier resisted.

As for Jackson, his inability to deal with the prospect of facing Ileane after the war and upon her reappearance decades later, along with his reaction to Belle's revelation about her father, marks him out as another 'grown-up child'. In the terms established by Erik Erikson's influential lifespan approach to psychosocial development, Jackson has not successfully negotiated the stage that involves a 'crisis of *intimacy*', a stage that Erikson associates with the early years of adulthood. Erikson claims that an inability to establish intimacy with others leads to '*distantiation*: the readiness to repudiate, isolate, and, if necessary, destroy those forces and people whose essence seems dangerous to one's own'. Erikson further observes that if a life is dominated by 'an impersonal kind of interpersonal pattern, a man can go far, very far, in life and yet harbor a severe character problem'.[43] For Jackson's part, in adulthood his instinctive reaction to a crisis is repeatedly to run away, in the same way that, as a child, he responded to his stepmother's 'fooling' by trying to run away from home. In other words, he appears condemned to a life of recursion. Before he abandons Belle, he thinks about her house 'and all the improvements' he has made to it, and later he makes what 'might be called improvements' to the building of which he becomes superintendent (193, 204). The juxtaposition of these material 'improvements' with the absence of psychosocial development in Jackson is striking. In that regard, the symbolism of the Mennonite boys whom, near the start of the story, Jackson mistakes for 'little men' in their buggy and whom, years later, he remembers in a dream is clear (180, 215). While the Mennonites have eschewed certain technological developments, Jackson is an anti-developmental figure in a different but similar sense. At the same time, the Mennonites' driving of the buggy stands in contrast with Jackson's train journeys to suggest the Mennonites have a control over their travels that Jackson literally lacks as a railway passenger and that he figuratively lacks more broadly.

Insofar as developmental narratives usually have behind them a model of causation – a sense of how and why things happen – it is notable that 'Train' remains agnostic in this regard. There is never any confirmation as to why Belle's father came to be hit by the train, and the effects of his death on Belle are never entirely clear. Given that she reveals her memory of the bathroom encounter only after surgery and sedation put her in what she calls an 'abnormal state', we do not even know for certain that her memory is accurate or complete (198). Jackson's motivations for abandoning Ileane and Belle are never wholly clear, either. However, the affective charge evident in his memory of his stepmother's 'fooling' suggests that the memory plays a fundamental role in his psyche. With reference to that memory, he asserts his belief that 'Things could be locked up, it only took some determination' (215). Given the assertion, one might also wonder what else he has locked up that he is not revealing. For instance, even though he never directly thinks about his war experiences, he characterizes his younger self as a 'nerve-racked soldier', and we discover that the young man who enlisted along with him died during the conflict (189, 210). Meanwhile, although Jackson calls himself 'a certain kind of man', readers are still left to wonder whether he might be homosexual or asexual. Accordingly, if the story's title encourages readers to think of Jackson's life as a train of episodes, the story itself leaves hidden the nature of the links between the episodes. Likewise, it resists providing a clear diagram of the engines driving Jackson. Models of development offered by psychoanalysis and trauma theory might provide a framework through which someone like Jackson can be understood, but Munro insists that there remains a stubborn indeterminacy with respect to the psychic mechanisms of such a person's life.

'A long chain of vital experience'

With that characterization of Jackson in mind, what if we were to read 'Train' as metafictionally commenting on Munro's own poetics? Jackson would seem to be an anti-Munrovian figure, insofar as he refuses to revisit events, in contrast with Munro's insistence on writing and reading as forms of return and review. Indeed, by revealing the stepmother's 'fooling' only late in the story and thereby providing a possible key to understanding Jackson's seemingly bizarre abandonments of Ileane and Belle, Munro prompts readers to revisit and even re-read 'Train' itself, thus turning them into the sort of retrospective agents that Munro foregrounds in her stories featuring first-person, memoirist narrators.

But if Jackson is an anti-Munrovian figure in certain respects, he also has affinities with Munro. In that regard, one might consider her 1985 introduction to the paperback edition of *The Moons of Jupiter*, in which she discusses her reluctance to look back at what she has published. She identifies in herself 'a queasiness, an unwillingness to look or examine' that she calls 'primitive and childish'. Of her stories, she says, 'I make them with such energy and devotion and secret pains, and then I wiggle out and leave them, to harden and settle in their place. I feel free. Next thing I know I've started assembling the makings; I'm getting ready to do the whole thing over again.'[44] With that self-characterization in mind, one might reconsider Jackson's repeated, compulsive embarkations on new endeavours. He is, in that respect, not so dissimilar to Munro and, indeed, to writers as a class, many of whom have admitted to being driven by a partly unconscious relationship to primal material that they end up recapitulating in their fiction.

That said, if there is one activity that repeatedly stands in Munro's stories as one fostering ameliorative self-development, it is a process of retrospection that, often enough, her stories associate with writing. Katherine J. Mayberry observes that Munro's work construes 'memory and narrative' as 'virtually equivalent faculties in that they both order past experience'.[45] As Munro's writer-narrators remember and review, they frequently gain a new perspective on their lives. At the same time, though, they often demonstrate the difficulty of achieving the deeper understanding and more mature perspective that they seek. By the end of 'Material' in *Something I've Been Meaning to Tell You*, the narrator is still struggling to forgive her ex-husband for his bad behaviour of several years before, while 'Gravel' in *Dear Life* concludes with the narrator still trying to make sense of her sister's mysterious drowning, though years have passed and answers seem as elusive as ever. Such narrators' attempts at recounting their lives can seem more symptomatic than therapeutic, shot through as they are with lingering resentments and score-settling. Yet their attempts at writing at least express a desire to see things differently, and this desire might itself might be considered a hopeful development.

In a 2001 speech given during an O. Henry Awards tribute night for her, Munro referred to the evening as 'a link in a long chain of vital experience'.[46] The metaphor of the chain resonates with that of the train in configuring life's moments as joined but not necessarily connected in a teleological manner, not necessarily producing change, much less moving towards a happy ending. Instead, her stories scrutinize everyday narratives that privilege and celebrate change. Challenging readers' investments in such narratives, Munro suggests that life is equally liable to feature stasis, continuation, repetition. Moreover, the pointed recursions of Munro's fiction encourage readers, as she puts it in the introduction to her *Selected Stories* (1996), repeatedly to see 'more than you saw the last time'.[47] With each return to Munro's fiction and to the characters inhabiting it – often startling in their resemblance to each other's lives and, sometimes, to our own – we gain another opportunity to explore those lives' shapes and complications. As we do so, the short story does become an apprentice form, after all, but it is we who are the novitiates, training for a trade that holds no greater reward than a transformation in how we understand the world and our journeys through it. The long train of Munro's career, with its fictions' refusal of complacency, their denial of neat endings, their endless resifting through their materials, and their self-reflexive insistence that there is always more to be discovered, suggests that the apprenticeship never ends.

Notes

1 Geoff Hancock, 'An Interview with Alice Munro', *Canadian Fiction Magazine* 43 (1982), 89.
2 In considering Munro and trains, I owe a debt to Aritha van Herk's talk on the subject at the 2014 Alice Munro Symposium at the University of Ottawa.
3 Alice Munro, *Open Secrets* (1994; London: Vintage, 1995) 41.
4 Alice Munro, *The Love of a Good Woman* (1998; London: Vintage, 2000) 161.
5 Alice Munro, 'What Is Real?', in *Making it New: Contemporary Canadian Stories*, ed. John Metcalf (Toronto: Methuen, 1982), 224.
6 Quoted in Alice Quinn, 'Go Ask Alice', *The New Yorker* (12 February 2001), available at www.newyorker.com.
7 Beverly J. Rasporich, *Dance of the Sexes: Art and Gender in the Fiction of Alice Munro* (Edmonton: University of Alberta Press, 1990), 77.
8 Alice Munro, *Dear Life* (2012; Toronto: Penguin, 2013) 255.
9 J. R. (Tim) Struthers, 'The Real Material: an Interview with Alice Munro', in Louis K. MacKendrick (ed.), *Probable Fictions: Alice Munro's Narrative Acts* (Toronto: ECW Press, 1983) 21.
10 Christian Lorentzen, 'Poor Rose', *London Review of Books* 35, 11 (6 June 2013), 11.
11 Coral Ann Howells, *Alice Munro* (Manchester University Press, 1998) 146.
12 Rasporich, *Dance of the Sexes*, 76.
13 Ajay Heble, *The Tumble of Reason: Alice Munro's Discourse of Absence* (University of Toronto Press, 1994) 75.
14 Lorentzen, 'Poor Rose', 12.
15 In Lisa Dickler Awano et al., 'Appreciations of Alice Munro', *Virginia Quarterly Review* 82, 3 (2006), 99.
16 Dennis Duffy, '"A Dark Sort of Mirror": "The Love of a Good Woman" as Pauline Poetic', in Robert Thacker (ed.), *The Rest of the Story: Critical Essays on Alice Munro* (Toronto: ECW Press, 1999), 172.
17 Quinn, 'Go Ask Alice'.
18 Edward W. Said, *On Late Style: Music and Literature against the Grain* (New York: Pantheon, 2006).
19 Coral Ann Howells, 'Double Vision', *Canadian Literature* 178 (2003), 160.
20 Robert Kastenbaum, 'The Creative Process: a Life-Span Approach', in Thomas R. Cole, David D. Van Tassel, and Robert Kastenbaum (eds.), *Handbook of the Humanities and Aging* (New York: Springer, 1992), 302.
21 James Grainger, 'Life and How to Live It', *Quill and Quire* 78, 9 (November 2012), 25.

22 Joyce Carol Oates, 'Who Do You Think You Are?', *New York Review of Books* 56, 19 (3 December 2009), 42.
23 Ailsa Cox, '"Age Could Be Her Ally": Late Style in Alice Munro's *Too Much Happiness*', in Charles E. May (ed.), *Critical Insights: Alice Munro* (Ipswich, MA: Salem Press, 2013), 276, 290.
24 David Galenson, *Artistic Capital* (New York: Routledge, 2006), 8–9.
25 John C. Van Rys, 'Fictional Violations in Alice Munro's Narratives', in Holly Faith Nelson, Lynn R. Szabo, and Jens Zimmermann (eds.), *Through a Glass Darkly: Suffering, the Sacred, and the Sublime in Literature and Theory* (Waterloo, Ont.: Wilfrid Laurier University Press, 2010), 272.
26 Alice Munro, *Dance of the Happy Shades* (1968; London: Vintage, 2000) 18.
27 Struthers, 'The Real Material', 24, 27, 12, 13.
28 Ibid., 9–10.
29 Peter Gzowski, 'You're the Same Person at 19 that You Are at 60', *The Globe and Mail* (29 September 2001), F5.
30 Jonathan Franzen, '"Runaway": Alice's Wonderland', *New York Times Book Review* (14 November 2004), 15.
31 Robert McGill, 'Somewhere I've Been Meaning to Tell You: Alice Munro's Fiction of Distance', *The Journal of Commonwealth Literature* 37, 1 (2002), 19–20.
32 Gzowski, 'You're the Same Person', F4.
33 Alice Munro, *The Moons of Jupiter* (1982; Toronto: Penguin, 1995), 109.
34 Alice Munro, *Who Do You Think You Are?* (1978; Toronto: Penguin, 1996), 125–6, 138.
35 Sara Jamieson, '"Surprising Developments": Midlife in Alice Munro's *Who Do You Think You Are?*', *Canadian Literature* 217 (2013), 55.
36 Munro, *Who Do You Think You Are?*, 256.
37 Alice Munro, *Something I've Been Meaning to Tell You* (1974; Scarborough, Ont.: Signet, 1975) 197.
38 Todd VanDerWerff, 'Where to Start with Alice Munro, the Newest Nobel Laureate for Fiction', *A.V. Club* (17 October 2013), available at www.avclub.com.
39 David Peck, 'Who Does Rose Think She Is? Acting and Being in *The Beggar Maid: Stories of Flo and Rose*', in May, *Critical Insights: Alice Munro*, 138.
40 Dante, *The Inferno of Dante*, trans. Robert Pinsky (New York: Farrar, Straus and Giroux, 1994), Canto XXVI, ll. 114–15.
41 Gabrielle-Suzanne Barbot de Villeneuve, 'The Story of the Beauty and the Beast', *Four and Twenty Fairy Tales: Selected from Those of Perreault and Other Popular Writers*, trans. J. R. Planché (London: Routledge, 1858).
42 Maria Tatar, 'Introduction: Beauty and the Beast', in Tatar (ed.), *The Classic Fairy Tales* (Cambridge, MA: Harvard University Press, 1999), 25.
43 Erik Erikson, *Identity: Youth and Crisis* (New York: Norton, 1968), 135, 136.
44 Munro, *The Moons of Jupiter*, xiii, xv–xvi.
45 Katherine J. Mayberry, '"Every Last Thing ... Everlasting": Alice Munro and the Limits of Narrative', *Studies in Short Fiction* 29 (1992), 540.
46 Alice Munro, 'Stories', www.randomhouse.com/knopf/authors/munro/desktop new.html.
47 Alice Munro, *Selected Stories* (1996; Toronto: Penguin, 1998), xvii.

9

HÉLIANE VENTURA

The female bard
Retrieving Greek myths, Celtic ballads, Norse sagas, and popular songs

Were it not for her own genealogy, an analogy between a contemporary Canadian female short story writer and the poets of ancient Celtic cultures, charged with the celebration of the heroic achievements of their people, would appear unlikely, but Alice Munro's bardic connection is hard to deny. It is inscribed in her bloodline: Munro is a collateral descendant of James Hogg, the Ettrick Shepherd, the Mountain Bard, who became famous with the publication of *The Private Memoirs and Confessions of a Justified Sinner* (1824), and of his mother, Margaret Laidlaw, who recited ballads which Walter Scott transcribed in his anthology of Scottish tales and poems: *Minstrelsy of the Scottish Borders* (1868).[1] In *The View from Castle Rock* (2006), she explicitly refers to both tutelary figures as well as to a number of other distinguished overseas ancestors, as if to inscribe her chronicle of family life in its transatlantic lineage. Like them, and like all ancient bards, Munro has a prodigious memory, which she endows on some of her characters, like Del Jordan in her recitation of facts learned from the encyclopedias her mother tried to sell. She has also more directly alluded to this prodigious capacity in the final four stories of her career (*Dear Life*, 2012), showing that it occasionally gave her trouble until she made up her mind to conceal her gift: 'I had learned to blank out even the prodigious memory I once had for reciting poetry, refusing to use it ever again for showing off.'[2]

As a true bard, Munro is geographically affiliated to the rural world, despite spending a large part of her adult life in the city before eventually returning to the small town environment into which she was born. Throughout her career, she has documented the lives of girls and women in rural southwestern Ontario in both the first and the second half of the twentieth century, via the Great Depression and the 1960s, to track their rise to emancipation. In occasional neo-Victorian pastiches, she has also depicted the way of life of the early settlers in Huron County and north Ontario. In writing about the progress of women from the nineteenth to the twenty-first century, she has infused historical memory into her contemporary narratives, turning 'story into history' while concomitantly reclaiming the literary inheritance of Romanticism and rural life.[3] She has transposed the *Anecdotes*, the *Tales*, and the *Sketches* of her ancestor, the Ettrick Shepherd, into short stories, and latched on to a world-wide movement of expression of imaginative truths based on the emotional directness of personal experience. This reclamation of a romantic ethos in the midst of the contemporary period is accompanied by the use of a distinctly self-reflexive mode, through which she interrogates the ways and processes of story-making and establishes relationships between the short story and the *lied*, the lay, the folktale, the poem in prose, and the popular song.

In this chapter, I shall explore Munro's reclamation of universal poetry, heroic, mythic, and popular, within the genre of the short story, and exhume and analyse her bardic affiliation through her covert or overt references to Homeric songs, Scottish minstrelsy, Nordic sagas, American folklore, and Canadian songs. I shall use the ambivalent term 'bardic' to describe Munro's prose, demonstrating that her testimony of things past, her format, her diction with its oral modes of address, incremental repetition, symmetries and parallelisms, her contestation of the doxa, and the complexity of her moral philosophy all have a patent connection with the heterodoxy and deceitfulness of the ancient bards' recitation. I shall argue that, from the personal to the metapoetic, Munro's art of storytelling rests upon a power of recall which revivifies historical and literary memory through a strategy of partially acknowledged and partially clandestine encoding of intertextual and intermusical references.

The resurgence of antiquity

Munro's first volume, published in 1968, borrows its title, *Dance of the Happy Shades*, from the opera by Christoph Willibald von Gluck, *Orfeo ed Euridice*. The different versions of this opera,[4] originally composed in 1762, reinterpret Orpheus' descent to the Underworld so as to provide the myth with a happy ending: against all odds, Orpheus manages to bring back Eurydice to the world of the living. In opposition to the established Orphic tradition dating from antiquity, the eighteenth-century composer allows the foredoomed couple to be reunited and to live happily together after the ordeal of the descent to the nether world. Through her allusion to this revised version of the myth in the title of her first volume, Munro simultaneously emphasizes and denies her allegiance to the myth of antiquity; instead of supporting unreservedly Orpheus' eventual separation from Eurydice, Munro sides with an operatic reinterpretation in the eighteenth century and, like the Italian librettist and the Bavarian composer, she allows the irreversible to become reversible. By paying allegiance to the opera rather than the myth, she reverses the most irreversible phenomenon of human life, death itself, with Eurydice's unexpected return from 'the other country'.

The reference which inaugurates Munro's work testifies to her ambivalent use of the canon, to her capacity to re-vision tradition, while simultaneously conforming, since Orpheus is probably one of the most conflicted mythical figures in the whole of the Greek Pantheon. At the same time crepuscular and luminous, he embodies the irreducible tensions of human experience. Munro concentrates on one major motif in the many variants of his myth: his role as a conqueror over the forces of night and destruction, who is reunited to his beloved through the power of his music. By alluding to Orpheus, the lyre player, from her inaugural volume of stories, Munro places her work in the oral tradition of poetry relying on the accompaniment of music. She reminds us of the presence of song and music at the origin of literature: she claims for her collection the bardic power of the lyre or cithara player, and she implicitly suggests a correspondence between the figure of the musician in antiquity and that of the contemporary writer who composes her tales with the formal technique of variations: repetition in an altered form.

Dance of the Happy Shades resonates with songs, not all of them explicitly derived from antiquity, but all testifying to Munro's reclamation of an oral tradition, implicitly or indirectly descended from the many variants in the myth of Orpheus and Eurydice. The young narrator in 'Boys and Girls' confesses to her fondness for singing and delights in her own performances, which occur at night, in her bed, before falling asleep: 'I loved the sound of my own voice, frail and supplicating, rising in the dark.'[5] The song she sings is called 'Danny Boy', a mournful song, generally associated with Irish communities, which is supposed to resonate from glen to glen and appears far removed from the Hellenistic world. However, like the myth of the lyre player who lost his beloved on his wedding day because she was bitten by a viper, it evokes the separation of lovers and their eventual reunion despite death:

> And all my grave will warmer, sweeter be,
> For you will bend and tell me that you love me,
> And I shall sleep in peace until you come to me![6]

The theme of the eventual reunion with the departed one is picked up in another story from the same collection. In 'The Time of Death', the young protagonist, Patricia Parry, performs in public two Gospel songs, 'May the Circle be Unbroken' and 'It is No Secret What God Can Do', shortly after her brother's accidental death. Both songs suggest the reunion of all the members of the family in the after-world and tacitly establish an intratextual

The female bard: myths, ballads, sagas, and songs

connection between apparently autonomous stories within the collection, as well as intertextual connections between various myths and songs belonging to far-removed spatio-temporal contexts. Through these recurring allusions to the reunion with the beloved, Munro covertly brings together Hellenistic myth, Irish ballad, and Gospel songs, and creates resonances between past and present, Greek mythology and Christian religion, traditional forms of lyrics and contemporary short stories.

In 'Walker Brothers Cowboy', the first story in the collection, her use of songs is even more extensive and ambivalently multi-layered. The narrator's father, Ben Jordan, is a silver-fox farmer turned travelling salesman on account of the Great Depression, who invents songs about his new job and entertains his children with his musical performances. Much more transgressively, he also sings one of his songs in front of Nora, the woman he loved but was prevented from marrying because of religious prejudices.

Clandestine references play a notable role in Munro's fiction and onomastics are particularly revelatory. The name chosen for the travelling salesman based on Munro's father is directly descended from a group of singers from the 1960s, the Walker Brothers, whose itinerary goes against the grain. Instead of crossing the Atlantic from the Old World to the North American continent, the Walker Brothers left New York in the 1960s to establish their fame in 'swinging London' as popular singers. The inverted journey or counter-epic which is allusively inscribed in the name given to the father is duplicated by the name given to his old flame. She is called Nora like Henrik Ibsen's female protagonist in *A Doll's House*: the Norwegian Nora makes up her mind to change her existence and, at the end of the play, walks out on her husband and children to find independence.[7] In Munro's story, Nora is jilted by Ben Jordan, who is intimidated by his family's diktats and marries an apparently more suitable woman. As a consequence of her abandonment by Ben, Nora leads a life of quiet desperation, caring for her blind mother and denying herself the right to lead a life of self-fulfilment. In Munro's story, Nora is the epitome of self-denial and sacrifice, whereas in Ibsen's play, she has come to epitomize an early version of the emancipation of women.

Through her covert references to the Walker Brothers and to Ibsen, Munro inscribes in the core of her story a shadow itinerary which seems to be exactly the opposite of Ben and Nora's. Instead of turning their back on their own unsatisfactory situation and seeking success in another direction, they appear to perform separate dancing and singing tricks and remain where they belong, the former with her blind mother, the latter with his migraine-suffering wife. The Walker Brothers and the Norwegian Nora come to constitute the shadow characters, the Happy Shades, which Munro enlists in her dance of references, to enhance, half secretly and half openly, the roads not taken, in the path of life. These allusions to popular culture of the 1960s and to nineteenth-century drama allow Munro to deflect attention from antiquity while simultaneously creating secret resonances with the myth of Orpheus and Eurydice. Instead of picking up the theme of the reunion of lovers as she does throughout 'Dance of the Happy Shades', 'The Time of Death', and 'Boys and Girls,' in the wake of Gluck and Calzabigi, she, on the contrary, returns to the theme of separation encapsulated in the original versions of the myth. When Ben Jordan descends upon Nora Cronin's farm with his children using his Walker Brothers tour as an alibi, he misses his chance to be reunited with her for a second time, in the same way that Orpheus found his way to the Elysian Fields but failed to bring back Eurydice from the underworld. During this belated visit to his old flame, Ben Jordan can be regarded as irreversibly separating from Nora, in the same way that Orpheus was denied reunion with Eurydice. Despite their talent for music and singing, both Orpheus and Ben Jordan eventually fail in their attempt at repairing a foredoomed situation.

The secret key to the understanding of a Munro story lies in a collaborative partnership, of the kind sought by bards of the past. Bards included references they did not need to elaborate because they were in common usage among their listeners, Munro resorts to half-clandestine allusions which require a vigilant attention from her readers because they expand the local situation into unexpected areas and create unsuspected correspondences. The references in her stories measure her characters against canonical or celebrated figures through implicit comparison. The travelling salesman who bears the name of the singers popular at the time when Munro wrote her story is also constructed as a singer descended from the ancient bards. He invents songs to describe his activity as a pedlar: 'he has a song about it, with these two lines: And have all linaments [sic] and oils / For everything from corns to boils ...'[8] These two lines are subsequently expanded in a prose sentence of epic dimension, relayed by the young narrator, a persona for Munro: 'He sells cough medicine, iron tonic, corn plasters, laxatives, pills for female disorders, mouth wash, shampoo, liniment, salves, lemon and orange and raspberry concentrate for making refreshing drinks, other spices, rat poison.' This long list of the pedlar's paraphernalia is very similar to a catalogue and can be envisaged as belonging to the genre of catalogue verse, common in epic poetry to record the heroes involved in battle or the genealogical information connected to the main figures. By allowing the young narrator to list such base items as laxatives or pills for female disorders, Munro actually turns the table. She transforms the description of the narrator's father's cornucopia of every kind of medicine into a mock-epic list, which employs a lofty style to record an undignified series of products connected to the generally unmentionable functions of the human body. The incongruity of the grand style used for a low subject testifies to Munro's attraction to the burlesque, but it nevertheless highlights her propensity for recycling the main features of bardic oratory art: the reciting of epic catalogues.

Munro's recurrent use of lists has been adumbrated by Marjorie Garson with specific reference to her second volume, *Lives of Girls and Women*, in which the narrator's mother, Addie Jordan, uses her daughter to rhyme off lists of facts. Of Del's performance, Garson says that it is 'like those of the ancient bards who recited epic catalogues, and it is one that Del initially enjoys in what she suggests is a childish way, finding it "an irresistible test ... like trying to hop a block on one foot" (66)'.[9] Garson convincingly demonstrates that Munro's use of 'the versatile figure of the epic catalogue' is mobilized 'in a highly self-conscious and by no means naively realistic way', and is associated 'less with documentary realism than with mythopoeic energy and performative aplomb'.[10]

The recurrent use of lists from volume to volume testifies to Munro's revivifying of classical topoi and endows her descriptions with the epic dimension of a ceremonial roster. She performs an inventory of the world which has epic undertones, remarkably exemplified in the closing lines to *The View from Castle Rock*, in which she makes a very discreet and oblique allusion to the Homeric songs by inserting a reference to the days of Troy:

> Now all these names I have been recording are joined to the living people in my mind, and to the lost kitchens, the polished nickel trim on the commodious presiding black stoves, the sour wooden drainboards that never quite dried, the yellow light of the coal-oil lamps. The cream cans on the porch, the apples in the cellar, the stovepipes going up through the holes in the ceiling, the stable warmed in winter by the bodies and breath of the cows – those cows whom we still spoke to in words common in the days of Troy. So bos. So bos. The cold wax parlor where the coffin was put when people died.[11]

In this paragraph Munro draws attention to her role as bard recalling genealogy and family history and she conspicuously inserts a melodic progression in her enumerative mode of writing which is strikingly reminiscent of oral recitation. For example, the series of nominal sentences which are progressively longer and based on periodic expansion include a perfectly symmetrical alliterative pattern which allows pairs of words to resonate against each other and prolong each other's effect: 'drainboards ... dried', 'light ... lamps', 'cream cans', 'warmed in winter', 'bodies and breath'. The duplication of the initial consonant in each sequence creates an echo: stylistics reinforce semantics, as the alliterative device underpins the reference to antiquity by mimicking the effect of an echo. The reader is made to hear the shepherds' call, echoing through the ages, from the days of Troy to contemporary southwestern Ontario.

This allusion to the days of Troy is striking on many accounts; it is a thinly veiled allusion to Homer's *Iliad* and *Odyssey*, but instead of being recondite or *recherché*, it is based on the words allegedly used by cowherds to call cows: 'So bos. So bos.' Such words which do not convey a particular meaning in a given language constitute the most rudimentary form of expression but also the most universal. These words are not noises, they are not strictly speaking onomatopoeias, and they are not pet names either. Their status is uncertain and indeterminate, all the more so as 'the line between onomatopoeic lexemes and noises is difficult to draw'.[12] The cowherd's call to the cow is a lexicalization of two syllables which are repeated, 'So bos. So bos', and read like an intriguing reclamation of the past. Stylistically they look like a palindrome, which reads the same forward and backward, but more accurately they are a boustrophedon, that is to say 'lines written alternately from right to left and from left to right, as in ancient Greek inscription'.[13] Boustrophedon in ancient Greek means 'ox turning' when ploughing up and down a field and, by formally using the figure of style called boustrophedon to transcribe the call to the cows, Munro gives a striking example of the literal use of a literary term. This instance becomes a clue for the reader to understand the type of odyssey or writing back that Munro has embarked on. Through the repetition of the call 'So bos. So bos', used by the cowboy from southwestern Ontario, Munro establishes resonances with her own Scottish ancestor, James Hogg, the Mountain Bard from the forest of Ettrick, and beyond him with other Hellenistic bards, primarily Homer, the blind bard who allegedly recorded the siege of Troy, but possibly the other bards in the *Iliad* and *Odyssey*, Phemios in Book 1, in Odysseus' own palace on Ithaca, and Demodokos in Book 8, at the court of King Alkinoos. Both Demodokos and Phemios are personae of Homer himself but other bards are also present in this epic song from the days of Troy. Through this reference to the universal language of cowherds existing since the days of Troy, Munro allusively includes not only all the bards in the *Iliad* and the *Odyssey*, but also all the other bards in antiquity, like Theocritus, who wrote bucolic songs when exiled from Arcadia, and Virgil, who transplanted the gods of Mount Olympus to the side of the Mincio. With this single allusion, she translocates the function of the cowherd to contemporary Ontario, through the forest of Ettrick, making the address to the cows resonate back and forth.

Supplementary resonances can be discovered in the cowherd's call she has chosen: 'So bos. So bos.' This call is a locus of singularity in which language allows truths that belong to the unconscious to be partially uttered. In this striking instance of homophony, there is an agency that thinks beyond the grasp of conscious thinking and enables the reader to hear other words than those which are uttered. In this call, we cannot but recognize the simultaneous attempt at glorifying and deriding the cow, which is attributed the status of 'boss' but simultaneously bossed about to return to the stables. The relationship between puns and the unconscious has been demonstrated by Freud, who has pointed out the secret scenarios which sometimes lurk beneath homophones. In the particular case of the cowherd's call to the cow, one cannot but remember that the volume entitled *The View from Castle Rock* was destined to pay homage to her ancestor, James Hogg, who himself was the butt of many jokes derived from the unfortunate homophony between his family name and the name of a wild pig. Through the cowherd's onomatopoeic call, which evidences a fall from rational language, Munro indulges in an ambiguous and cryptic act. She celebrates the pastoral and the life of cowherds, glorifying at the same time the personal, the historical, and the literary, Homer and Hogg, Hogg and herself, and establishing the heroic lineage of bards from time immemorial. More allusively, she also fuses the addressor and the addressee, the human and the animal in an apparent elevation, which is ironically diffident and deprecatory.

The cowherd's connection with the cows is imbued with particular disquieting expressiveness because it evidences a return to an infantile or archaic and pre-symbolic form of address, through a puzzling and impenetrable arrangement of sounds. By resorting to onomatopoeia as universal language used by shepherds from time immemorial, Munro postulates a connection between antiquity and contemporaneity, between the Mediterranean and the North American, and between the shepherds of the past and those of the present. But beyond the connection and continuity between the activities of country people from time immemorial, she also erases the frontiers between animals and humanity. Through the use of this strange call, she suggests a closeness between the living species, she reminds us of the lost intimacy between animals and human beings, of the solidarity of their common destiny: she recalls a more archaic temporality, a time characterized by a more primordial relationship between species. Using articulate language to highlight the fact and the process of transmission of narratives, she also lays stress on the residue of language or its origins in inarticulate ejaculation: she reconnects the reader with the origins of language at the same time as the origins of storytelling.

Scottish minstrelsy

Among the original forms of storytelling, the ballad occupies pride of place, and Munro has incorporated more or less clandestinely a number of Scottish ballads in her stories, appropriating the themes and transforming them by occasionally reversing their consequences. For instance, in 'Friend of my Youth' from the eponymous collection (1986), she organizes the plot around two sisters, Flora and Ellie Grieves.[14] Flora is courted by the hired man, Robert Deal, and yet he marries Ellie, the younger sister. This is a plot, inspired by the traditional Scottish ballad 'The Twa Sisters of Binnorie', which is sometimes anthologized as 'The Cruel Sister'. In this ballad the knight courts the elder but loves the younger sister:

> He courted the elder with glove and ring,
> But he loved the younger beyond all thing;
> He courted the elder with brooch and knife,
> But he loved the younger as his life.[15]

The ballad describes the elder sister's jealousy and her felony. She entices the younger sister to the river strand and pushes her into the water where she drowns. Munro starts with the same original situation but transforms the knight into a hired man and reverses the elder sister's reaction to her suitor's defection. Once Robert has married Ellie, Flora dedicates her life to the sister who has deprived her of her suitor. Instead of drowning her, she provides her with nursing and caring, for the younger sister soon develops a terminal illness. Munro's recasting of the traditional ballad is at the same time conservative and contestatory: she preserves the memory of the ancient song, but she challenges the cliché of the vengeful woman by changing vindictiveness into fortitude.

After the younger sister's death, when the hired man deserts Flora a second time to marry the professional nurse, the elder sister displays anew a fortitude and a self-righteousness which are profoundly intriguing and challenging. Although this second desertion is not part of the original ballad, it constitutes a form of 'cumulative' argument, inspired by the construction of traditional songs based upon repetitive reinforcement. Munro's appropriation and transformation of Scottish Borders ballads represents a type of writing back which elaborates on traditional plots through creative and fabulous invention. It highlights her commitment to a moral philosophy which rises above conformity to the moral values of the community or those exemplified in traditional narratives. Through her intriguing manipulation of plots, she commits herself to more complex and more covert ethical principles, of which surprise, wonder, and subversion are significant components.

In 'Hold Me Fast, Don't Let Me Pass' from the same volume, she explicitly rewrites the 'Ballad of Tam Lin', some excerpts of which are even recited by an old lady who bears a striking resemblance to Margaret Laidlaw, Munro's own Scottish ancestor from the valley of Ettrick. The ballad revolves around Tam Lin's rescue from the Queen of Fairies by his beloved Jenet, while the short story denies the character such victory and happy end. The contemporary solicitor, Dudley Brown, is entangled in two complex love relationships from which there is apparently no rescuing. He loves Antoinette, the owner of the Royal Hotel, but cannot marry her because she is still married to a man she cannot divorce, having lost track of his whereabouts. He also loves his mother's hired girl, Judy, an illegitimate child, with whom he has had a daughter, but he is equally prevented from marrying her through social prejudice.

Munro's recasting of the ballad in a narrow-minded, socially prejudiced Scottish border town acquires an uncommon expansion because of the historical framework provided. The story of modern day Tam Lin is narrated by a Canadian widow whose former husband, a pilot, was stationed in Great Britain during the Second World War and had a love relationship with the same Antoinette from the Royal Hotel. On the legendary chronotope of the ballad, which allegedly took place near Selkirk in the Scottish Borders, Munro superimposes two historical references, that of the battle of Philiphaugh which took place in 1645, and that of the Second World War in 1945. Thus, she synchronizes the battle with the fairies with the local battle of Philiphaugh, and with the air raids of the Second World War. To her fictional drama, she aggregates legendary love stories and historical conflagrations. She collapses the frontiers between private affairs, legends, and world diplomacy by dramatizing and aggrandizing to heroic proportions the minuscule lives of girls and women from the contemporary world.

In her volume explicitly dedicated to Scotland, *The View from Castle Rock*, Munro has ironically commented upon this tendency towards aggrandizement by envisaging it as a life-instinct she shares with some members of her family:

> Self-dramatization got short shrift in our family. Though now that I come to think of it, it wasn't exactly that word they used. They spoke of calling attention. Calling attention to oneself. The opposite of which was not exactly modesty but a strenuous dignity and control, a sort of refusal. The refusal to feel any need to turn your life into a story, either for other people or for yourself. And when I study the people I know about in the family, it does seem that some of us have that need in large and irresistible measure – enough so as to make the others cringe with embarrassment and apprehension.[16]

There is in this paragraph a contradictory presence of markers of connection based on association and identification, and markers of disconnection, suggesting dissociation and rejection, but there is also a syntax of repetition and amplification. There might be no future in repetition, but there is arguably one in amplification and one can suggest that, leaning on her patrilineal descent, absorbing and recycling James Hogg's manner and memoirs, Munro paradoxically uses the short story as the means and the medium for her bardic amplification and expansion, redefining in the process the genre of the short story and its meaningfulness in contemporary literature.

In the paragraph just quoted, stylistic amplification is first achieved through the repetition of the last words of one sentence at the beginning of the next: 'They spoke of calling attention. Calling attention to oneself', 'a sort of refusal. The refusal', a process which is called anadiplosis: 'a device of repetition to gain a special effect'.[17] Amplification is also achieved performatively and self-reflexively; by repeating the words 'calling attention to oneself', she calls attention to herself and knowingly enforces the process of self-dramatization. She knowingly transgresses the family rule of dignity and control: through infringement, through violation of the law, she brings her stories into the world. Like Defoe, who makes Crusoe disobey his father's injunction, and like Rousseau, Munro initiates the process of written confession and private memoirs with Original Sin. And true to her stylistic strategy, she amplifies the process by drawing other members of her family into the ranks of sinners: 'And when I study the people I know about in the family, it does seem that some of us have that need in large and irresistible measure.' The guilt-bearing subject belongs to a community of justified sinners, a community which refuses self-denial, which refuses 'the refusal to feel any need to turn your life into a story'.

This last sentence, just as the one which repeats 'Calling attention to oneself', exemplifies a paradoxical use of the nominal sentence which highlights both repression and expression. Munro paradoxically constructs nominal sentences with verbs; 'calling attention' is the gerundive form of the verb 'to call' and 'The refusal to feel any need to turn your life into a story' is a verbal expansion of the nominal syntagm: 'the refusal'. Emile Benvéniste has famously described the nominal sentence as being beyond all temporal or modal localization and beyond the subjectivity of the speaker, while Ernst Cassirer associates it with the languages of early and 'primitive' peoples who employ the nominal sentence, 'lacking … a copula in our logical-grammatical sense' and perceptually having 'no need of one'.[18] The former establishes an absolute, whereas the latter suggests an existential, sensuous reality linked with the use of nominalization. Both philosophers' response to the significance of the nominal sentence is useful for our understanding of Munro's recurrent use of it.

In the paragraph under study Munro is using the nominal sentence to designate the moral and psychological framework through which she operates. She posits the foundational impulses which feed her paradoxical, ambiguous, and ironic engagement with writing. She posits the dualism between self-indulgence and self-denial, between exhibitionism which is implicit in calling attention to oneself and an inhibition derived from Presbyterianism which subtends the refusal to feel any need to turn life into a story. Through this dichotomy, which can productively be envisaged as 'life narcissism' on the one hand and 'death narcissism' on the other, to pick up André Green's categories, Munro is at once trying to render sensuously present and absolute the contradictory moral and psychological framework within which she operates.[19] Through the use of nominal sentences, she ambiguously legitimizes self-aggrandizement and de-legitimizes self-denial.

To vindicate her ways to the reader, and justify the life narcissism she has chosen, she leans on the authority of genealogical precedents. This is how James Hogg begins *The Memoirs of the Author's Life*:

> I like to write about myself: in fact there are few things I like better; it is so delightful to call up old reminiscences. Often have I been laughed at for what an Edinburgh editor styles my good-natured egotism, which is sometimes anything but that; and I am aware that I shall be laughed at again. But I care not: for this important memoir, now to be brought forward for the fourth time, at different periods of my life, I shall narrate with the same frankness as formerly; and in all, relating either to others or to myself speak fearlessly and unreservedly out.[20]

Throughout her oeuvre, Munro takes up Hogg's foundational and programmatic pronouncement, repeatedly speaking about herself and her family and ceaselessly submitting her life to examination, repetition, and amplification. Munro annexes the function of bard and legitimizes her annexation by publicly revealing her literal kinship to the Bard of Ettrick. She takes it upon herself to prolong the bardic tradition she has inherited from Hogg and his mother, Margaret Laidlaw. She performs a re-appropriation of inheritance to transform her status as a writer from the border with the United States into a writer descended from the Scottish Borders.

This repositioning is based on an act of reclamation of James Hogg and Walter Scott's legacy, but also of European Romantic poetry. In 'What Do You Want to Know For?' (2006), she resorts to German culture and German language, providing quotations in the original German without entirely translating them and without entirely elucidating their origins. One of them allegedly comes from the epitaph which the narrator and her husband eventually find on a crypt in Grey County, Ontario:

> Das arme Herz hienieden
> Von manches Sturm bewegt
> Erlangt den renen Frieden
> Nur wenn es nicht mehr schlagt.[21]

This so-called epitaph contains a mistake noted by the narrator. The German adjective *reinen* meaning pure is spelt *renen*; it is therefore rendered impure through a blemish, encrypting self-reflexively the process of contamination that the narrator, possibly afflicted with a lethal tumour, is believed to have undergone. The epitaph also conceals its real nature to the reader. What Munro deceitfully presents as a self-contained German epitaph she found in a Lutheran cemetery in a half-deserted part of Canada happens to be an excerpt from a poem of 1788 written by Johann Gaudenz von Salis-Seewis (1762–1834) and set to music by Schubert in a *lied* entitled 'The Grave' he wrote in 1816. Munro resorts to a clandestine strategy of inclusion and refrains from providing her sources. She curtails the poem by inserting only the last stanza and passes it off as an epitaph.

Several questions are raised by this clandestine and incomplete introduction of a *lied* written in German in the last story of a collection explicitly dedicated to Munro's transatlantic affiliation and explicitly identified as rendering homage to her Scottish ancestors. One possible answer may be linked to the nature of a *lied*: a German folksong, particularly 'a German art song of the nineteenth century (as by Schubert, Hugo Wolf) in which a lyric text is set to a well-considered usu. through composed melody and accompaniment, with all three elements contributing nearly equally to the total effect' (Webster's Dictionary). As a Romantic genre set to folk music, the *lied* claims a kinship to the ballad, a poem in fixed form Hogg and Margaret Laidlaw excelled at, Hogg writing poetry and his mother reciting ballads to Sir Walter Scott. Walter Scott himself translated songs from the German and included them in his collection of ancient and modern Scottish ballads.

That Munro should have chosen to incorporate or to encrypt a *lied* in her story is further evidence of her strategy of appropriation of a bardic role. Her strategy is reticulated and rhizomatic. She does not follow a single thread or expand a single centre. The homage she pays to her ancestors, the peasant poet, the Ettrick shepherd, and his mother, the ballad singer, consists in extending indirectly their spatial and temporal zone of influence by suggesting possible convergences with other historical, geographical, or literary contexts, convergences which were already part of the European-wide Romantic movement. Epitaphs were a characteristic Romantic preoccupation, forming the subject of Wordsworth's essay of 1810, and being used in a number of novels in the nineteenth century, notably *The Master of*

Ballantrae (1889) by Robert Louis Stevenson, which concludes with the narrator chiselling an epitaph on the monument of two Scottish brothers who spent their lives hating and pursuing each other.

The use of a recovered epitaph in the closing story of Munro's volume is also a striking reminder of Sir Walter Scott's own use of the renewing of inscriptions on gravestones performed by Old Mortality in the opening pages of the eponymous novel. There, Pattieson encounters Old Mortality seated on the monument of the covenanters: 'An old man was seated upon the monument of the slaughtered Presbyterians, and busily employed in deepening, with his chisel, the letters of the inscription, which, announcing, in scriptural language, the promised blessings of futurity to be the lot of the slain, anathematized the murderers with corresponding violence.'[22]

Munro's inserting one stanza from a German *lied* into her own story is a similar act of curation and preservation of the past. It is also an act of generic affiliation to Romantic aesthetics, an explicit endorsement of a literary inheritance which claims its kinship with minstrels and bards. By performing the introduction of a German Romantic *lied* chiselled on a grave within a contemporary Canadian short story, Munro positions herself in world literature as reclaiming the oral origin of literature, and implicates a network of related texts and authors, from the twelfth- and thirteenth-century philosopher Michael Scott mentioned in Dante's *Divine Comedy* and also born in the Ettrick Valley, to the most famous or most obscure of her own ancestors and ballad singers from the Scottish Borders. She highlights the transmission of literature as a process of genealogic descent and generic affiliation. She lays the stress on the generative and regenerative dimension of storytelling. Through the choice of a *lied*, she dramatizes the oral origins of literature and through the choice of its inscription on a grave, she suggests the continuance of the song beyond the limits of the individual living experience. It might even be argued that by embedding a poem entitled 'The Grave' in a text which describes a grave, she performs a *mise en abyme*, or specular insertion, which is curative and regenerative because it consists in transmitting the word beyond death.

Norse saga and skaldic poetry

Munro's reclamation of Romanticism is not only based on inclusion in her short stories of epitaphs in German, but also upon the introduction of references to Nordic mythology in the original Norse language. In the story entitled 'White Dump', which is the last story in *The Progress of Love* (1986), she includes a citation of two lines in Old Norse and she appends a translation but refrains from elucidating precisely their origin since the title of the poem is not given. Denise, the narrator, picks up the book left open by the main character, Sophie, an assistant professor of Scandinavian languages, and reads the end of a poem, which serves as a conclusion to the story:

> Seinat er at segia;
> svà er nu ràdit.
> (it is too late to talk of this now: it has been decided).[23]

Munro refrains from indicating that these lines belong to the 'Lay of Atli', a lay which is part of the heroic poems of the *Codex Regius* dating back to the thirteenth century.[24] The lay describes the disastrous fate of Gudrun: she marries Atli (Attila), has two sons by him, whom she roasts and feeds to her husband in revenge for his murder of her brothers, and she later attempts to commit suicide. With this allusion to the 'Lay of Atli', Munro establishes intertextual links with Scandinavian oral poetry as well as the pagan antiquity of Germanic Europe, as she recasts her contemporary Canadian story against the life stories of Brynhildr, Gudrun, and Sigurdt in the 'Lay of Atli', and against those of Brunhilde, Gudrun, and Siegfried in the corresponding *Nibelungen* tales. Her strategy remains discreet and clandestine. Far from explicitly tracing the genealogy of her contemporary characters, she requires the reader to identify the allusions, maintaining thus an aesthetic transaction with the reader, of the type that the bard or the skald indulged in, in their oral recitations.

The reading of a story by Munro is not only transactional but also transferential. Through onomastics, Munro provides clues to the reader which are to be interpreted across cultures. For the character of Sophie to be fully grasped, the reader must bear in mind the allusive implications encapsulated in her names. She is jokingly called 'the Old Norse' by her son Laurence and her daughter-in-law, Isabel, because she reads the *Poetic Edda* in the original language.[25] Sophie means 'wisdom' in ancient Greek and, among several other meanings, Edda is also linked with a female deity, the symbolic ancestor of humankind, mother of all science and mythic as well as heroic history of the world, of gods and human beings.[26] By having her character called simultaneously Old Norse and Sophie, Munro increases and deflects her dimension as the original mother of wisdom, because she bifurcates her genealogy and leads the two references to somehow collide with one another. The surfeit of wisdom is less a replenishment than a debunking, all the more so as Laurence and Isabel play games around the secret name they have attributed to Sophie and these games contribute to ironize her status as a formidable woman.

Munro's strategy in this story is simultaneously one of reverence and irreverence, of appropriation and repudiation of the mythological legacy associated with the *Poetic Edda*. By quoting the 'Lay of Atli' and refraining from identifying it, she simultaneously stresses and conceals, suggests and problematizes the possible connections between the fate of the two women who have lived under Sophie's roof, Isabel and Magda, and the fate of the two women in the 'Lay of Atli': Brynhildr and Gudrun. Munro entrusts the reader with the responsibility of transferring meaning from one context to another and linking the stories of today with the stories of the past. This transactional and transferential activity has far-reaching consequences: it is a covert and tricky reconfiguration of experience, allusively hypothesized although unacknowledged, through which a middle-class divorce in the mid-twentieth century in Ontario becomes connected to the history of Attila the Hun and to the Nordic myth of Siegfried. Munro clandestinely historicizes fiction and mythologizes history in her contemporary short stories. She synchronizes the personal, the factual, and the fabulous by irreverently suggesting the possibility of an equation between her local plot and the history of the world and of world literature.

Another prominent example of her use of Norse mythology is to be found in the collection *Hateship, Friendship, Courtship, Loveship, Marriage* (2001), which includes an acclaimed story, 'The Bear Came over the Mountain', turned into a film by Sarah Polley in 2006. The male protagonist of the story, Grant, is a professor of Anglo-Saxon and Nordic literature and, because he reads skaldic poetry aloud to his students, he is simultaneously allowed to cut the figure of the emblematic Icelandic poet or skald.[27] The magnificent ode which is mentioned by the narrator as being read aloud in class by Grant is one of the most famous, the *Hofuolausn* by Egill Skallagrímsson, whose life and works are preserved in the *Egils Saga* attributed to Snorri Sturluson.

When referring to the *Hofuolausn* or 'Head-Ransom' as recited by Grant in front of his students, Munro highlights the miraculous power of poetry to transform a death sentence into a gift of life:

> he risked reciting and then translating the majestic and gory ode, the head-ransom, the Hofuolausn, composed to honor King Eric Blood-axe by the skald whom that king had condemned to death. (And who was then, by the same king – and by the power of poetry – set free.)[28]

By reciting aloud the *Hofuolausn*, Egill saved his head because the beauty of his words moved the heart of the king who, in return, granted him his life. By taking up Egill's words and reciting them in front of his class, Grant turns into the skald and, like him, remains unpunished, despite his repeated misconduct and improper behaviour. Grant is endowed with the power of a skaldic poet who casts a spell over his students and ensures the remission of his sexual sins.

Munro takes up explicitly and literally Egill Skallagrímsson's life story and the theme of the redemption brought about by the power of poetry, which it encapsulates, to transfer it to Grant's life story. By equating Grant to Egill, Munro performs a heroic aggrandizement of the contemporary professor's status which is matched by her transformation of the status of her female protagonist, Fiona. Fiona is Grant's wife and she is afflicted with a degenerative disease, gradually losing her words, but the moment of final lapse into silence is eventually deferred thanks to Grant's empathy and self-denial. In what will probably remain one of the most unorthodox stories in her oeuvre, Munro represents Grant in the process of permitting his wife to enjoy a restorative relationship with a male inmate from the medical institution where she lives. In other words, Grant procures a lover for his newly wanton wife: through homophony, Fiona embodies Friia, also called Frigg or Frija (in German) and Frea. She is the goddess of love, the very same goddess who is called Aphrodite by the Greeks and Venus by the Romans. At the end of the story, the wanton wife struggles to find her words and proves capable of restoring her grammar: '"You could have just driven away," she said. "Just driven away without a care in the world and forsook me. Forsooken me. Forsaken."'[29]

The elderly protagonist is undeniably in the grip of a degenerative disease but Munro does not resign herself to depicting her lapse into inarticulateness; the story latches on to the *Egils Saga* to suggest indirectly the means of redemption. By making Fiona learn language again at the end of her life with a youthful and transgressive gusto, the story brings together degeneracy and recovery, old age and infancy, sanity and dementia, infidelity and loyalty. Through the allusion to skaldic poetry, and through the transferential activity she suggests between the stories of the past and the stories of the present, Munro celebrates the empowerment brought about by language.

Folksongs and popular culture

Alongside erudite references to the *Codex Regius* and to Norse mythology, Munro includes allusions to popular culture and 'The Bear Came over the Mountain' is a case in point since its title is directly taken from American folklore:

> The bear went over the mountain,
> The bear went over the mountain,
> The bear went over the mountain,
> To see what he could see.
> And what do you think he saw?
> And what do you think he saw?

> The other side of the mountain,
> The other side of the mountain,
> The other side of the mountain,
> Was all that he could see.

By introducing in the same story a skaldic poem, the 'Head-Ransom' by Snorri Sturluson, and an American folksong, Munro uses, once more, a strategy of synchronization of distinct categories in order to establish connections between apparently remote or even irreducible experiences. The American folksong self-reflexively epitomizes the obliteration of frontiers: the other becomes the same through a disquieting tautology. As demonstrated by Jean Jacques Lecercle in his study of nonsense, tautology is fraught with rhetorical power.[30] It guarantees the values of the world we live in: boys will be boys. The other side of the mountain is the other side of the mountain. The assertion is extremely sensible at the same time as it refrains from conveying meaning. It confirms the real world, the existence of which is clearly posited: the other side of the mountain exists and the bear has been able to find its location, which is to be accepted as part and parcel of the real world, but this real world is simultaneously questioned because it is reduced to a self-parodic play on words. By narrating the story of a woman afflicted with a degenerative disease and making a reference to an empowering ode as well as a tautological folksong, Munro simultaneously confirms and denies the reality of degeneracy, which is ambiguously acknowledged but circumvented. Fiona's disease, which is never given a definite label, is fictionalized because it is framed by a reference to a folksong and, at the same time, it is counteracted through its synchronization with an ode which displays redemption through language.

With a rejuvenating impertinence, Munro's story attributes to language a power and a performativity which keeps degeneracy and final dissolution at bay: it transgresses the threshold between reality and fiction and orchestrates the collapsing of the difference between the greatest ode in the *Codex Regius* and the reciting of the irregular verbs of English grammar or the most tautological of American folksongs.

The collapsing of the difference between high culture and low culture is Munro's signature, to be found throughout her work. In what will probably be her last book, *Dear Life*, the four closing stories are defined by Munro herself as 'the first and last – and the closest – things I have to say about my own life'.[31] Paradoxically enough, these self-avowedly most autobiographical stories are also the most intertextual ones, which create infinite reverberations through world literature, but also give pride of place to the humblest and most decried of popular songs. This set of stories is implicitly inspired by E. T. A. Hoffmann's tales, in the volume entitled *Die Nachtstücke*

(*The Night Pieces*) from 1817, if only because the title of Munro's first two stories, 'The Eye' and 'Night', directly echo the first story in the volume of 1817, 'The Sandman'.³² In the first story of Hoffmann's *Night Pieces*, the young Nathanael lives in fear of having his eyes burnt by the sandman, a fear which becomes a self-fulfilling prophecy since he eventually sees the eyes of the sandman in the crowd and jumps from on high to his death, in order to be reunited with his evil seducer, his last words being 'pretty eyes, pretty eyes'.

In Munro's story entitled 'The Eye', the first one in this set of four, the young narrator recalls that, when she looked at the body of a dead young girl for the last time, she saw her eyelid move. She convinced herself that the dead girl was looking out through her lashes and she remained under that delusion for several years, until she reached the age of experience and eventually dismissed such misconception. This very disquieting story based upon a hardly concealed revisitation of Hoffmann's 'The Sandman' provides a description of the hired girl who worked for the Laidlaw family at the time when Alice was a little child. The young Alice was full of admiration for Sadie, the hired girl, because she also happened to be a singer for the local radio. Munro depicts her voice in a striking manner: 'her voice was strong and sad and she sang about loneliness and grief'.³³ The repeated initial and terminal consonant 's' which echoes through this line creates an uncanny alliteration, with a sibilant sound, which is reinforced by the repetition of the coordinating conjunction, 'and'. This repetition, called polysyndeton, underpins the melancholy strain of Sadie's song by making the reader hear the mournful melody, a melody strongly reminiscent of Wordsworth's poem 'The Solitary Reaper':

>Will no one tell me what she sings?
>Perhaps the plaintive numbers flow
>For old, unhappy, far-off things,
>And battles long ago:
>Or is it some more humble lay,
>Familiar matter of to-day?
>Some natural sorrow, loss, or pain,
>That has been, and may be again?
>
>Whate'er the theme, the Maiden sang
>As if her song could have no ending;
>I saw her singing at her work,
>And o'er the sickle bending;—
>I listened, motionless and still;
>And, as I mounted up the hill,
>The music in my heart I bore,
>Long after it was heard no more.

The female bard: myths, ballads, sagas, and songs

In his poem about the solitary Highland lass, Wordsworth similarly evoked the natural sorrow, loss, or pain the maiden gave expression to in the vale profound of the Hebrides. The last line of Wordsworth's poem is borrowed verbatim from Thomas Wilkinson. In his manuscript, *Tours to the British Mountains* (1824), Wilkinson recorded the events of his rambles in nature and wrote: 'Passed a female who was reaping alone: she sung in Erse as she bended over her sickle; the sweetest human voice I ever heard: her strains were tenderly melancholy, and felt delicious, long after they were heard no more.'[34]

With the character of Sadie, evoked in the first story of her final set, Munro does not provide the reader with the plaintive sound of a reaper in the oat fields of the Hebrides. She provides the first stanza of a sad ballad sung by a New World cowgirl:

> Leanin' on the old top rail
> In a big corral.
> Looking down the twilight trail
> For my long lost pal.[35]

This elegiac transposition of the song of the solitary reaper results from a literary migration from the Hebrides to North America. Munro has taken up the figure of the solitary reaper and she has playfully Canadianized it: she has transformed her into a cowgirl of the Western World.

One could use this instance of the transformation of a figure borrowed from one poet, who himself borrowed it from another, as the exemplary instance of Munro's own appropriation of the literary memory of Romantic Europe. Munro is not only transmitting the personal memories of her family migration to Canada from the vale of Ettrick; her stories exemplify the transperipheral processes of literary migration of the bardic tradition from Scotland to Ontario, and it is small wonder that she should have chosen for her last group of stories to focus on the voice of a domestic help or hired girl.

Etymologically a minstrel is employed by the landlord for the entertainment of his household: 'ministralis means a dependant'.[36] The presence of dependants or domestic help or hired girls is particularly remarkable in Munro's stories. Their presence can be taken as a further sign of her ironic recasting of the figure of the minstrel in the twentieth century in Ontario. In characteristic fashion Munro proceeds through symbolic inversion; she replaces the invalid, often blind, male singer of yesteryear with an alert young maid who is not only employed by Munro's parents but vicariously represents her own self. During the summer of 1948, Munro worked as a kitchen help in the homes of a well-to-do family in Toronto and on Georgian

Bay.[37] This experience has been recorded in at least two of her stories – 'Sunday Afternoon' (1968) and 'The Hired Girl' (2006) – and gives ample proof that Munro's writing is not to be considered metaphorically or literally as 'white writing', to borrow a metaphor from Coetzee, implicitly sympathetic to the cultural mission of empire. Munro's writing emanates from a rural background and bears the challenging ambivalence of its bardic affiliation. As it recycles and reverses the myths of the Hellenistic world or the Romantic poems of the margins of the English-speaking world, and as it re-visions German and Scandinavian legacies, it constructs itself as a site of indexation to imperial ideology, at the same time as a site of resistance to and revision of the traditions and literary genres of the British Empire and the western canon.

As demonstrated by Trumpener, the figure of the bard is a catalyst for 'literary counter-representations and the articulation of an oppositional nationalist aesthetics'.[38] Munro's transformation of myths, of ballads, and of Nordic sagas, and her appropriation of opera as well as popular songs, not only evidences the contestatory dimension of her poetics but also testifies to the vitality of the continuance of an oral tradition based on a female song.

In the marvellous folktales of the western tradition, the hero who is engaged in a quest comes up against a number of qualifying ordeals before he reveals his heroic stature and completes his journey satisfactorily with the discovery of the object he was looking for. An object looms up with particular import at the end of *The View from Castle Rock*. This object is presented in the closing lines of the Epilogue entitled 'Messenger':

> And in one of these houses – I can't remember whose – a magic door stop, a big mother of pearl sea shell that I recognised as a messenger from near and far, because I could hold it to my ear – when nobody was there to stop me – and discover the tremendous pounding of my own blood and the sea.[39]

This single concluding line is at once a nominal and a hypotactic sentence which conjoins opposites: it evokes closure to foster aperture since it features a door stop which is meant to keep the door ajar; it suggests proximity through an ordinary object but it makes room for distance; it provides a fragment to conjure up totality; it describes the self only to dissolve the individual in an oceanic flux. In her conclusion to her 'special set of stories', Munro provides a further clue to the allegory of self-discovery to which she has committed herself throughout her writing life. By choosing a natural object to transform it into a cultural one, she generates resonances, echoing with intertextual references. In Golding's

Lord of the Flies (1954), a sea conch is used as an emblem of democracy and a preserver of civilization on the island on which the teenagers are stranded. That the volume entitled *The View from Castle Rock* should finish on the image of a preserved sea shell is particularly revelatory, should we remember that in the same novel by Golding the decay of civilization and the rise of tyranny are symbolized by the shattering of the sea conch and the settlement of the tribe in the part of the island called Castle Rock. Munro's re-appropriation of the historical Scottish Castle Rock for the title of the collection and her finishing on the sound from the intact sea shell as an oceanic messenger perform a metonymic reclamation of the past which is regenerative.

With this highly suggestive object offered to the reader at the end of her twelfth volume, she confirms her endorsement of the role of female bard by activating an apparently traditional image of womanhood. The giant opalescent sea shell is a metaphor for women as 'delicate vessels of natural and cultural transmission', a celebrated image that George Eliot used in *Daniel Deronda*.[40] Munro's treatment of 'the image of woman as vessel of containment for the essence of humanity'[41] bears the ambivalent mark of her reappropriation: it is founded on a homely object, a door stop, which is also an icon of western art, to be found in the Musée d'Orsay in Paris through the painting by Odilon Redon entitled 'The Seashell' (1912).[42] With this multi-layered reference, Munro pays implicit homage to the maternal function of generation and produces an emblem of the engendering of self and stories through the ages.

From *Dance of the Happy Shades* to *Dear Life*, through fourteen volumes of short stories, Munro does not develop a series of disconnected stories or even partially connected ones, but a single song of herself, a long epic poem based on the counter energy of return,[43] which may in the final analysis be compared to a *chanson de geste* or *gesta*. A *chanson de geste* is a song of deeds, for *gesta* in Latin means deeds or accomplishments. From the eleventh to the fourteenth century, the *gesta*, written in lines of ten or twelve syllables, at first with assonance then rhymed, constituted the traditional tale of adventure based on the achievements of male heroes of superhuman stature.[44] Munro's minor stories based on the minuscule anecdotes of women's lives which clandestinely latch on to the most canonical narratives in the western world represent a type of counter-text which simultaneously appropriates and ironizes the bardic tradition with self-reflexive inventiveness and irreverence. Through the ceaseless reiteration of the adventures of her life in the form of direct or indirect autobiographical vignettes, relentlessly or clandestinely self-centred, she makes us glimpse infinity in mother-of-pearl.

Notes

1. James Hogg, *The Private Memoirs and Confessions of a Justified Sinner* [1824], edited by Karl Miller (London: Penguin, 2006); Walter Scott, *Minstrelsy of the Scottish Border: Historical and Romantic Ballads* [1802] (London: Ward, Lock, 1868).
2. Alice Munro, *Dear Life* (New York: Alfred A. Knopf, 2012), 288.
3. Adrian Hunter, 'Story into History: Alice Munro's Minor Literature', *English* 53 (2004), 219–38.
4. There are at least three versions of this opera. The first one was performed in Vienna on 5 October 1762, with a libretto by Ranieri de Calzabigi. It was then adapted for French taste and performed in Paris in 1774; the libretto was translated into French by Pierre Louis Moline. Almost a century later, in 1859, Hector Berlioz took up the work by Gluck, which he considered exemplary, and proposed a longer and revised version. See Michel Noiray, 'Gluck Christoph Willibald', *Encyclopaedia Universalis* 10 (1990), 523–4.
5. Alice Munro, *Dance of the Happy Shades* (Toronto: McGraw-Hill Ryerson, 1968), 113.
6. Fred Weatherly, *Piano and Gown* (London and New York: G. P. Putnam's Sons, 1926), 277–9.
7. Henrik Ibsen, *Four Major Plays : A Doll's House ; Ghosts ; Hedda Gabler ; and The Master Builder*, translated by James McFarlane and Jens Arup (Oxford University Press, 2008).
8. Munro, *Dance of the Happy Shades*, 4.
9. Marjorie Garson, '"I Would Try to Make Lists": the Catalogue in *Lives of Girls and Women*', *Canadian Literature* 150 (1996), 56.
10. Ibid., 46.
11. Alice Munro, *The View from Castle Rock* (Toronto: McClelland & Stewart, 2006), 348.
12. Bernard Dupriez, *A Dictionary of Literary Devices*, translated by Albert W. Halsall (University of Toronto Press, 1991), 311.
13. J. A. Cuddon, *Dictionary of Literary Terms* (Harmondsworth: Penguin, 1979), 89.
14. Alice Munro, *Friend of my Youth* (London: Vintage, 1990).
15. Robert Graves, *English and Scottish Ballads* [1957] (London: Heinemann, 1977), 3.
16. Munro, *The View from Castle Rock*, 20.
17. Cuddon, *Dictionary of Literary Terms*, 38.
18. Emile Benvéniste, *Problèmes de linguistique générale*, vol. I (Paris: Gallimard, 1966), 151–75; Ernst Cassirer, *La philosophie des formes symboliques*, translated by Jane Lacoste and Ole Hansen-Love, vol. I (Paris: Minuit, 1972), 314–15.
19. André Green, *Narcissisme de vie, narcissisme de mort* (Paris: Minuit, 1983).
20. James Hogg, *Memoirs of the Author's Life* [1806] (London: Chatto & Windus, 1972), 3.
21. Munro, *The View from Castle Rock*, 324. This epitaph can be translated as 'The poor heart, here on earth / moved by many storms / reaches true peace / only when it beats no more.' The poem was set to music by Schubert in 1816 and 1817 as a *lied*, and carries *Deutsch Katalog* numbers 330 (First setting), 377 (Second setting), and 569 (Third setting). The date of D. 330, 377 is 1816 and of 569 is 1817. The poem itself does not seem to have been first published until

1788, in the *Goettinger Musenalmanach* magazine. John Reed, *The Schubert Song Companion* (Manchester: Mandolin, 1997), 75–7.
22 Walter Scott, *Old Mortality* [1816], edited by Angus Calder (Harmondsworth: Penguin, 1974), 63.
23 Alice Munro, *The Progress of Love* (Toronto: McClelland & Stewart, 1986), 309.
24 Andrew Dennis, Peter Foote, and Richard Perkins (eds.), *The Codex Regius of Grágás with Material from Other Manuscripts* (Winnipeg: University of Manitoba Press, 2006).
25 Ursula Dronke, *The Poetic Edda Mythological Poems* (Oxford: Clarendon Press, 1996).
26 Scholars do not agree upon the signification of the word Edda. Its meaning is linked with the act of composing poetry and it is also used to refer to two works which date back to the thirteenth century: the Elder Edda and the Younger Edda. Régis Boyer, 'EDDAS', *Encyclopædia Universalis*, available at www-universalis-edu-com.nomade.univ-tlse2.fr/encyclopedie/eddas/; accessed 22 November 2014.
27 Unlike anonymous Eddaic poetry, skaldic oral court poetry, which originated in Norway but was developed chiefly by Icelandic poets from the ninth to the thirteenth century, could be attributed to single identifiable characters. 'Skaldic poetry', *Encyclopædia Britannica* (Chicago: Ultimate Reference Suite, 2007).
28 Alice Munro, *Hateship, Friendship, Courtship, Loveship, Marriage* (Toronto: McClelland & Stewart, 2001), 302.
29 Ibid., 322.
30 Jean Jacques Lecercle, *Le dictionnaire et le cri* (Nancy: Presses Universitaires de Nancy, 1995), 49.
31 Munro, *Dear Life*, 255.
32 E. T. A. Hoffmann, *The Sand-Man and Other Night Pieces* [1817], translated by J. T. Bealby (Leyburn: Tartarus Press, 2008).
33 Munro, *Dear Life*, 259.
34 *William Wordsworth*, edited by Stephen Gill (Oxford University Press, 2010), 757.
35 Munro, *Dear Life*, 259.
36 Robert Graves, *English and Scottish Ballads* [1957] (London: Heinemann, 1977), xiv.
37 Robert Thacker, *Alice Munro: Writing Her Lives* (Toronto: McClelland & Stewart, 2005), 81.
38 Katie Trumpener, *Bardic Nationalism: the Romantic Novel and the British Empire* (Princeton University Press, 1997), xii.
39 Munro, *The View from Castle Rock*, 349.
40 Peter Brooks, *Body Work: Objects of Desire in Modern Narrative* (Cambridge, MA: Harvard University Press, 1993), 248.
41 Ibid.
42 Odilon Redon, *La coquille: en bas à droite petit coquillage, dans l'ombre*. 1912. Pastel, 52 x 57.8 cm. Musée d'Orsay, Paris.
43 Salman Rushdie has noted this tendency of the migrant, the exile, the emigrant, 'to be haunted by some sense of loss, some urge to reclaim, to look back, even at the risk of being mutated into pillars of salt'. Salman Rushdie, *Imaginary Homelands: Essays and Criticism, 1981–1991* (London: Penguin, 1992), 10.
44 Chris Baldick, *The Concise Oxford Dictionary of Literary Terms* (Oxford University Press, 1990), 33.

10

ELIZABETH HAY

The mother as material

I've had the notion over the years that among Alice Munro's stories were a select number about her own mother that spoke directly to me, offering a deeper and more personal truth than I was used to finding in fiction. I read them avidly, wished there were more, sometimes wished she would write about nothing else. They were stories about the complex of emotions aroused by having an invalid mother and leaving her behind. It seemed to me I was picking up the scent of the real mother inside the fiction, a mother who came from the Ottawa Valley in eastern Ontario, as did mine. And what was the truth the stories revealed? It had to do with the way intimate yet tentative knowledge about one's mother leads to unsparing self-knowledge.

Let me start with 'The Ottawa Valley', a relatively early story. 'I think of my mother sometimes in department stores,' the narrator begins, or 'when I see somebody on the street who has Parkinson's disease, and more and more often lately when I look in the mirror. Also in Union Station, Toronto...'[1] And she goes on to recall the summer during the Second World War when her mother took her by train to visit 'her old home in the Ottawa Valley' (182), the place that formed a woman given to categorical, sentimental, prim, easily mocked statements – an oversimplifying, self-deceiving mother. Here is the truth about the Ottawa Valley: 'It was no valley' (183). For it is the daughter's job, the writer's job, to deflate the mother and insert the plain, unsentimental truth.

The problem of 'the mother' for a daughter who writes about her is fundamental to Munro's work. There are stories, such as this one, where she deals with its moral and emotional dimensions directly, but I think it fair to say that the problem hovers in the background of everything she writes, for in order to become a writer Munro had to abandon her ill and needy mother, who then became the subject to which she irresistibly returned. Over her long career she probes it, branches out from it, leaves it behind, returns to it once again. Just as she pressed against the limitations her mother imposed on her life, she presses against the limitations of the subject in her fiction, coming at it from many angles and mining it for meaning.

In 'The Ottawa Valley' Munro gets at the problem sideways by first giving us the mother's colourful relatives in deft, unforgettably sharp strokes: the jilted cousin, Dodie, whose every sentence ends in a laugh; the brother who gets even with his domineering wife by keeping her continually pregnant; the sister-in-law who won't let her children go near the grandmother in case they catch her cancer; the poverty greater than any the narrator has known. In contrast the mother seems a mere bystander until another unsentimental truth lands, sudden as a tombstone. A medical definition interrupts the story: '*The onset is very slow and often years may pass before the patient or his family observes that he is becoming disabled*' (189).

From the first paragraph we've seen the mother's disease coming, and here it is. 'Just her left forearm trembled. The hand trembled more than the arm. The thumb knocked ceaselessly against the palm' (190). Now the mother moves to the centre of the story. It is Sunday morning, the daughter and her mother are about to enter the local church when the daughter's underpants give way, the elastic breaks. She badgers her mother for a safety pin, but the only pin to be had is already at work, fastening the strap of the slip under the mother's good dress. Much against her will, the mother sacrifices her own appearance for her daughter's, yielding up the pin. 'My mother set out boldly to join Aunt Dodie and my sister in a pew near the front. I could see that the gray slip had slid down half an inch and was showing in a slovenly way at one side' (193). The child is embarrassed by her mother, aware of her own ingratitude, unable to make up for it. Later, she will question her mother ruthlessly. Will her arm ever stop shaking? Her mother doesn't answer. She 'went on as if she had not heard, her familiar bulk ahead of me turning strange, indifferent. She withdrew, she darkened in front of me' (195).

On display here is Munro's power to see people as they are, which means not at their best. It's a marvellous surprise, then, when she doesn't end with the daughter hunting the mother in her weakness, pursuing her as she walks on ahead (though it's a fine ending, where most writers would have stopped). Instead, as it closes, the story opens into an evening on the porch during which the mother and her relatives recite poetry back and forth. They are allowed the fullness of their own memories, long ago imprinted by poetry learned by heart. Munro extends this generosity to the mother, and to the reader, and to herself. Then comes a curious, explicit last paragraph, in which Munro confesses that this isn't 'a proper story', but 'a series of snapshots' (197). Confesses that if she had been making a proper story she would indeed have ended 'with my mother not answering and going ahead of me across the pasture'. But she 'wanted to find out more, remember more. I wanted to bring back all I could' (197).

So, standing slightly to one side, inside yet outside the story, Munro takes issue with what she has written and with herself, letting us into her working mind and thereby making the story even more personal yet more encompassing. We are left with the categorical mother's resistance to being categorized by her daughter: she will not be pinned down and neither will her ever-shifting illness. She withdraws, she darkens, she eludes, she tantalizes. She is, in her way, magnetic; the kind of character who demands another sequel and another.

Now is a good moment to say that it is incredible how much Munro knows and to try to describe the particular flavour of her knowing. 'It was no valley', she writes in her deadpan way. There is an edgy, undercutting humour to her truth-seeking. Often it seems less a matter of what she knows than the more complicated matter of what she knows about what she knows, for hers is a restless kind of knowing, no less shifting and unpredictable than her mother's mysterious illness, always working away at itself and revealing one facet after another. Aunt Dodie, for instance, 'laughed at me, to cheer me up. In her thin brown face her eyes were large and hot ... flashing malice and kindness at me, threatening to let out more secrets than I could stand' (195). This is how families operate, though most of us are so confused by the malice and so seduced by the kindness that we can't make sense of either or see that such things coexist. Captured in this sentence is the tension that flows from Munro's kind of knowledge: that of being in the know yet never knowing enough.

Munro is all too aware that the one character in 'The Ottawa Valley' who doesn't come clear is her mother, the very one she has taken this narrative journey to reach. In that last paragraph, she confesses that she had wanted 'to mark her off, to describe, to illumine, to celebrate, to *get rid*, of her; and it did not work, for she looms too close' (197). By addressing the failure of the mother to come clear, Munro makes the problem come clear: things very close to us are hard, if not impossible, to know, yet more than anything else they are what we need to know, and for that reason we return to them again and again.

There is a special irony here. The kind of material a writer wants to get rid of is the material that recurs, and it is always rich and troubling. The subject of her mother is what Munro called in a *Paris Review* interview in 1994 'my central material in life'.[2]

The loaded question of a writer's material is what Munro delves into in the story she calls simply 'Material'. Here the narrator is the jaded ex-wife of a writer named Hugo, one of those vain, quarrelsome, self-serving men who

The mother as material

take no responsibility for their real-life cruelties. 'You filthy moral idiot',[3] she calls him savagely and hilariously when they are still together. 'You should have shut up, Hugo' (25). Now he has done something unexpected. He has written an excellent story about a woman they both knew, Dotty, someone they used to call the 'harlot-in-residence' (26), and the story 'is an act of magic ... you might say, of a special, unsparing, unsentimental love'. Dotty, unaccountably, 'has passed into Art' (35). 'Material' is both funny and bruising. It ends with the narrator about to write a thank-you letter to Hugo for his story, then jabbing down these words instead: *'This is not enough, Hugo. You think it is, but it isn't. You are mistaken, Hugo'* (36). What she cannot bear, she admits, is how Hugo, and her current husband in his own way, have got everything figured out to their advantage, 'what attitude to take, how to ignore or use things'. She says, 'I do blame them. I envy and despise' (36). They have a lot to answer for, she is saying. And so does art.

However, the question begs to be asked: what *would* be enough to justify the way artists use real people as their material? Hugo has made the only reparation he can make by writing so well that he does Dotty justice. To the reader-narrator it is not enough. But then in her mind nothing will ever be enough to make up for Hugo's shortcomings as a human being.

And surely this is why Munro keeps writing about her mother. What she writes isn't enough and never can be enough, not for a daughter aware of her own shortcomings.

It is tempting to read 'Material' as a self-accusing story, at least in part. It ends with the narrator's bitter mood of envious despising, though in her realistic and humorous way she says she'll get over it. The confession at the end of 'The Ottawa Valley', on the other hand, opens into a lifetime of trying to get closer to something and always failing. Munro is compelled to write about her mother and condemned to being dissatisfied. Does she really want to use up this resource (this material) as Hugo used up Dotty? She can't and she doesn't. She never uses up her mother in her fiction. Neither does she use up the mother figure upon whom she works variation after variation.

Munro had an astonishing epiphany when she was fifteen. She was in the public library in Wingham, Ontario when she looked out the window and saw in the falling snow a team of horses pulling a sleigh on to the town weigh scales. The scene gave her 'something like a blow in the chest', she has written in her Introduction to her *Selected Stories*. The people, she realized, 'are moving through a story which is hidden, and now, for a moment, carelessly revealed'.[4]

The epiphany gives us a beautiful clue as to how Munro gains access to the stories she tells. It would seem a curtain is pulled back and she sees what has been there all along. No barrier exists between her and this discovery. She is *inside* the characters, inside the drama, inside the irony. And so is the reader.

There can be a great gaiety, a wonderful thrill in her stories as secrets get revealed, since secrets are fun and allow you to feel superior; but knowledge in Munro never promises superiority for long. At a crucial point in the unfolding of events, it becomes frightening and hard to bear. In 'The Peace of Utrecht', the narrator, Helen, has 'been at home now for three weeks and it has not been a success'.[5] Here we have one of Munro's first-person reminiscent stories in which a daughter returns for a visit to the small town in southwestern Ontario in which she grew up, in this case the fictional town of Jubilee. Helen and her older sister, Maddy, have been getting along during these three weeks of summer by not talking about anything that matters. 'No exorcising here, says Maddy in her thin, bright voice with the slangy quality I had forgotten, we're not going to depress each other. So we haven't' (170).

The present tense of the visit then moves into the past, 'the dim world of continuing disaster, of home' (170) from which Helen escaped but Maddy did not, and we come to the real subject of the story, their mother's death a year earlier after a long incurable illness. 'I find that people stop me in the street to talk about my mother', says Helen. Formerly, when her mother was alive, the very words 'your mother' were enough to make her 'whole identity ... come crumbling down'. Now that her mother is dead those words have lost their shame-inducing sting, for the town has claimed her mother's disease-riddled life as one of its 'oddities, its brief legends' (173).

We learn that it was Maddy who looked after their mother for the final ten years of her life, 'Maddy was the one who stayed' (173), while Helen did not even come home for the funeral. Helen's complicated burden of guilt cuts her off from other emotions and from the place itself. She is suffering from 'a puzzled lack of emotional recognition' (175) and is afflicted by her teenage memories of the mother as 'a sickly child' with whom she dealt in a 'remorselessly casual' (176) way, followed by what she calls 'parodies of love. But we grew cunning, unfailing in cold solicitude; we took away from her our anger and impatience and disgust, took all emotion away from our dealings with her, as you might take away meat from a prisoner to weaken him, till he died' (177).

This harrowing admission has been arrived at slowly, quietly, lethally. Everything in the story has slowed down to match the sick mother's 'very slow and mournful voice that was not intelligible or quite human; we would have to interpret. Such theatricality humiliated us almost to death; yet now I think that without that egotism feeding stubbornly even on disaster she might have sunk rapidly into some dim vegetable life' (177). And we know that without her own egotism Helen would have been swallowed up like her sister Maddy. We understand that the story is a deeply felt working out of the problem of 'the mother' as stumbling block to an independent self.

Then one day during this summer visit she is recounting, Helen is in her old bedroom, looking around, when she opens the drawer of the washstand and discovers that it is 'crammed full of pages from a loose-leaf notebook' (178). On one page she reads 'The Peace of Utrecht, 1713, brought an end to the War of the Spanish Succession' (179), written in her own hand, a long-ago school assignment. The words have 'a strong effect' on her. They cause something momentous to happen: her old life reassembles around her and so does the town, 'curiously meaningful for me, and complete' (179). This written evidence of earlier life – her younger self as well as a world that existed before she was ever born – engenders a momentary saving vision of the whole town in its largeness and then in its detail. 'Also: we wore ballerina shoes, and full black taffeta skirts.' In this moment everything vividly registers as itself, including 'Maddy; her bright skeptical look; my sister' (179).

Munro reaches these depths of perceptive feeling by having her character unexpectedly come upon earlier parts of herself, parts of herself that she had forgotten and now rediscovers in the light of the present. It's a movement characteristic of many of her stories and it echoes her epiphany in the library, that moment when what was hidden was 'carelessly revealed'. Figures and truths are not super-imposed; they emerge from a background whose mysterious life has been going on for a long time.

The story has a second half. Helen visits her ancient aunts and one of them, Annie, insists on trying to pass on the pressed and mended clothes of 'your mother' (183). Rebuffed, Aunt Annie goes further. She tells Helen about her mother's final days: '"*Did you know your mother got out of the hospital?*"' Helen's reaction is 'a vague physical sense of terror, a longing not to be told – and beyond this a feeling that what I would be told I already knew, I had always known' (184). And from the frail and implacable aunt we get the details of the mother's flight in the snow followed by her confinement, 'the board across her bed'. Helen is forced to hear the truth and the truth harrows her. These old aunts 'making sure the haunts we have contracted for are with us, not one gone without' (185). The final scene is between the sisters, Helen telling her sister not to be guilty, to seize her life, '"Take it."' Yet the shattering final line is Maddy's: '"But why can't I, Helen? *Why can't I?*"' (187)

The journey from knowledge of the mother to self-knowledge has brought us to this helpless, anguished cry that has no answer. And we are with the poet Elizabeth Bishop realizing that if you tasted the cold Atlantic 'it would first taste bitter, / then briny, then surely burn your tongue. / It is like what we imagine knowledge to be: / dark, salt, clear, moving, utterly free, / drawn from the cold hard mouth / of the world.'[6] We are with the great Russian novelists who strip their characters bare. We are with Munro as she reaches an ending that leaves us staggered by Maddy's knowledge that she cannot *begin*. Staggered by the sisters' finally inescapable and overwhelming self-knowledge. Though it is this mutual extremity that allows them finally to connect.

There is a line in 'Miles City, Montana' that speaks of the narrator's 'real work, which was a sort of wooing of distant parts of myself'.[7] That phrase, 'wooing distant parts of myself', gets to the very heart of Munro's genius. The narrator here is a mother herself who has 'a dread of turning into a certain kind of mother ... solemn with trivial burdens' (312), and she is also a writer, looking for places to hide, where she can do her real work. In that wooing of herself she remembers a scene from childhood, a boy who was drowned, and brings it into view even as she doubts the memory, 'I don't think so. I don't think I really saw all this' (308). She recreates the boy, the funeral, the feeling about her parents that is hard to describe – that 'thin, familiar misgiving' (309). The story she then relates about the near-drowning of her own daughter will bring her to similar misgivings about herself as a parent 'trusting to be forgiven, in time, for everything that had first to be seen and condemned by those children: whatever was flippant, arbitrary, careless, callous – all our natural, and particular, mistakes' (324). The list of parental mistakes also happens to be a list of what Munro works hard to avoid in her writing. In her Afterword to Ethel Wilson's *The Equations of Love*, she spells it out: 'I'm on the alert for a self-indulgent flippancy, for that betrayal of the characters – a faintly giddy contempt for them – which is a pitfall waiting for so light-footed and ironic a writer ... I bristle at a threat of condescension to a poorer, or serving, class.'[8]

Munro's wooing of herself seems to me quite different from the self-satisfied love-of-one's-material that writers often claim to have. Her wooing is a ceaseless, subtle getting-to-know that has something trance-like and heightened about it. She woos her childhood, her adolescence, her early life as a mother; she woos her mother and father, their childhoods, their ancestors, their pasts; she gives her undivided attention in order to draw distant things close. The writing this wooing produces is physical in turn: vital, concrete, sensuous, and full of unexpected pleasures. Above all, it is urgent and real.

To return to 'The Ottawa Valley'. You read this story and feel that you're getting Munro's own voice talking about Munro's own life; the machinery of narrator, invention, plot does not press upon you or distract. Something about the texture of the story gives the impression of unvarnished truth. It isn't seamless, there are patches that come from elsewhere, threads not brought to a typical fictional close. And Munro never blinks; she doesn't turn away from human heartlessness. Neither, and equally important, does she overstate it. What you have in her formidable intelligence is a mind that puts everything in question again and again. She is the opposite of a know-it-all. The reader trusts this communing, self-distrustful yet confident voice that doesn't pretend to know everything, even as knowing is held in the highest regard.

Helen remarks casually in 'The Peace of Utrecht' that she occasionally has dreams in which her mother is nearly her old self, only her hands are trembling, 'and I think, why did I exaggerate so to myself, see, she is all right' (178). In the later 'Friend of My Youth', this thread is picked up and taken further. 'I used to dream about my mother,' the story begins, but then 'the dream stopped, I suppose because it was too transparent in its hopefulness, too easy in its forgiveness'.[9] Too easy a fiction, in other words. 'Friend of My Youth' then drops farther back into the past to a time when the mother was an unmarried teacher in the Ottawa Valley. The story has her boarding with a strictly religious family who live in a divided house: in one half the jilted and saint-like older sister, Flora; in the other half, the man she was supposed to marry, married instead to the younger sister whom he got pregnant while he was courting Flora. In her *Paris Review* interview Munro speaks of having been told by a friend about just such a religious family and how in pondering their situation 'the whole story of my mother closed around it, and then me telling the story closed around my mother, and I saw what it was about'. It's about hidden truths coming out, the full truth of the younger sister's pregnancy, the limited truth about what we can ever know about anyone. The narrator's schoolteacher mother refuses to see Flora as anything but admirable, while the narrator takes joy in concocting more convincing versions of what really happened in that strangely divided house. 'I saw through my mother's story and put in what she left out' (20). Mainly sex. Bold and heated sex in Munro's stories always sets the daughter off from the 'gloomy caution' (22) and prim narrowness of the mother. Desperately, the narrator-daughter uses her powers of invention to break free of the 'great fog of platitudes and pieties lurking, an incontestable crippled-mother power, which would capture and choke me' (20).

But versions of the truth keep coming because no one version can ever be enough, until Flora, the character herself, 'is weary of it, of me and my idea of her, my information, my notion that I can know anything about her'. Similarly elusive is the mother herself 'as she was in those dreams ... showing options and powers I never dreamed she had'. The mother shakes off the daughter with a display of lightness and indifference and 'changes the bitter lump of love I have carried all this time into a phantom – something useless and uncalled for, like a phantom pregnancy' (26). These real and invented people, the author's material, in the end outsmart and outdistance her, leaving her disconcerted, fumbling for more, amused, and discomfited.

In the wide-ranging stories of what might loosely be called her middle period, Munro works many variations on the mother figure, giving us unmarried mothers, substitute mothers, runaway mothers, invalid mothers, and motherless or poorly mothered or over-mothered children, these last becoming the unreachable children of some of her late stories. She often picks a moment in the past into which she drops and it becomes the present tense (the present tense of the past), which then joins with the future tense that is the present. Or she drops into a story that was set in motion years ago, as small-town stories are (people having known each other a long time, if not their whole lives), or as a daughter's relationship to her mother is – a lifelong, subtly changing, inherently dramatic affair.

For me the sweep of time in Munro's stories reflects the lifelong nature of her 'central material'. A mother changes over time (changes frighteningly and dramatically, in the case of Munro's mother) and so does the daughter who becomes a mother herself, left behind in turn by her children. Working with this material, Munro shows how self-knowledge comes slowly, insidiously, frighteningly. The movement is a long-range movement towards dismay, either on the part of the characters or on the part of the reader.

In the extraordinarily chilling 'Vandals', we gradually come to understand over the course of the story's several parts that Bea, the apparently innocuous substitute-mother figure, has made a bargain with herself not to see what is going on with Ladner, her lover and the sexual predator of two motherless children across the road. Therefore, she is useless to the children, this woman who 'could spread safety, if she wanted to';[10] useless, because what she 'has been sent to see, she doesn't see' (545). Munro harrows us with the horror of adult complicity in the ruination of children.

In 'The Love of a Good Woman', the starting point is a box of optometrist's instruments donated anonymously to a local museum; some person chose to bestow but not to divulge. This story, we are being told, will be a drama about knowing and not telling. It flows outward, we'll discover, through tributaries of knowledge to a conclusion in which an unusual daughter learns what her mother and most people in this part of the world have known all along: a kind of common wisdom about the uses of keeping one's mouth shut.

At first we are with a trio of boys moving through the countryside. It's a Saturday morning in the spring of 1951 and everything is seen with a boy's fascination. Their aim is to swim in the river before the snow is off the ground, but they make a discovery instead. They spot a 'little English car'[11] under water; they see the body of Mr Willens in the car. The optometrist's hand, floating up through the open panel in the roof, 'rode there tremulously and irresolutely, like a feather, though it looked as solid as dough' (7). A poet is writing these pages, a poet's hallucinatory vision is at work. 'The boys squatted down on the bank, then lay on their stomachs and pushed their heads out like turtles, trying to see' (6). The boys in their world are, like Munro herself, self-forgetful, possessed by a place.

On the way to the river the boys behave as they did whenever 'they got clear of town. They talked as if they were free' (10), not needing to address each other by name, discussing 'useful finds that might be made or had been made in past years' (9), and what they might do with them, liberated by being in their natural element. 'The wind was warm; it was pulling the clouds apart into threads of old wool, and the gulls and crows were quarrelling and diving over the river' (8). On the way back to town, however, they walk fast, bearing their astonishing news. They re-enter the town and its ritualized interactions and then they are at home, in time for lunch, and they are no longer free. How do you bring what you know, what you've discovered on your own, into the foreign land of the family? A land populated by mothers, fathers, sisters, who behave in their own peculiar, irritating, dangerous ways. Cece Ferns, the boy with the drunken father, finds his ill, bathrobe-clad mother in the kitchen, cradling her abdominal pain; Bud Salter arrives at a house presided over by his tolerating mother and saturated in his older sisters' clothes, makeup, paraphernalia, endless vanity, female moods; Jimmy Box returns to a crowded, multi-generational house defined by handicaps, mental and physical, and by unfailing courtesy: 'complaints were as rare as lightning balls in that house' (21). The great, overflowing Russian novelists do no more than Alice Munro when she constructs in a few paragraphs a complete and separate life for each of the three boys and their families. We feel the complexity of their knowing something no one else knows as we follow them having their lunch, not telling, then reconvening outside, heading to the police station, being forestalled, and so on, until the information finally slips out, as information so often does: Bud, the boy with the most normal mother, 'looked at comic books for an hour or so and then he told her' (30).

The story shifts in part two to one of Munro's invalid mothers, dying Mrs Quinn, cared for by Enid, the unusual daughter and good woman who becomes a substitute mother for Mrs Quinn's two small children. Soon enough, Enid sees the sick woman's viciousness towards her small daughters and her husband. More gradually, she learns about the dying woman's connection with the drowned optometrist. 'Mrs Quinn might crack and crack, but there would be nothing but sullen mischief, nothing but rot inside her' (38). And as certain revulsions ripen, certain intimacies creep shyly into view. Enid and Mrs Quinn's husband, Rupert, went to school together (their small-town lives overlapping), and late one summer evening, whispering so as not to wake the children, they have a conversation that is abbreviated and delicately charged. It reminds Enid of their senior year in high school when Rupert sat behind her in class and they developed a discreet and almost courtly way of communicating with each other and 'she felt forgiven' then for her cruel teasing of him as a boy. 'In a way, she felt honored. Restored to seriousness and respect' (47). In the kitchen, by candlelight, she works a crossword and he helps her. Underlying her feelings for him is not a burial ground (at first) but a learning ground – of school and the surprising things they had studied: Latin, trigonometry, the *History of the Renaissance and Reformation*. And she feels 'a tenderness and wonder. It wasn't that they had meant to be something that they hadn't become ... Just that they had not understood how time would pass and leave them not more but maybe a little less than what they used to be' (48). In this remarkable scene, with its lovely echo of moments in the kitchen between Adam and Dinah in *Adam Bede*, a certain kind of knowledge, innocent, high-minded, moral in its tenderness, draws them together and gives them a way to be with each other. 'Bread of the Amazon? ... Seven letters ... Cassava?' (48–9) Knowledge here is an oasis, it's the stillness you come to in any Munro story when there is a slowing down to fully observe and register something astounding.

The stillness renews the story's energy for its next development: Mrs Quinn, hankering to do harm in the last hours before she dies, tells Enid what she knows about the death of the optometrist. Then in a lurid flashback we see how the death happened: Mr Willens pays one of his salacious visits to Mrs Quinn, Rupert catches them in the act, and bangs in the 'horny old devil's' (59) head. Enid's initial reaction to what she's been told is to orchestrate in her mind a melodramatic scene in which she elicits Rupert's confession. It takes time for another possibility to occur to her, that of not saying a word. 'Through her silence, her collaboration in a silence, what benefits could bloom. For others, and for herself' (76). And now we appreciate that Munro has been telling a story about not telling a story. What we do with what we know, whether learned in school or later, is not what we expect.

The final lines return us to pregnant summer stillness: 'everything for a long way around had gone quiet' (78). As if the soul of the Ontario landscape that for a moment revealed one of its stories has provided this merciful exit.

In the later 'Dimensions' Munro goes even further with her mother-haunted material and does something altogether staggering. It's hard to do justice to the imaginative genius of this story. It begins in the stunned present and works backwards into the past that produced it. Doree is on a bus. To get where she is going, she will need to take three buses in all. She works as a chambermaid in the Blue Spruce Inn, scrubbing and cleaning, 'content to do what she did. She didn't want to have to talk to people.'[12] On the bus she is heading to 'the facility' (1), where her husband, Lloyd, has been imprisoned for murdering their three children in an act of horrific violence that was meant to punish her.

What dignity Munro gives her characters as the story unfolds and we relive the recent and more distant past. The gradual buildup of that past mirrors the buildup of Lloyd's controlling violence. 'It got worse, gradually' (12). And Doree's haunting reconnection with him builds in the same way, for he is her only link to her dead children, this man who had been 'the closest person in the world to her' (14). Post-catastrophe, she has no life, beyond having 'the heaves' (6) and trying not to think. Following one of her visits to the prison, Lloyd writes to her. Letters in Munro's narratives often contain revelations of character that move the story forward and they do so here. What Lloyd writes is partly predictable – 'there seemed to be some trace of the old bragging' (27) – and partly dumbfounding. He reveals that he has seen the children and talked to them. They exist in *'another Dimension'* where they are *'happy and smart'* (25). He wants to give Doree 'this *information – the Truth – and in telling you I have seen them, I hope that it will make your heart lighter'* (26). And indeed this is what happens. Not immediately but after a time, the thought that the children 'were in what he had called their Dimension' brings 'a light feeling to her, not pain'. And who had brought her this relief? Not the social worker, but 'Lloyd that terrible person, that isolated and insane person' (27).

At the end of the story Doree is on the bus again, heading to the facility outside London, Ontario (it occurs to me that the several parts into which Munro often divides her stories are like the separate but connected segments of a bus ride down main roads and secondary roads leading to a place on the outskirts, and this is the place the writer and the reader go back to, and where they meet up with uncomfortable self-truths) when in front of them a pickup truck rockets across the road into the ditch, sending its driver flying through the air. 'The boy was lying on his back, arms and legs flung out, like somebody making an angel in the snow. Only there was gravel around him, not snow' (29). Doree crouches beside him, she lays her hand on his chest, applies mouth-to-mouth resuscitation, and then she stays with the boy she has brought back to life. His breath is 'a sweet obedience in the chest', utterly remarkable words in the context, for they take the obedience demanded of Doree in her abusive marriage and make it independent, of its own volition, and life-giving. Doree assures the bus driver that the bus can go on without her, she doesn't need to get to London. '"You don't have to get to London?"' (31) And the story ends on the downbeat of her no.

Nothing in 'Dimensions' is categorical. In this way it forms a bookend to the categorical mother in 'The Ottawa Valley'. It forms a bookend to any all-knowing, definitive view of the world. What we have instead is *possibility* and from the unlikeliest source, 'that terrible person'. It's a story that makes you hold your breath until the last moment, and the last moment allows you to breathe as if for the first time.

I return to Munro's epiphany in the library, that 'blow in the chest' which filled her lungs, if you like, with literary oxygen. She has an extra sense, a sixth sense or a seventh, of what lies hidden, yet is fully alive, waiting to transfigure us. Perhaps the recurring stories about her mother, stories in which her mother wrestles free of her as much as Munro wrestles free of her mother, were what allowed her to write this altogether remarkable story about a man who confirms and then defies our worst preconceptions, throwing into question everything we might think we know.

I want to return as well to her wooing of the past. In the openly autobiographical 'Working for a Living' a glimpse of sumacs beside an empty country store jogs Munro's memory and takes her back to her mother in her prime, before her body turned against her. Suddenly we are in the 1940s when Munro's mother was selling American tourists silver-fox capes in a last-ditch effort to save the family from financial ruin. As ever, Munro settles into her noticing ways, her working ways, ranging far and wide, an outward focus that might owe some of its intensity to how fed up she became with her ill mother's inward gaze, how 'sick of her self-absorption'.[13] Her details are working details. 'The white weasel does not attain its purity until around the tenth of December' (108). Her perceptions are working perceptions. 'Whenever she had to deal with the problem of my grandmother's touchiness my mother brightened up, as if she had got back some competence or importance in our family' (124). The structure is a working structure that gets the most out of her material by turning it and turning it again, seeing it from new angles, revisiting it in a series of returns, each of which produces a new crop of understandings and revelations.

In 'Home', another story about wooing the personal past and one that Munro worked on and revised for thirty years, we meet her irrepressible stepmother, a salty interloper who has remade the family home in her own image, displacing the dead mother and her books and tastes and 'embarrassing ambitions'[14] and embarrassing illness. Now it is the father who is ill and dying. The narrator has made one of her visits home, 'travelling on three buses' (227), and towards the end of the story she finds herself alone in the barn and pictures herself as she would have been had she never left, 'like one of those misfits, captives', imprisoned in a time and place, living in 'a surly trance' (248). Then on the final page, thinking later 'about all this', another awareness comes over her. Where she had been standing in the stable, spreading the hay and surrendering to panic, was 'the scene of the first clear memory of my life'. The memory comes back in trance-like detail: she is in the corner, sitting on the first or second step of the flight of steps going up to the hayloft and 'watching my father milk the black-and-white cow' that 'died of pneumonia in the worst winter of my childhood, which was 1935'. It's a recollection that restores the narrator to her earliest self and then brings her forward through time and place, steadying and deepening her as it steadies and deepens the reader. The memory holds the many strands of life and death that flowed from 'the cold of that extraordinary winter which killed all the chestnut trees, and many orchards' (250).

All the juices of life that flow so abundantly through Munro's body of work become still waters of a profound kind in the several autobiographical stories at the end of her last collection, *Dear Life*. The last story closes – like a bell tolling – with the central haunting fact of her life: 'I did not go home for my mother's last illness or for her funeral.'[15] There were reasons, and she gives them. Then the final two lines state the unsparing self-knowledge it has taken a lifetime to adequately measure and do so in a voice that is distinctly hers: sober, chastened, wise, and not unkind.

> We say of some things that they can't be forgiven, or that we will never forgive ourselves. But we do – we do it all the time. (319)

Notes

1 'The Ottawa Valley', in *Something I've Been Meaning to Tell You* (Scarborough, Ont.: New American Library, 1975), 182.
2 Alice Munro, 'The Art of Fiction', *The Paris Review* 36, 131 (summer 1994), 237.
3 'Material', in *Something I've Been Meaning to Tell You*, 33.
4 Alice Munro, 'Introduction', in *Selected Stories* (New York: Vintage, 1997), xvi.
5 'The Peace of Utrecht', in *Dance of the Happy Shades* (Toronto: Penguin Canada, 2005), 169.
6 Elizabeth Bishop, 'At the Fishhouses', in *The Complete Poems* (New York: Farrar, Straus and Giroux, 1992), 66.
7 'Miles City, Montana', in *Selected Stories* (Toronto: McClelland & Stewart, 1996), 311.
8 Alice Munro, 'Afterword', in Ethel Wilson, *The Equations of Love* (Toronto: McClelland & Stewart, 1990), 262.
9 'Friend of My Youth', in *Friend of My Youth* (New York: Knopf, 1990), 3.
10 'Vandals', in *Selected Stories* (Toronto: McClelland & Stewart, 1996), 544.

11 'The Love of a Good Woman', in *The Love of a Good Woman* (Toronto: McClelland & Stewart, 1998), 6.
12 'Dimensions', in *Too Much Happiness* (Toronto: McClelland & Stewart, 2009), 1.
13 'Working for a Living', in *The View from Castle Rock* (Toronto: Penguin Canada, 2010), 124.
14 'Home', in *The View from Castle Rock*, 231.
15 'Dear Life', in *Dear Life* (Toronto: McClelland & Stewart, 2012), 319.

BIBLIOGRAPHY

Although Alice Munro's writings have appeared throughout the world in various manners and in many translations, I have listed only the first appearance of her books in Canada.

Dance of the Happy Shades. Foreword by Hugh Garner. Toronto: Ryerson, 1968.
Lives of Girls and Women. Toronto: McGraw-Hill Ryerson, 1971.
Something I've Been Meaning to Tell You: Thirteen Stories. Toronto: McGraw-Hill Ryerson, 1974.
Who Do You Think You Are? Toronto: Macmillan, 1978.
The Moons of Jupiter. Toronto: Macmillan, 1982.
The Progress of Love. Toronto: McClelland & Stewart, 1986.
Friend of My Youth. Toronto: McClelland & Stewart, 1990.
Open Secrets. Toronto: McClelland & Stewart, 1994.
The Love of a Good Woman. Toronto: McClelland & Stewart, 1998.
Hateship, Friendship, Courtship, Loveship, Marriage. Toronto: McClelland & Stewart, 2001.
Runaway. Toronto: McClelland & Stewart, 2004.
The View from Castle Rock. Toronto: McClelland & Stewart, 2006.
Too Much Happiness. Toronto: McClelland & Stewart, 2009.
Dear Life. Toronto: McClelland & Stewart, 2012.

In addition, there have been four selections of her stories published in Canada:

Selected Stories. Toronto: McClelland & Stewart, 1996.
No Love Lost. Selected and with an afterword by Jane Urquhart. Toronto: McClelland & Stewart, 2003.
Alice Munro's Best: Selected Stories with an Introduction by Margaret Atwood. Toronto: McClelland & Stewart, 2006.
Family Furnishings: Selected Stories 1995–2014. Toronto: McClelland & Stewart, 2014.

Then there are Munro's own commentaries and critical studies, which include the following:

'Remember Roger Mortimer: Dickens' "Child's History of England" Remembered', *Montrealer* (February 1962), 34–7.

'Author's Commentary', in John Metcalf (ed.), *Sixteen by Twelve* (Toronto: Ryerson, 1970), 125–6.
'The Colonel's Hash Resettled', in John Metcalf (ed.), *The Narrative Voice* (Toronto: McGraw-Hill Ryerson, 1972), 181–3.
'An Open Letter', *Jubilee* 1 [1974], 5–7.
'Everything Here Is Touchable and Mysterious', *Weekend Magazine (Toronto Star)* (11 May 1974), 33.
'On Writing "The Office"', in Edward Peck (ed.), *Transitions II: Short Fiction* (Vancouver: Commcept, 1978), 259–62.
'Working for a Living', *Grand Street* 1, 1 (1981), 9–37.
'Through the Jade Curtain', *Chinada: Memoirs of the Gang of Seven* (Dunvegan, Ont.: Quadrant, 1982), 51–5.
'What Is Real?' in John Metcalf (ed.), *Making it New: Contemporary Canadian Stories* (Toronto: Methuen, 1982), 223–6.
'Going to the Lake', in *Ontario: a Bicentennial Tribute* (Toronto: Key Porter, 1983), 51–2.
'An Appreciation [of Marian Engel]', *Room of One's Own* 9, 2 (1984), 32–3.
'Foreword' in Robert Weaver (ed.), *The Anthology Anthology: a Selection from 30 Years of CBC Radio's 'Anthology'* (Toronto: Macmillan, 1984), ix–x.
'On John Metcalf: Taking Writing Seriously', *Malahat Review* 70 (1985), 6–7.
'Introduction', in *The Moons of Jupiter* (Markham, Ont.: Penguin, 1986), vii–xvi.
'The Novels of William Maxwell', *Brick* 34 (fall 1988), 28–31.
'Afterword', in Lucy Maud Montgomery, *Emily of New Moon* (Toronto: McClelland & Stewart, 1989), 357–61.
'Contributor's Note', in Margaret Atwood and Shannon Ravenal (eds.), *Best American Short Stories 1989* (Boston: Houghton Mifflin, 1989), 322–3.
'Take a Walk on the Wild Side', *Canadian Living* 38 (October 1989), 41–2.
'Afterword', in Ethel Wilson, *The Equations of Love* (Toronto: McClelland & Stewart, 1990), 259–63.
'What Do You Want to Know For?' in Constance Rooke (ed.), *Writing Away: the PEN Canada Travel Anthology* (Toronto: McClelland & Stewart, 1994), 203–20.
'Changing Places', in Constance Rooke (ed.), *Writing Home: a PEN Canada Anthology* (Toronto: McClelland & Stewart, 1997), 190–206.
'Contributor's Note', in Larry Dark (ed.), *Prize Stories 1997: the O. Henry Awards* (New York: Anchor, 1997), 442–3.
'Introduction', in *Selected Stories* (New York: Vintage, 1997), xiii–xxi.
'Golden Apples', *Georgia Review* 53 (1999), 22–4.
'Contributor's Note', in Larry Dark (ed.), *Prize Stories 1999: The O. Henry Awards* (New York: Anchor, 1999), 404.
'Lying Under the Apple Tree', *The New Yorker* (17/24 June 2002), 88–90, 92, 105–8, 110–14.
'The Second Sweet Summer of Kitty Malone', in Graeme Gibson et al. (eds.), *Uncommon Ground: a Celebration of Matt Cohen* (Toronto: Knopf, 2002), 91–4.
'Good Woman in Ireland', in Gary Stephen Ross (ed.), *Prize Writing* (Toronto: Giller Prize Foundation, 2003), 57–64.
'Maxwell', in Charles Baxter, Michael Collier, and Edward Hirsch (eds.), *A William Maxwell Portrait: Memories and Appreciations* (New York: Norton, 2004), 34–47.

'Writing. Or, Giving Up Writing', in Constance Rooke (ed.), *Writing Life: Celebrated Canadian and International Authors on Writing and Life*. (Toronto: McClelland & Stewart, 2006), 297–300.

Books on Alice Munro

Balestra, Gianfranca, Ferri, Laura, and Ricciardi, Caterina (eds.) *Reading Alice Munro in Italy* (Toronto: The Frank Iacobucci Centre for Italian Studies, 2008).
Besner, Neil K. *Introducing Alice Munro's Lives of Girls and Women: a Reader's Guide* (Toronto: ECW Press, 1990).
Bigot, Corinne, and Lanone, Catherine (eds.) *'With a Roar from Underground': Alice Munro's Dance of the Happy Shades* (Paris: Presses Universitaires de Paris Ouest, 2015).
Blodgett, E. D. *Alice Munro* (Boston: Twayne, 1988).
Bloom, Harold (ed.) *Alice Munro* (New York: Bloom's Literary Criticism, 2009).
Buchholtz, Miroslawa and Sojka, Eugenia (eds.) *Alice Munro: Reminiscence, Interpretation, Adaptation and Comparison* (Frankfurt am Main: Peter Lang, 2015).
Carrington, Ildiko de Papp. *Controlling the Uncontrollable: the Fiction of Alice Munro* (DeKalb, IL: Northern Illinois University Press, 1989).
Carscallen, James. *The Other Country: Patterns in the Writing of Alice Munro* (Toronto: ECW Press, 1993).
Cox, Ailsa. *Alice Munro* (Tavistock: Northcote House, 2004).
Cox, Ailsa, and Lorre, Christine. *The Mind's Eye: Alice Munro's Dance of the Happy Shades* (Paris: Fahrenheit, 2015).
Dahlie, Hallvard. *Alice Munro and Her Works* (Toronto: ECW Press, 1984).
Duncan, Isla. *Alice Munro's Narrative Acts* (New York: Palgrave Macmillan, 2011).
Guignery, Vanessa (ed.) *The Inside of a Shell: Alice Munro's Dance of the Happy Shades* (Newcastle upon Tyne: Cambridge Scholars, 2015).
Heble, Ajay. *The Tumble of Reason: Alice Munro's Discourse of Absence* (University of Toronto Press, 1994).
Hooper, Brad. *The Fiction of Alice Munro: an Appreciation* (Westport, CN: Praeger, 2008).
Howells, Coral Ann. *Alice Munro* (Manchester University Press, 1998).
McCaig, Jo Ann. *Reading in Alice Munro's Archives* (Waterloo, Ont.: Wilfrid Laurier University Press, 2002).
MacKendrick, Louis K. *Some Other Reality: Alice Munro's Something I've Been Meaning to Tell You* (Toronto: ECW Press, 1993).
MacKendrick, Louis K. (ed.) *Probable Fictions: Alice Munro's Narrative Acts* (Downsview, Ont.: ECW Press, 1983).
Martin, W. R. *Alice Munro: Paradox and Parallel* (Edmonton: University of Alberta Press, 1987).
May, Charles E. (ed.) *Critical Insights: Alice Munro* (Ipswich, MA: Salem 2013).
Miller Judith (ed.) *The Art of Alice Munro: Saying the Unsayable* (Waterloo, Ont.: University of Waterloo Press, 1984).
Munro, Sheila. *Lives of Mothers and Daughters: Growing Up with Alice Munro* (Toronto: McClelland & Stewart, 2001).

Rasporich, Beverly J. *Dance of the Sexes: Art and Gender in the Fiction of Alice Munro* (Edmonton: University of Alberta Press, 1990).
Redekop, Magdalene. *Mothers and Other Clowns: the Stories of Alice Munro* (New York: Routledge, 1992).
Ross, Catherine Sheldrick. *Alice Munro: a Double Life* (Toronto: ECW Press, 1992).
Smyth, Karen E. *Figuring Grief: Gallant, Munro and the Poetics of Elegy* (Montreal: McGill-Queen's University Press, 1992).
Steele, Apollonia, and Tener, Jean F. (eds.) *The Alice Munro Papers: First Accession* (University of Calgary Press, 1986).
Steele, Apollonia, and Tener, Jean F. (eds.) *The Alice Munro Papers: Second Accession* (University of Calgary Press, 1987).
Thacker, Robert. *Alice Munro: Writing Her Lives* (Toronto: McClelland & Stewart, 2005; revised edition 2011).
Thacker, Robert (ed.) *The Rest of the Story: Critical Essays on Alice Munro* (Toronto: ECW Press, 1999).
Zehelein, Eva-Sabine (ed.) *For (Dear) Life: Close Readings of Alice Munro's Ultimate Fiction* (Zurich: LIT, 2014).

INDEX

Albania, 3, 33, 138
Alberta, 9, 35
American South, 3, 12–13, 112
Amos, Janet, 18
Andersen, Hans Christian, 10
Atlantic Monthly, 117
Atwood, Margaret, 1, 4, 14, 60, 91, 96–114
Australia, 3, 7, 33–4, 73, 125, 127
Australia Council, 18
autobiography. *See* non-fiction

Barber, Virginia, 18, 118
Benstock, Shari, 80
Beran, Carol L., 60
Bishop, Elizabeth, 183
Blaise, Clark, 131
Blyth, 9, 13
Blyth Festival, 18
Bradbury, Ray, 112
British Columbia, 7, 40, 82
Brontë, Emily, 3, 11–12, 89
Burne-Jones, Edward, 65

Calgary (Alberta), 20
Callaghan, Morley, 12
Canada Council, 14
Canada Council Senior Arts Grant, 16
Canada-Australia Literary Prize, 18
Canadian Booksellers' Award, 16
Canadian Short Stories, 14
Carleton Place (Ontario), 9
Carman, Bliss, 128
Celtic culture, 154, 162–7
Chamney, Anne Clarke, 9, 13, 80, 178–91
Chapman, L. J., 90
Chatelaine, 117, 121
Chekhov, 1, 17
China, 20

Church of England, 9
Cixous, Hélène, 61–2, 88
    écriture féminine, 62, 75
Clinton, 3, 7–10, 17, 19, 23, 40
Close, Ann, 118, 124
Codex Regius, 177
    'Lay of Atli', 168
Conron, Brandon, 16
Corelli, Marie, 106

Dante, 146–7, 167
Dickens, Charles, 46, 53
    Oliver Twist, 108
Duffy, Dennis, 140

Eaton's Department Store, 13
Eliot, T. S., 5
Engel, Marian, 20
Englund, Peter, 2
Erikson, Erik, 149
experimental writing, 139
External Affairs, Department of, 18

fairy tales, 10, 62, 64–6, 113, 147
Faulkner, William, 12
    Sound and the Fury, The, 112
female body, 71–4
feminism, 4, 60–76
Fitzgerald, F. Scott, 86
Folio, x, 13
Franzen, Jonathan, 1, 142
Fremlin, Gerald, 17, 19, 23
    National Atlas of Canada, 17, 40

Gibson, Douglas, 118, 124
Gibson, Graeme, 96
    Eleven Canadian Novelists, 96, 100, 112, 114
Gide, André, 67

197

INDEX

Gilbert and Sullivan, 103
Giller Prize, 2, 21
Glover, Douglas, 3, 45–59, 90, 92
Gluck, Christoph Willibad von, 155
  Orfeo ed Euridice, 155
Golding, William, 174
  Lord of the Flies, 175
Gothic, 12, 101, 112
Grand Street, 79, 87, 117
Great Lakes, 7
Greek myth, 155–61
Grey, Zane, 11

Hadley, Tessa, 1
Halifax (Nova Scotia), 20, 125
Herk, Aritha van, 60
Hodgins, Jack, 19
Hoffmann, E. T. A., 171
  Night Pieces, The, 172
Hogg, James, 160, 164
  Memoirs of the Author's Life, The, 165
  Private Memoirs and Confessions of a Justified Sinner, 154
Homer, 5, 146–7
How I Met My Husband, 18
Howells, Coral Ann, 4, 64, 65, 75, 79–93, 139, 140
Hugo, Victor, 128
Humber School for Writers, 17
Huron County (Ontario), 3, 7–10, 19, 23, 32, 40, 42, 121, 125, 154
Huron, Lake, 7–8, 27, 36–7

Ibsen, Henrik, 157
  Doll's House, A, 157
Indonesia, 3, 33

James, Henry, 86
Japan, 14
Joyce, James, 4, 48, 114

Kertes, Joseph, 17
Kingston (Ontario), 3, 32, 35
Kitchener (Ontario), 3, 37
Künstlerroman, 4, 96, 143

Laidlaw, Margaret, 154, 163, 165–6
Laidlaw, Mary Etta, 13
Laidlaw, Robert, 9, 87
  Macgregors, The, 13, 87
Last of the Mohicans, The, 11
Laurence, Jack, 15

Laurence, Margaret, 15, 99
  This Side Jordan, 15
life writing. *See* non-fiction
London (Ontario), 16, 18, 37, 71, 189–90
Lorentzen, Christian, 139

McCullers, Carson, 12, 112
McGrath, Charles, 118, 139
McGraw-Hill, 15
Macmillan, 87, 117
Maitland River, the, 9, 29, 36–7
maps, 37, 39–42, 90
Maps as Mediated Seeing: Fundamentals of Cartography, 41
Marian Engel Award, 20
Metcalf, John, 82
Mezei, Kathy, 82
Mill on the Floss, The, 98
Miller, Joaquin, 128
Montgomery, Lucy Maud, 3, 10–11
  Anne of Green Gables, 10, 98
  Emily of New Moon, 10, 20
Morocco, 14
Morris-Turnberry Township, 28, 42
motherhood, 5, 61, 66–8, 143
Munro, Alice
  collections
    Carried Away, 97
    Dance of the Happy Shades, 2, 5, 26, 37, 68, 96, 131, 138–9, 141, 155–6, 175
    Dear Life, 2, 5, 21, 23, 37, 65, 81, 85, 136–7, 139, 142, 145, 151, 154, 171, 175
    Friend of My Youth, 20, 26, 61, 138–9
    Hateship, Friendship, Courtship, Loveship, Marriage, 21, 32, 63–4, 66, 69, 140, 143
    Lives of Girls and Women, 15, 19, 40, 47, 68, 87, 138, 159
    Moons of Jupiter, The, 4, 14, 20, 72, 116–33, 139, 143, 150
    Open Secrets, 21, 32, 65, 93, 136, 138–9
    Progress of Love, The, 20, 32–3, 67, 72, 139, 167
    Runaway, 1, 21–2, 33, 37, 67, 70, 137, 140
    Selected Stories, 1, 151, 181
    Something I've Been Meaning to Tell You, 16, 23, 32, 68, 71, 136, 151
    The Love of a Good Woman, 21, 29, 37, 66, 136
    Too Much Happiness, 21, 32, 36, 67, 71, 117, 145

INDEX

View from Castle Rock, The, 21, 28, 30, 40-1, 63, 79, 117, 139, 154, 159, 161, 163, 175
Who Do You Think You Are?, 18, 22, 28, 33-4, 37, 62, 137, 141, 143-5
screenplay
  1847: the Irish, 18
stories
  'A Queer Streak', 31
  'A Real Life', 33
  'A Trip to the Coast', 33
  'Accident', 117, 124-5, 130-1, 143
  'Albanian Virgin, The', 32-3
  'Amundsen', 37, 145
  'An Ounce of Cure', 64, 96
  'Baptizing', 47-59
  'Bardon Bus', 72-3, 117, 124-5, 127, 130-1
  'Bear Came Over the Mountain, The', 39, 147
  'Beggar Maid, The', 65
  'Boys and Girls', 62, 156, 158
  'Carried Away', 65, 136, 147
  'Chaddeleys and Flemings', 30, 117-19, 121-3, 131, 133
  'Chance', 33, 137
  'Changes and Ceremonies', 106-7
  'Child's Play', 145
  'Children Stay, The', 39, 66-7
  'Connection', 117, 120-1
  'Corrie', 142
  'Dance of the Happy Shades', 97, 102, 158
  'Deep Holes', 67
  'Dimensions', 71, 188
  'Dulse', 117, 124-5, 131
  'Eskimo', 34
  'Eye, The', 172
  'Family Furnishings', 31, 69
  'Ferguson Girls Must Never Marry, The', 117
  'Friend of My Youth', 92, 162, 185-6
  'Gravel', 151
  'Hard-Luck Stories', 117, 125, 128, 130-1
  'Haven', 37, 68-70
  'Hired Girl', 38, 80, 174
  'Hold Me Fast Don't Let Me Pass', 163
  'Home', 32, 36, 38, 79, 81, 190
  'Images', 15, 27
  'Jack Randa Hotel, The', 138
  'Labor Day Dinner', 117, 125, 130-1
  'Lives of Girls and Women', 3, 107-9
  'Love of a Good Woman, The', 138-9, 186
  'Lying Under the Apple Tree', 63, 80-1, 87-9
  'Material', 32, 68, 99, 151, 180-1
  'Memorial', 71
  'Meneseteung', 28, 99, 138
  'Messenger', 41, 87, 174
  'Miles City, Montana', 33, 67, 184
  'Mischief', 36, 66, 143
  'Moons of Jupiter, The', 117, 123, 128
  'Mrs. Cross and Mrs. Kidd', 117, 125, 131
  'My Mother's Dream', 32, 67
  'Nettles', 38, 63, 66
  'Night', 86, 172
  'Office, The', 15, 32, 68
  'Oh, What Avails', 34, 40
  'Open Secrets', 36
  'Oranges and Apples', 61
  'Ottawa Valley, The', 5, 19, 36, 92, 136, 144, 178-80, 184, 190
  'Peace of Utrecht, The', 5, 92-3, 96, 182-5
  'Pictures of the Ice', 33
  'Postcard', 15
  'Powers', 70
  'Privilege', 63
  'Prue', 117, 125, 127, 131
  'Queenie', 32
  'Red Dress – 1946', 63
  'Royal Beatings', 18
  'Save the Reaper', 34, 136
  'Simon's Luck', 35
  'Soon', 67
  'Spaceships Have Landed', 28
  'Stone in the Field, The', 117, 121-3, 126, 129, 131
  'Sunday Afternoon', 174
  'Ticket, The', 81
  'Time of Death, The', 156, 158
  'To Reach Japan', 37, 145
  'Train', 137, 145-50
  'Tricks', 39, 70
  'Turkey Season, The', 117-18, 121, 125, 132
  'Vandals', 186
  'Visitors', 34-5, 117, 125-6, 130-2
  'Voices', 80
  'Walker Brothers Cowboy', 15, 21, 27, 141
  'Wenlock Edge', 32

199

INDEX

Munro, Alice (cont.)
  'What Do You Want to Know For?',
    40-1, 81, 89-91, 165
  'What Is Real?', 6, 116
  'White Dump', 32, 75, 167
  'Wild Swans', 33, 137
  'Wilds of Morris Township, The', 42, 87
  'Wood', 36, 117
  'Working for a Living', 80-1, 85-7, 117, 190
Munro, Andrea, 13
Munro, Catherine, 13
Munro, Jenny, 13
Munro, Jim, 13-14, 16
Munro, Sheila, 13, 67
  Lives of Mothers and Daughters, 67
Munro's Books, 13-14

New Canadian Library, 20
New Canadian Stories, 79
New Yorker, The, 18, 93, 117-18, 123-4, 138-9, 142
New, William, 20, 116-33
Newcomers, The, 18
Nobel Prize, 1-2, 5, 22, 51, 60
non-fiction, 3-4, 15-16, 92-3, 138
Norse myth, 5, 167-75
Norway, 20
Notre Dame University, 16

Oates, Joyce Carol, 140
O'Brien, Tim, 17
O'Connor, Flannery, 12
Ondaatje, Michael, 18
Ottawa (Ontario), 3, 32

Paris Review, 180, 185
Parkinson's disease, 13, 86, 92, 178
PEN/O. Henry Prize, 142, 151
Phillips, Anne, 61
place in Munro's fiction, 26-42
Porter, Katherine Ann, 12
postmodernism, 139
Pound, Ezra, 5
Presbyterianism, 9, 13, 165, 167
Pride and Prejudice, 64
Protestantism, 13
Proust, Marcel, 85
Putnam, D. F., 90
  Physiography of Southern Ontario, The, 90

Rabinovitch, Jack, 21
Richler, Mordecai, 14, 21

Roberts, Charles G. D., 12
Ryerson Press, 15

Said, Edward, 140
  On Late Style, 140
Salis-Seewis, Johann Gaudenz von, 166
Saturday Night, 117
Scandinavia, 7, 174
Schubert, Franz, 166
Scobie, Stephen, 87
Scotch Corners, 9
Scotland, 3, 33, 163, 173
Scott, Michael, 167
Scott, Walter, 154, 165-7
  Minstrelsy of the Scottish Borders, 154
Seton, Ernest Thompson, 12
sex/sexuality, 16, 18, 61, 81, 185
Shakespeare, William, 23
  Hamlet, 98
Shawn, William, 117-18
Shields, Carol, 17, 79, 84
short story, 22, 47, 60, 136, 152, 155, 163-4
Shorter Poems, 129
Stevenson, Robert Louis, 167
Stratford (Ontario), 3, 37
style, 45-59
Sweden, 20

Tamarack Review, 14, 117
Tate, Allen, 5
Tennyson, Alfred Lord, 64, 98, 103-4, 109, 112
  'Mariana', 64, 112
  'The Beggar Maid', 65
  'The Lady of Shalott', 98
  'The Princess', 103
Thacker, Robert, 82, 119
Tolstoy, Leo, 23
Toppings, Earle, 15
Toronto (Ontario), 3, 13, 16, 20, 31-2, 99, 117, 145, 148, 173, 178
Toronto Life, 117
trains, 136-7
Trillium Book Award, 20

United Church, 13
University of British Columbia, 14
University of New Brunswick, 21
University of Ottawa, 19
University of Western Ontario, 13, 16-18, 40

INDEX

Vancouver (British Columbia), 3, 13, 15, 20, 30, 32–3, 36, 82, 92, 131
Vancouver Public Library, 13
Vanderhaeghe, Guy, 20
Victoria (British Columbia), 3, 13, 16, 20, 32

Wachtel, Eleanor, 80
Wawanash (Ontario), 27, 36, 38, 49, 100, 105–14
Weaver, Robert, 14
Welty, Eudora, 3, 12

Wilkinson, Thomas, 173
Tours to the British Mountain, 173
Wilson, Ethel, 14, 184
Wingham (Ontario), 3, 28–42, 96, 181
Wingham Advance Times, 8
Woolf, Virginia, 84–5, 92, 98
Moments of Being, 84–5
Wordsworth, William, 84, 166, 172

York University (Ontario), 16

201

Cambridge Companions to …

AUTHORS

Edward Albee edited by Stephen J. Bottoms

Margaret Atwood edited by Coral Ann Howells

W. H. Auden edited by Stan Smith

Jane Austen edited by Edward Copeland and Juliet McMaster (second edition)

Beckett edited by John Pilling

Bede edited by Scott DeGregorio

Aphra Behn edited by Derek Hughes and Janet Todd

Walter Benjamin edited by David S. Ferris

William Blake edited by Morris Eaves

Boccaccio edited by Guyda Armstrong, Rhiannon Daniels, and Stephen J. Milner

Jorge Luis Borges edited by Edwin Williamson

Brecht edited by Peter Thomson and Glendyr Sacks (second edition)

The Brontës edited by Heather Glen

Bunyan edited by Anne Dunan-Page

Frances Burney edited by Peter Sabor

Byron edited by Drummond Bone

Albert Camus edited by Edward J. Hughes

Willa Cather edited by Marilee Lindemann

Cervantes edited by Anthony J. Cascardi

Chaucer edited by Piero Boitani and Jill Mann (second edition)

Chekhov edited by Vera Gottlieb and Paul Allain

Kate Chopin edited by Janet Beer

Caryl Churchill edited by Elaine Aston and Elin Diamond

Cicero edited by Catherine Steel

Coleridge edited by Lucy Newlyn

Wilkie Collins edited by Jenny Bourne Taylor

Joseph Conrad edited by J. H. Stape

H. D. edited by Nephie J. Christodoulides and Polina Mackay

Dante edited by Rachel Jacoff (second edition)

Daniel Defoe edited by John Richetti

Don DeLillo edited by John N. Duvall

Charles Dickens edited by John O. Jordan

Emily Dickinson edited by Wendy Martin

John Donne edited by Achsah Guibbory

Dostoevskii edited by W. J. Leatherbarrow

Theodore Dreiser edited by Leonard Cassuto and Claire Virginia Eby

John Dryden edited by Steven N. Zwicker

W. E. B. Du Bois edited by Shamoon Zamir

George Eliot edited by George Levine

T. S. Eliot edited by A. David Moody

Ralph Ellison edited by Ross Posnock

Ralph Waldo Emerson edited by Joel Porte and Saundra Morris

William Faulkner edited by Philip M. Weinstein

Henry Fielding edited by Claude Rawson

F. Scott Fitzgerald edited by Ruth Prigozy

Flaubert edited by Timothy Unwin

E. M. Forster edited by David Bradshaw

Benjamin Franklin edited by Carla Mulford

Brian Friel edited by Anthony Roche

Robert Frost edited by Robert Faggen

Gabriel García Márquez edited by Philip Swanson

Elizabeth Gaskell edited by Jill L. Matus

Goethe edited by Lesley Sharpe

Günter Grass edited by Stuart Taberner

Thomas Hardy edited by Dale Kramer

David Hare edited by Richard Boon

Nathaniel Hawthorne edited by Richard Millington

Seamus Heaney edited by Bernard O'Donoghue

Ernest Hemingway edited by Scott Donaldson

Homer edited by Robert Fowler

Horace edited by Stephen Harrison

Ted Hughes edited by Terry Gifford

Ibsen edited by James McFarlane

Henry James edited by Jonathan Freedman

Samuel Johnson edited by Greg Clingham

Ben Jonson edited by Richard Harp and Stanley Stewart

James Joyce edited by Derek Attridge (second edition)

Kafka edited by Julian Preece
Keats edited by Susan J. Wolfson
Rudyard Kipling edited by Howard J. Booth
Lacan edited by Jean-Michel Rabaté
D. H. Lawrence edited by Anne Fernihough
Primo Levi edited by Robert Gordon
Lucretius edited by Stuart Gillespie and Philip Hardie
Machiavelli edited by John M. Najemy
David Mamet edited by Christopher Bigsby
Thomas Mann edited by Ritchie Robertson
Christopher Marlowe edited by Patrick Cheney
Andrew Marvell edited by Derek Hirst and Steven N. Zwicker
Herman Melville edited by Robert S. Levine
Arthur Miller edited by Christopher Bigsby (second edition)
Milton edited by Dennis Danielson (second edition)
Molière edited by David Bradby and Andrew Calder
Toni Morrison edited by Justine Tally
Alice Munro edited by David Staines
Nabokov edited by Julian W. Connolly
Eugene O'Neill edited by Michael Manheim
George Orwell edited by John Rodden
Ovid edited by Philip Hardie
Petrarch edited by Albert Russell Ascoli and Unn Falkeid
Harold Pinter edited by Peter Raby (second edition)
Sylvia Plath edited by Jo Gill
Edgar Allan Poe edited by Kevin J. Hayes
Alexander Pope edited by Pat Rogers
Ezra Pound edited by Ira B. Nadel
Proust edited by Richard Bales
Pushkin edited by Andrew Kahn
Rabelais edited by John O'Brien
Rilke edited by Karen Leeder and Robert Vilain
Philip Roth edited by Timothy Parrish
Salman Rushdie edited by Abdulrazak Gurnah
Shakespeare edited by Margareta de Grazia and Stanley Wells (second edition)
Shakespearean Comedy edited by Alexander Leggatt

Shakespeare and Contemporary Dramatists edited by Ton Hoenselaars
Shakespeare and Popular Culture edited by Robert Shaughnessy
Shakespearean Tragedy edited by Claire McEachern (second edition)
Shakespeare on Film edited by Russell Jackson (second edition)
Shakespeare on Stage edited by Stanley Wells and Sarah Stanton
Shakespeare's History Plays edited by Michael Hattaway
Shakespeare's Last Plays edited by Catherine M. S. Alexander
Shakespeare's Poetry edited by Patrick Cheney
George Bernard Shaw edited by Christopher Innes
Shelley edited by Timothy Morton
Mary Shelley edited by Esther Schor
Sam Shepard edited by Matthew C. Roudané
Spenser edited by Andrew Hadfield
Laurence Sterne edited by Thomas Keymer
Wallace Stevens edited by John N. Serio
Tom Stoppard edited by Katherine E. Kelly
Harriet Beecher Stowe edited by Cindy Weinstein
August Strindberg edited by Michael Robinson
Jonathan Swift edited by Christopher Fox
J. M. Synge edited by P. J. Mathews
Tacitus edited by A. J. Woodman
Henry David Thoreau edited by Joel Myerson
Tolstoy edited by Donna Tussing Orwin
Anthony Trollope edited by Carolyn Dever and Lisa Niles
Mark Twain edited by Forrest G. Robinson
John Updike edited by Stacey Olster
Mario Vargas Llosa edited by Efrain Kristal and John King
Virgil edited by Charles Martindale
Voltaire edited by Nicholas Cronk
Edith Wharton edited by Millicent Bell
Walt Whitman edited by Ezra Greenspan
Oscar Wilde edited by Peter Raby
Tennessee Williams edited by Matthew C. Roudané
August Wilson edited by Christopher Bigsby
Mary Wollstonecraft edited by Claudia L. Johnson

Virginia Woolf edited by Susan Sellers (second edition)

Wordsworth edited by Stephen Gill

W. B. Yeats edited by Marjorie Howes and John Kelly

Zola edited by Brian Nelson

TOPICS

The Actress edited by Maggie B. Gale and John Stokes

The African American Novel edited by Maryemma Graham

The African American Slave Narrative edited by Audrey A. Fisch

African American Theatre by Harvey Young

Allegory edited by Rita Copeland and Peter Struck

American Crime Fiction edited by Catherine Ross Nickerson

American Modernism edited by Walter Kalaidjian

American Poetry Since 1945 edited by Jennifer Ashton

American Realism and Naturalism edited by Donald Pizer

American Travel Writing edited by Alfred Bendixen and Judith Hamera

American Women Playwrights edited by Brenda Murphy

Ancient Rhetoric edited by Erik Gunderson

Arthurian Legend edited by Elizabeth Archibald and Ad Putter

Australian Literature edited by Elizabeth Webby

British Literature of the French Revolution edited by Pamela Clemit

British Romanticism edited by Stuart Curran (second edition)

British Romantic Poetry edited by James Chandler and Maureen N. McLane

British Theatre, 1730–1830, edited by Jane Moody and Daniel O'Quinn

Canadian Literature edited by Eva-Marie Kröller

Children's Literature edited by M. O. Grenby and Andrea Immel

The Classic Russian Novel edited by Malcolm V. Jones and Robin Feuer Miller

Contemporary Irish Poetry edited by Matthew Campbell

Creative Writing edited by David Morley and Philip Neilsen

Crime Fiction edited by Martin Priestman

Early Modern Women's Writing edited by Laura Lunger Knoppers

The Eighteenth-Century Novel edited by John Richetti

Eighteenth-Century Poetry edited by John Sitter

Emma edited by Peter Sabor

English Literature, 1500–1600 edited by Arthur F. Kinney

English Literature, 1650–1740 edited by Steven N. Zwicker

English Literature, 1740–1830 edited by Thomas Keymer and Jon Mee

English Literature, 1830–1914 edited by Joanne Shattock

English Novelists edited by Adrian Poole

English Poetry, Donne to Marvell edited by Thomas N. Corns

English Poets edited by Claude Rawson

English Renaissance Drama, second edition edited by A. R. Braunmuller and Michael Hattaway

English Renaissance Tragedy edited by Emma Smith and Garrett A. Sullivan Jr.

English Restoration Theatre edited by Deborah C. Payne Fisk

The Epic edited by Catherine Bates

European Modernism edited by Pericles Lewis

European Novelists edited by Michael Bell

Fairy Tales edited by Maria Tatar

Fantasy Literature edited by Edward James and Farah Mendlesohn

Feminist Literary Theory edited by Ellen Rooney

Fiction in the Romantic Period edited by Richard Maxwell and Katie Trumpener

The Fin de Siècle edited by Gail Marshall

The French Enlightenment edited by Daniel Brewer

The French Novel: from 1800 to the Present edited by Timothy Unwin

Gay and Lesbian Writing edited by Hugh Stevens

German Romanticism edited by Nicholas Saul

Gothic Fiction edited by Jerrold E. Hogle

The Greek and Roman Novel edited by Tim Whitmarsh

Greek and Roman Theatre edited by Marianne McDonald and J. Michael Walton

Greek Comedy edited by Martin Revermann

Greek Lyric edited by Felix Budelmann

Greek Mythology edited by Roger D. Woodard

Greek Tragedy edited by P. E. Easterling

The Harlem Renaissance edited by George Hutchinson

The History of the Book edited by Leslie Howsam

The Irish Novel edited by John Wilson Foster

The Italian Novel edited by Peter Bondanella and Andrea Ciccarelli

The Italian Renaissance edited by Michael Wyatt

Jewish American Literature edited by Hana Wirth-Nesher and Michael P. Kramer

The Latin American Novel edited by Efraín Kristal

The Literature of the First World War edited by Vincent Sherry

The Literature of London edited by Lawrence Manley

The Literature of Los Angeles edited by Kevin R. McNamara

The Literature of New York edited by Cyrus Patell and Bryan Waterman

The Literature of Paris edited by Anna-Louise Milne

The Literature of World War II edited by Marina MacKay

Literature on Screen edited by Deborah Cartmell and Imelda Whelehan

Medieval English Culture edited by Andrew Galloway

Medieval English Literature edited by Larry Scanlon

Medieval English Mysticism edited by Samuel Fanous and Vincent Gillespie

Medieval English Theatre edited by Richard Beadle and Alan J. Fletcher (second edition)

Medieval French Literature edited by Simon Gaunt and Sarah Kay

Medieval Romance edited by Roberta L. Krueger

Medieval Women's Writing edited by Carolyn Dinshaw and David Wallace

Modern American Culture edited by Christopher Bigsby

Modern British Women Playwrights edited by Elaine Aston and Janelle Reinelt

Modern French Culture edited by Nicholas Hewitt

Modern German Culture edited by Eva Kolinsky and Wilfried van der Will

The Modern German Novel edited by Graham Bartram

The Modern Gothic edited by Jerrold E. Hogle

Modern Irish Culture edited by Joe Cleary and Claire Connolly

Modern Italian Culture edited by Zygmunt G. Baranski and Rebecca J. West

Modern Latin American Culture edited by John King

Modern Russian Culture edited by Nicholas Rzhevsky

Modern Spanish Culture edited by David T. Gies

Modernism edited by Michael Levenson (second edition)

The Modernist Novel edited by Morag Shiach

Modernist Poetry edited by Alex Davis and Lee M. Jenkins

Modernist Women Writers edited by Maren Tova Linett

Narrative edited by David Herman

Native American Literature edited by Joy Porter and Kenneth M. Roemer

Nineteenth-Century American Women's Writing edited by Dale M. Bauer and Philip Gould

Old English Literature edited by Malcolm Godden and Michael Lapidge (second edition)

Performance Studies edited by Tracy C. Davis

Piers Plowman by Andrew Cole and Andrew Galloway

Popular Fiction edited by David Glover and Scott McCracken

Postcolonial Literary Studies edited by Neil Lazarus

Postmodernism edited by Steven Connor

The Pre-Raphaelites edited by Elizabeth Prettejohn

Pride and Prejudice edited by Janet Todd

Renaissance Humanism edited by Jill Kraye

The Roman Historians edited by Andrew Feldherr

Roman Satire edited by Kirk Freudenburg

Science Fiction edited by Edward James and Farah Mendlesohn

Scottish Literature edited by Gerald Carruthers and Liam McIlvanney

Sensation Fiction edited by Andrew Mangham

The Sonnet edited by A. D. Cousins and Peter Howarth

The Spanish Novel: from 1600 to the Present edited by Harriet Turner and Adelaida López de Martínez

Textual Scholarship edited by Neil Fraistat and Julia Flanders

Theatre History by David Wiles and Christine Dymkowski

Travel Writing edited by Peter Hulme and Tim Youngs

Twentieth-Century British and Irish Women's Poetry edited by Jane Dowson

The Twentieth-Century English Novel edited by Robert L. Caserio

Twentieth-Century English Poetry edited by Neil Corcoran

Twentieth-Century Irish Drama edited by Shaun Richards

Twentieth-Century Russian Literature edited by Marina Balina and Evgeny Dobrenko

Utopian Literature edited by Gregory Claeys

Victorian and Edwardian Theatre edited by Kerry Powell

The Victorian Novel edited by Deirdre David (second edition)

Victorian Poetry edited by Joseph Bristow

Victorian Women's Writing edited by Linda H. Peterson

War Writing edited by Kate McLoughlin

Women's Writing in Britain, 1660–1789 edited by Catherine Ingrassia

Women's Writing in the Romantic Period edited by Devoney Looser

Writing of the English Revolution edited by N. H. Keeble

PORTLAND PUBLIC LIBRARY
5 MONUMENT SQUARE
PORTLAND ME 04101

MANEW $89.99

WITHDRAWN